PSYCHOLOGICAL REALITY

ADVANCES IN PSYCHOLOGY
26

Editors

G. E. STELMACH

P. A. VROON

NORTH-HOLLAND
AMSTERDAM · NEW YORK · OXFORD

PSYCHOLOGICAL REALITY

Kenneth P. HILLNER

Department of Psychology
South Dakota State University
Brookings, S.D., U.S.A.

1985

NORTH-HOLLAND
AMSTERDAM · NEW YORK · OXFORD

© ELSEVIER SCIENCE PUBLISHERS B.V., 1985

ISBN: 0 444 87741 x

Publishers:
ELSEVIER SCIENCE PUBLISHERS B.V.
P.O. Box 1991
1000 BZ Amsterdam
The Netherlands

Sole distributors for the U.S.A. and Canada:
ELSEVIER SCIENCE PUBLISHING COMPANY, INC.
52 Vanderbilt Avenue
New York, N.Y. 10017
U.S.A.

Library of Congress Cataloging in Publication Data

Hillner, Kenneth P.
  Psychological reality.

  (Advances in psychology ; 26)
  Bibliography: p.
  Includes indexes.
  1. Psychology--Philosophy. 2. Psychology, Applied--
Philosophy. 3. Reality--Psychological aspects.
I. Title. II. Series: Advances in psychology (Amsterdam,
Netherlands) ; 26.
BF38.H535 1985   150'.1   85-4513
ISBN 0-444-87741-X

PRINTED IN THE NETHERLANDS

DEDICATION

This book is dedicated to the memory of my late father, Everett Charles Hillner. I also wish to pay homage to Aleksandr I. Solzhenitsyn and countless other victims of the Gulag Archipelago.

CONTENTS

PREFACE

The discipline of psychology exists both as an end in itself and as a means to other ends. As an end in itself, psychology is an independent, institutionalized, academic discipline (intellectual endeavor) concerned with the nature of psychological reality. As a means to other ends, psychology is a professional discipline (delivery system) seeking to apply established psychological doctrine to problems believed amenable to solution by active psychological intervention.

Psychology, as an intellectual endeavor, derived from the synthesis of epistemological philosophy, experimental physiology, and sensory psychophysics. This synthesis was accomplished in Germany around 1880 under the aegis of Wilhelm Wundt, who established the first recognized system of experimental psychology, known as structuralism.

Psychology, as an applied entity, derives from our perennial interest in human nature and the general cultural belief that interventionist actions are beneficial. The establishment of psychology as a profession outside the confines of academia is implicit in Freudian psychology (roughly 1885); but the specific subvarieties of professional psychology now known as clinical, industrial, vocational, and the like are of more recent origin.

        Ideally, academic psychology serves as the con-
ceptual basis of applied psychology. How the academic psychologist construes the nature of psychological reality determines the appropriateness of
specific psychological interventionist techniques.

        The task of resolving the nature of psycholog-
ical reality, i.e., constructing a specific psychological reality, is both a rational and arbitrary
endeavor, such that it must be viewed as a philosophical exercise. One of the primary features of
academic psychology is that no consensus exists as
to what constitutes the proper psychological universe. Various models of psychological reality exist and implicitly compete with each other for the
right to be called the psychology: for instance,
descriptive behaviorism, cognitive psychology, humanism, dialectical psychology, and depth psychology of which psychoanalysis is one version.

        Since the germinal phase of the evolution of
academic psychology is over and the era of the
classical schools of psychology now is a part of
history, many psychologists are becoming quite de-
fensive about their discipline's failure to resolve
the nature of the psychological universe. The lack
of a consensus is viewed negatively, especially by
those who like to compare psychology with such more
formalized and established sciences as physics and
chemistry, in which competing versions of an ultimate physical reality no longer exist. Such psychologists as Deese (1972), Koch (1975), Kendler
(1981), and Staats (1983) even like to argue that
psychology currently is in a state of crisis or

conflict.

There also is a current tendency (Robinson,
1979) to assume that psychology should be an atheoretical endeavor and practiced at a strictly parametric level, such that every issue that psychology
faces, whether conceptual or pragmatic, can be resolved by accumulation of further experimental data.
But this is not a realistic reaction to psychology's
lack of paradigmatic coherence, because academic
psychology is nothing if not an applied philosophy.
No psychological truth exists independently of a
given model of psychological reality.

In my opinion, academic psychology's perennial
metaphysical pluralism should be accepted at face
value with an evaluatively neutral stance, so that
the task of constructing a model of psychological
reality can be objectively assessed. Such an assessment would demonstrate four moderating characteristics of psychology's conceptual predicament:

1. The pluralism of psychology is a function of
various historical and philosophical factors that
by and large are immutable.

2. Much of psychology's pluralism is superficial or semantically based.

3. The same basic set of problems must be faced
by every proposed model of psychological reality.
The various conceptions of the psychological universe have more in common than is usually realized,
and this has a general leavening effect on the content of psychology.

4. Any possible evaluation of the many different models of psychological reality must be conducted on a nonpsychological basis. The decision to

accept or reject a given brand of psychology is a
value judgment, determined by factors external to
the discipline of psychology itself.

*   *   *   *

The purpose of this book is to present one possible
conceptual analysis of the task of constructing a
model of psychological reality, so that psychology's
pluralistic state can be put in proper perspective.
It consists of five parts:

   1. Chapters 1 and 2 specify the essential input assumptions of the analysis, establish the boundary conditions of the treatise, preview the kinds
of decisions involved in the construction process,
and present some necessary background information.

   2. Chapters 3 through 5 collectively abstract
out possible psychological universes and recount the
dominant classical and contemporary models of psychological reality in the context of a common analytical framework.

   3. Chapters 6 through 9 focus on the philosophical input into psychology, especially as related to the nature of humanity, the mind-body problem, scientific explanation, and the discipline's
two fundamental analytical categories--behavior and
experience.

   4. Chapters 10 through 12 highlight many of the
cultural and pragmatic constraints imposed on any
model of psychological reality by considering the
applied, contextual, and relational aspects of psychology.

   5. Chapter 13 provides some final perspective
on the task of constructing a model of psychological
reality.

The book can be used profitably in any conceptually oriented psychology course at either the un-
dergraduate or graduate level: senior seminar, systems of psychology, psychological theory, concepts
of psychology, or overview of the discipline. The
level of exposition does presume that the reader has
been exposed to a traditional introductory psychology course. Some rudimentary knowledge of philosophy also would be helpful for appreciating the
analysis, but is not required for an understanding
of the basic arguments presented in the text. The
individual chapters are by and large self-contained
and can be read in any order that is desired; however, an initial perusal of the first part is rec-
ommended so as to prevent any misconceptions about
the tenor and tone of the succeeding chapters.
*   *   *   *
Some preliminary notes on the terminological usages
and classificational assumptions employed in the
analysis follow.

1. The phrases "psychological reality" and
"psychological universe" are used equivalently to
refer to the specific aspect of reality or the universe that is of endemic concern to the psychologist. They are analogous to the notions of physical
reality and physical universe in the physical science context.

2. The terms "model" and "system or school"
are used interchangeably to refer to specific conceptions of psychological reality, such as behaviorism, functionalism, and psychoanalysis. The analysis will make no formal distinction between a system and subsystem.

3. The term "orientation" is used to refer to the specific manner in which a psychologist constructs a model of psychological reality: for instance, objective, subjective, or mixed. The notion of orientation is employed in Chapter 3 as a derivational tool for mapping the major classical schools and contemporary systems of psychology onto a postulated psychological space.

4. The phrase "psychological space" denotes the didactic classification system used to represent the many different models of psychological reality.

5. The phrase "type of psychology" is used informally to categorize certain systems that possess one or more critical features in common: for instance, action, epistemological, or understanding psychology.

6. Most systems of psychology have originated in an academic context. One glaring exception is depth psychology, of which Freudian psychoanalysis is the primary example. Most academic systems subsume some kind of experimental psychology; they identify with science as practiced by the physical scientist. One glaring exception is humanistic psychology, which is empirically oriented, but not experimental in the traditional sense.

7. The phrase "professional psychology" is used to refer to the practice of psychology in an applied context, such as clinical, industrial, or educational. Much, but not all, applied psychology is an extension of the academic experimental systems.

ACKNOWLEDGMENTS

A Skinnerian likes to argue that one does what one finds reinforcing. A humanist likes to point out that certain activities contribute to one's self-realization. There is no doubt that I enjoy writing and use it as a means of professional expression. Nonetheless, this book could never have been written without the sacrifice, understanding, or encouragement of each of the following: my family, the Psychology Department, the Arts and Science College, Dr. K. Michielsen of North Holland, and the Series Editors George Stelmach and Pieter Vroon. Special acknowledgment is extended to the hundreds of South Dakota State University students who tolerate my classroom behavior as a means of coming to terms with life and the universe. More generally, I am very appreciative of a set of personal circumstances that affords both the philosophical freedom and opportunity for reflection requisite for psychological exposition. As one ages, one gets more sentimental. I hope that the content of this book aids in making the discipline more tolerant. Psychology certainly has a central role to play in twentieth century life; however, it is one that must respect the diversity, intelligent awareness, and dignity of its focus of interest: humankind.

CHAPTER 1

INTRODUCTION

As a consequence of paradigmatic heterogeneity (see
Preface), no internal or external (relational) question about the nature of contemporary psychology is
resolvable independently of the specific model of
psychological reality that is used as the evaluative
reference point.

Examples of internal matters include (1) object
of study, (2) purpose, (3) key psychological processes and mechanisms, (4) acceptable methodology,
(5) locus of causation, and (6) standards of sufficient explanation.

Relational matters constitute an open-ended, indeterminate set; but the following questions serve
as a representative sampling:

1. How does psychology differ from other disciplines and endeavors also concerned with our nature
and condition, such as art, religion, literature, the
theatre, law, medicine, economics, sociology, political science, and history?

2. What is our nature, or in what sense are we
an object of psychological analysis?

3. Is psychology a science? If so, what kind:
biological, social, humanistic? Or, where is psychology located in the hierarchy of sciences?

4. Are psychological phenomena reducible to

physiological phenomena or strictly emergent in nature?

     5. Does psychology possess significant practi-
cal application value, or has psychology contributed
to our progress?

     6. Is psychology relevant for ethics and mor-
ality?

     7. Does psychology have to be taken into ac-
count in any rational consideration of the meaning
of life?

     The irresolvability of these internal and ex-
ternal matters cannot be meaningfully evaluated independently of an objective analysis of the task of
constructing a model of psychological reality; however, such an analysis cannot be performed in a conceptual vacuum. We must attempt some specification
of the common ground that every psychologist accepts, regardless of theoretical persuasion. This
common ground can best be abstracted in terms of a
set of input assumptions that will both constrain
and color our analysis.

     A set of boundary conditions also must be adop-
ted so that the domain of the analysis is continuous
with that of prior analyses (such as Deese, 1972;
Koch, 1975; Kendler, 1981; Staats, 1983) and is congruent with the current spectrum of interests of the
American psychological establishment (see Nelson and
Stapp, 1983).

     This chapter introduces seven input assumptions
and four representative boundary conditions, pre-
paratory to "doing psychology" in the next chapter.
INPUT ASSUMPTIONS

     The input assumptions relate to (1) the exis-

tential reality level of psychology, (2) the language function, (3) the interminable provinciality of
psychology, (4) the infinite or generic nature of
psychology, (5) models as all-or-none packages, (6)
the change imperative, and (7) psychology as a component of the economic system. No claim is made
that the assumptions are of equal importance or are
entirely mutually exclusive of each other. Some of
them may seem obvious; others may seem surprising
and thus appear to be more relevant and insightful.
But they all are necessary and constitute a minimal
set of conditions for conducting an objective analysis.

EXISTENTIAL REALITY LEVEL OF PSYCHOLOGY Human
knowledge is one of the many facets of human experience. Knowledge per se presupposes a living organism who is conscious of the existence of a physical
universe that is independent of the self. In this
context, psychology comprises one type of human
knowledge and serves as one possible conceptual approach to organizing human experience.

Psychology exists only because the human being
exists. Psychology only has meaning for a self-
aware and self-descriptive organism. Psychology is
one possible or only one possible way of conceptualizing and organizing the content of consciousness
and its descriptions.

It could be argued that any science or academic discipline is a property of human experience and
serves to organize reality: for instance, physics,
art, or history. But the object of analysis of many
of these disciplines, especially the physical sciences, would still exist even if the human being did

not exist. If you take the human being out of the
world, the objects of analysis of physics, chemistry, astronomy, geology, and the like still remain.
Such is _not_ the case with psychology.

This fact has a crucial consequence for constructing a _psychological_ reality, in comparison
with the task of constructing a _physical_ reality.
The physical scientist must attempt to model the
physical world, devoid of any human component. For
instance, the physicist seeks descriptions and explanations of the behavior of inanimate objects, uncontaminated by the fact that they exist in the consciousness of the human being. The physicist operates in a formal, objective, externally sourced reference system, such that physical events constitute
impersonal entities.

Psychologists have a choice when it comes to
modeling the psychological universe; that is, they
have a choice with respect to the existential reality level of psychology. They can imitate the
physical scientist and attempt an objective, externally based reconstruction, much as behaviorists do;
or they can make the human presence a critical component of psychological reality, yielding the subjective approach characteristic of humanistic, existential, or phenomenological psychologists.

The phenomenal growth of psychology began in
the late nineteenth century once the assumptions and
methods physical scientists used to model _physical_
reality were applied to the problems of constructing
a _psychological_ reality. Specifically, Wundt and
the structuralists attempted to analyze and catalogue the content of human consciousness empirically
in a consistent fashion. This initial focus of

experimental psychology was later expanded to include (1) the utility of consciousness and the adaptive function of mental activity under the influence
of the functionalists and (2) the formal observation
of organismic behavior under the stimulus of the
classical behaviorists. The dominance of the objective, externally based orientation in experimental
psychology began to wane at mid twentieth century
when the philosophical underpinnings of the physical
sciences, especially physics, came under severe
scrutiny: for instance, logical positivism, opera-
tionism, and the existence of a mechanistic, Newton-
ian universe.

The subjective orientation to psychology has a
long and detailed history, but only recently has
made significant inroads in the mainstream of American academic psychology. At a pragmatic level, the
subjective orientation always has been of greater
value for the applied psychologist, especially one
engaged in some type of interventionist therapeutic
endeavor.

Note that this initial input assumption results
in a distinction between objectively oriented psychology and subjectively oriented psychology. This
distinction will assume major importance in the next
two chapters.

THE LANGUAGE FUNCTION Given the fact that psychology is one possible approach to conceptualizing
and organizing the content of our conscious experience, the primary feature of any aspect of our consciousness is that it is most readily expressible in
terms of language. A model of psychological reality
must exist in linguistic form. The physicalization

of a system of psychology embodies both the knowledge and use of some natural language, such as English.

    This fact is highlighted by the tremendous dif-
ficulty that is associated with attempting to translate a system constructed in one language into another language. The best example of this historically is Gestalt psychology, originally expressed in
German (Wertheimer, 1912; Koffka, 1922). Another
example is the attempt to express Pavlov's (1927)
Russian "psychophysiology of higher nervous activity" in English. The usual English derivative merely subsumes functional classical conditioning phenomena (Hillner, 1978, 1979).

    The only reason psychology exists in the first
place is that we possess the language function. We
have various sensory systems, response modalities,
and bodily needs; but they are not responsible for
the creation of a psychological reality. Psychology
exists because we can transform the events occurring
in our inner and outer worlds of experience into
verbal form. In fact, there would be no experience
at all without language.

    Psychology is a component of our symbolic life.
Psychology is not a property of the physical, external universe, independent of us. Psychology was one
of the last components of our symbolic life to be
formally identified and codified. We constructed
models of physical, chemical, and biological reality
long before we constructed models of psychological
reality using strictly psychological terms and categories.

    Language delimits the kinds of distinctions

psychologists can make and categories psychologists
can use. While scores of different psychological
systems and subsystems exist, they are relatable to
each other because they all must make reference to
the same basic set of verbal distinctions and categories: for instance, conscious experience versus
behavior, nomothetic versus idiographic, external
environmental versus internal organismic events,
transcendence versus nontranscendence, determinism
versus free will, mechanism versus mentalism, dualism versus monism, constructional laboratory settings versus given natural settings, and priority
of the psychological subject versus posteriority of
the psychological subject.

     This is why the same basic set of problems must
be faced by every proposed model of psychological
reality and why the various conceptions of the psychological universe have more in common than is usually realized. Most systems of psychology, especially contemporary ones, make informal provision via
conversion statements for those psychological phenomena that are explicitly excluded from the system
by its metaphysical categories. For instance, Skinnerian descriptive behaviorism (Skinner, 1974) denies the existence of mental events, but readmits
such events into psychology by conceptualizing them
as private, covert stimulus and response events to
which only the individual observer has direct access. Likewise, it is merely a matter of semantics
whether humanistic psychology (Maslow, 1971; Rychlak, 1977) deals with conscious experience or behavior.

     How the various orientations to the task of

constructing a model of psychological reality conceptualize the language function will be described
in Chapter 13.

INTERMINABLE PROVINCIALITY OF PSYCHOLOGY   Under
the assumption that no absolute reality exists (or,
if there is, it is unknowable), a given system of
psychology can be viewed as an attempt to model reality.   The immediate question arising in the context of this assumption is why is psychology so pro-
vincial: why has psychology spawned so many systems
and subsystems?   Beyond considerations regarding the
idiosyncrasies of the respective founders of these
systems and the specific social/cultural demands under which the founders operated, we can appeal to a
glaring conceptual fact: there is no meaningful way
of arbitrating among the many different systems of
psychology.   The postulation of a given system of
psychology does not generate an evaluation technique
that is independent of the assumptions and content
of the model of psychological reality proposed by
the system.

A given psychologist adopts a particular model
of psychological reality on a nonrational basis: for
instance, esthetic or intellectual preference, past
training influences, or imitation of various respec-
ted role models.   Models of psychological reality
cannot be proven right or wrong, correct or incorrect, by any objective criterion.   Models can only
be assessed in a pragmatic sense, according to a set
of idiosyncratic goals or a set of socially acclaim-
ed criteria originating outside the confines of psychology.   For instance, descriptive behaviorism
(Skinner, 1974) is useful to the extent that it

allows the control of behavior, assuming the latter
is a worthy goal; humanistic psychology (Maslow,
1971; Keen, 1975) is useful to the extent that it
allows a resolution of the psychological world of
the individual person, assuming the latter is a worthy goal.

Any possible evaluation of the many different
models of psychological reality must be conducted on
a nonpsychological basis. The decision to accept or
reject a given brand of psychology is a value judgment, determined by factors external to the discipline of psychology itself.

INFINITE OR GENERIC NATURE OF PSYCHOLOGY There
is no facet of human activity and experience that
does not have some psychological aspect associated
with it. The psychological universe is infinite in
nature, regardless of the model of psychological reality used to represent it. Any model of psychological reality must be capable of dealing with an infinite number of events. Both the phenomena of interest to psychology and the possible determinants
of these phenomena are infinite in number. A laboratory experiment can be conducted in an infinite
number of ways; so-called naturalistic observation
involves an infinite number of environments; a therapy session admits of infinite variation; a specific
practical application technique can be physically
realized in an infinite number of ways.

Because psychologists must deal with a potentially infinite domain, they are forced to use class
or generic concepts. The denotation of any psychological term, regardless of whether it refers to an
operation, a piece of behavior, an experiential

event, a process, or even a theoretical construct, is generic in nature. No psychological term refers to just one entity, but to a class of related entities; no psychological concept is physically realizable in only one way, but in a number of related ways. For instance, at the operational level, Skinnerian operant conditioning (Skinner, 1938, 1953) is a generic term for a host of procedures involving response-contingent delivery of positive reinforcement; structuralist introspection (Wundt, 1873-1874; Titchener, 1901, 1905) is a generic term for a host of procedures involving self-report on the content of immediate conscious experience. For reasons of convenience, certain variants of a technique tend to be used more often than others and come to constitute the prototypical case.

A generic term is usually defined in terms of other generic terms, which in turn are defined in terms of other generic terms, ad infinitum. The higher the level and more abstract a specific psychological concept is, the more open-ended it is. In behaviorism (Hillner, 1984), concepts such as stimulus and response that constitute the primary metaphysical units of analysis possess virtually infinite interpretive possibilities. In humanism (Hillner, 1984), a concept such as the self or self-actualization is infinitely descriptive.

Creators of models of psychological reality make no serious attempt at universality and exhaustiveness. Rather, a specific situation or process is focused on arbitrarily, raised to a hallowed status, assumed to be the key aspect of psychological reality, treated as the most representative psycho-

logical phenomenon, and used as a "model" for the
rest of the psychological universe. For descriptive
behaviorism (Watson, 1916; Skinner, 1953), learning
in general and conditioning in particular serve as
the "model" for the rest of the psychological universe. Many versions of humanism (see Rogers, 1961)
regard "flowering" or growth as the key aspect of
psychological reality. Depth psychology (Munroe,
1955) especially is famous for getting an excessive
amount of mileage from a few key constructs. Freud
(1939, 1949) is accused of reducing everything to
sex, Adler (1959) to a striving for superiority, and
Horney (1950) to a basic anxiety. Cognitive behaviorism (Lindsay and Norman, 1977) uses the computer as the basic metaphor for every significant
aspect of the psychological universe.

     The fact that the psychologist must deal with a
potentially infinite domain helps to maintain the
provinciality of the discipline, explains why any
model of psychological reality can only be an approximation, and should lead to a cautious attitude
on the part of any potential detractor of a given
system of psychology.

     MODELS AS ALL-OR-NONE PACKAGES The substance
of a model of psychological reality can be viewed
from either of two perspectives: (1) a model is a
consistent, coherent _metaphysical_ interpretation of
the subject matter, units of analysis, methodology,
locus of causation, and explanatory entities of psychology; or (2) a model is an _epistemological_ combination of data, fact, methodology, and theory.

     In the context of either view, many psycholo-
gists implicitly assume that the existential sub-

components of a model constitute independently ad-
dressable entities. For instance, subject matter
and locus of causation are independent; data and
theory are independent. But such is not the case.
The components of a model, whether metaphysical or
epistemological in nature, are mutually interdependent and codetermined entities. Subject matter and
locus of causation never constitute independent
items of observation. No fact is independent of
data; no datum is independent of methodology; no
methodology is independent of theory.

The components of a model comprise an indivisible whole; the substance of a model constitutes an
all-or-none package. Our analysis must take cognizance of the interrelationship of all the components
of a model.

CHANGE IMPERATIVE A model of psychological
reality must allow for the possibility of change,
either in a descriptive, mechanical sense or in a
normative, ethical sense. A system of psychology
must assume that the relevant psychological aspects
of the organism are malleable, whatever they may be.
Granted that the various models of the psychological
universe postulated over the past one hundred years
bear differing degrees of approximation and commitment to this imperative, no system postulates a psychological reality that excludes any kind or degree
of change. If the psychological state of the organism were immutable, psychology would be irrelevant
and have no metaphysical reason for being.

The descriptive imperative to change encompasses the operational change mechanisms comprising the
content of a given model of psychological reality.

The normative imperative to change is related to the
explicit end goals of the model. Although there is
no hard and fast division between these two kinds of
change principles, the descriptive one is more related to and justifies academic, experimental psychology, while the normative one is more related to
and justifies applied, professional psychology. The
change imperative motivates everything from the development of a new form of therapy to philosophical
speculation about the nature of Utopia.

The normative change principle is more comprehensive than the descriptive change principle, because it implies the existence of an ought, in addition to the existence of an is. It implies that an
ideal psychological reality exists that is not only
worthwhile, but also attainable. The trend in the
more recently developed systems of psychology, such
as latter-day depth psychology (Rapaport, 1959), humanism (Rogers, 1961), and dialectical psychology
(Riegel, 1979), is toward a more explicit recognition of and emphasis on the normative change principle.

Although the initial philosophical input into
psychology related to the nature of the human mind
in the context of structuralism (Hillner, 1984), the
continued relevance of philosophy for psychology relates more directly to principles of action and the
change imperative (Wheeler, 1973): to what degree
should the organism be controlled; what constitute
ethical forms of psychological intervention; what
constitutes the content of ideal end-states; or is
the use of punishment and other aversive techniques
ever justifiable?

The change imperative is relevant for an analysis of the task of constructing psychological reality because it constitutes one of the nonpsychological dimensions on which the viability of a given
model can be judged. The success rate of the specific form of the change principle embodied by a
model of psychological reality can be objectively
evaluated.

PSYCHOLOGY AS A COMPONENT OF THE ECONOMIC SYS-
TEM One of the most commonly overlooked aspects of
the task of constructing a model of psychological
reality is the fact that both the construction process itself and the resulting model must bear a
meaningful relationship to the physical means of
production currently characteristic of a given society and culture. Psychology could not exist as an
independent discipline unless it operated as a component of the economy of a given society/culture.
This fact can be stated in various ways:

1. Psychology must serve as a source of livelihood.

2. Psychology must contribute to the vast store
of capital accumulated by a given society/culture,
even if it is only symbolic and intellectual in nature.

3. A psychological transaction must possess
some economic value.

4. A psychological service must be exchangeable
for money or some other commodity of economic value.

Experimental psychology is possible because
society both supports institutions of higher learning that accumulate vast stores of symbolic capital
and encourages knowledge acquisition and transmis-

sion as a profession.   Applied psychology is possible only because society is willing to put an economic value on a psychological transaction or an
exchange value on a psychological service.

CONCEPTUAL SUMMARY   The seven assumptions in-
puting into our conceptual analysis of the task of
constructing a model of psychological reality can be
briefly summarized, as follows:

1. Psychology comprises one type of human knowledge and serves as one possible conceptual approach
to organizing human experience.   Unlike the case of
the physical scientist, the psychologist has the
choice of modeling psychological reality from an objective orientation or from a subjective orientation.

2. Psychology is a central part of our symbolic
life, and a model of psychology is both physically
realized and constrained by the language function.
This fact has a general leavening effect on the content of psychology.

3. The provinciality of psychology is due, in
large part, to the fact that the postulation of a
given system of psychology does not generate an
evaluation technique that is independent of the assumptions and content of the model of psychological
reality proposed by the system.   Any possible evaluation of the many different models of psychological
reality must be conducted on a nonpsychological
basis.

4. The domain of psychology is infinite, such
that models of psychological reality must employ
generic constructs.   The modeling of an infinite
psychological universe is usually accomplished by

"modeling" the model of psychological reality in terms of some presumably highly representative psychological phenomenon.

5. A model of psychological reality constitutes an indivisible whole, either at the metaphysical or epistemological level, in the sense that its components are mutually interdependent and codetermined.

6. A model of psychological reality must entail the change imperative, either at the descriptive or normative level. An immutable psychological universe would be vacuous at a metaphysical level.

7. Both the process of constructing a model of psychological reality and the resulting model itself must bear a meaningful relationship to the physical means of production characteristic of a given society or culture. At a more general level, psychology must be a viable component of the economic system.

BOUNDARY CONDITIONS

The four boundary conditions can be denoted as (1) Western psychology, (2) classical and contemporary models, (3) models as possible paradigms, and (4) psychological subspecialties and processes. These entities respectively establish (1) spatial, (2) temporal, (3) conceptual, and (4) constitutive constraints on the domain of our analysis. It will soon become apparent that the first two constraints specify what is included in the analysis and the last two indicate what is excluded.

WESTERN PSYCHOLOGY Our analysis will be strictly limited to attempts at modeling psychological reality arising in the context of the Western European or American intellectual tradition (Bronowski and Mazlish, 1960). The primary feature of this type of psychology is its empirical base and treatment of the human organism as a real-space and real-time entity.

What is explicitly excluded from the analysis by this boundary condition is various Eastern or Oriental psychologies that have a strong theological flavor and contain many mystical and revelational components (Akhilananda, 1953; Suzuki, 1956).

CLASSICAL AND CONTEMPORARY MODELS   The history of academic psychology is commonly subdivided into two phases: (1) the era of the classical schools (1880-1930) and (2) the post 1930 contemporary system era (Hillner, 1984).   Classical schools of academic psychology include the many variants of structuralism, functionalism, Gestalt psychology, and classical behaviorism.   Examples of contemporary systems include the many variants of post Watsonian behaviorism, latter-day functionalism, humanism, existential psychology, and dialectical psychology. Freudian psychology, the classic psychoanalytic approach, is missing from this dichotomy because it is a nonacademic system that transcends the two historical phases.   Although orthodox Freudian psychoanalysis still has many adherents, it has given rise to newer forms of depth psychology, as promulgated by both neo-Freudians and anti-Freudians, such as Adler and Jung.

The classical schools constitute part of the historical and contextual background of contemporary psychology.   Significant and interesting differences exist between a classical school and a contemporary system (see Chapter 2).   Our analysis cannot be limited to the contemporary systems.

Freudian psychoanalysis, as the canonical form
of depth psychology, must be included in the analysis and will be treated as a contemporary system in
Chapter 5. Other versions of depth psychology will
be referred to only where relevant.

MODELS AS POSSIBLE PARADIGMS In order to prevent the analysis from becoming a case study in the
philosophy of science, we are not going to be concerned with Thomas Kuhn's (1970) paradigmatic view
of the evolution of science and its possible application to psychology. Although it is popular currently to treat the classical schools as preparadig-
matic in nature and then argue about whether any
contemporary system has achieved the status of a
paradigm, we are not going to consider the issue,
for two basic reasons:

1. The notion of a paradigm is indigenous to
sciences that model physical reality, such as physics, chemistry, and astronomy. The relevance of its
application to psychology is tenuous at best.

2. Consideration of the paradigm issue would in
no way clarify our analysis of the task of constructing a model of psychological reality. In fact, it
would force us to introduce some assumptions that
detract from the goal of illuminating the model construction process.

In sum, attempting to account for the pluralistic nature of contemporary psychology in terms of
Kuhn's conception of science is not germane to our
analysis.

PSYCHOLOGICAL SUBSPECIALTIES AND PROCESSES The
structure of psychology, both as an academic and
professional discipline, is usually abstracted in

terms of subspecialties: for instance, perceptual
psychologist, learning psychologist, clinical psychologist, and industrial psychologist (Harré and
Lamb, 1983). Also, the content of psychology, as an
academic curriculum, is usually abstracted in terms
of various processes, such as perception, learning,
motivation, and development (Harré and Lamb, 1983).
These subspecialties bear differing relationships to
the various models of psychological reality, and one
or more of the basic set of psychological processes
constitutes a necessary component of every model of
psychological reality. But our analytical focus
will not be on the subspecialties and processes per
se, such that the substantive content areas of psychology do not constitute units of analysis. They
only are referred to where necessary for illuminating the current model under consideration.

        CONCEPTUAL SUMMARY The four boundary condi-
tions constricting the domain of our analysis of
the task of constructing a model of psychological
reality establish the classical and contemporary
systems of Western psychology as focal points of interest, exclude Eastern or Oriental psychology and
the paradigm issue from any consideration, and reduce the substantive psychological content areas to
ancillary phenomena.

CHAPTER 2

DOING PSYCHOLOGY

The human organism is confronted with certain natural
phenomena that it attempts to understand. Certainly
since at least the mid nineteenth century, the scientific approach has served as the preferred mode of
understanding. But the various physical, biological,
and social sciences merely cross-classify the same
phenomena from different perspectives. The unique or
indigenously characteristic property of a given natural event is not an absolute property residing in
the event; it merely is an abstraction relative to
the particular conceptual scheme used to analyze and
classify the event.

In this context, practically everyone claims
they know what the term "psychological" means and can
recognize instances of psychological events when they
occur. Yet it is impossible to give a technical
specification to psychological phenomena that would
be acceptable to every professional psychologist.
The unique or indigenously characteristic property of
a psychological event is a philosophical question,
not admissable to final resolution.

Psychology, as we know it today, began once explicit models of psychological reality were developed
under the impetus of a materialistic or mechanistic
conception of the universe, in which the psychologi-

cal aspects of organisms were assumed amenable to
scientific analysis. Constructing an explicit model
of psychological reality (doing psychology) is both
a rational and arbitrary endeavor, such that it must
be viewed as a philosophical exercise. The construction process is rational in the sense that it
is reducible to a number of discrete decisions. It
is arbitrary in the sense that any one psychologist's decisions involve all sorts of subjective and
idiosyncratic considerations. It is a philosophical
exercise because doing psychology is nothing if not
an applied philosophy: The process of constructing
a model of the psychological universe is the process
of creating a psychological reality. Any system of
psychology is a combined epistemological and metaphysical, or ontological, statement about the nature
of psychological reality.

    The purpose of this chapter is two-fold: (1) to
analyze just what decisions are involved in doing
psychology, i.e., constructing psychological reality, and (2) to present three additional assumptions
germane to our analysis. The discussion serves a
transitional function, bridging the gap between the
input assumptions covered in Chapter 1 and the actual derivation of the dominant models of psychological reality accomplished in Chapter 3.

DECISIONS INVOLVED IN CONSTRUCTING A MODEL OF PSY-
CHOLOGICAL REALITY

    The creator of a model of psychological reality
must make decisions concerning at least eight separate matters: (1) nature of the human being, (2) the
mind-body problem, (3) goal or purpose, (4) content
of observation, (5) methodology, (6) standards

and/or form of explanation, (7) the notion of a key
psychological process or mechanism, and (8) the notion of a prototypical psychological situation or
activity.

The first two matters primarily are philosophical in nature. The question of goal or purpose
possesses both philosophical and procedural aspects.
The content of observation is a multifaceted issue,
but will be classified here, along with methodology,
as primarily being procedural in nature. Explanation has both philosophical and procedural aspects.
The final two matters are indigenously psychological
in nature and determine, in large part, the content
psychology associated with a given system.

NATURE OF THE HUMAN BEING The construction of
a model of psychological reality is only relevant in
the context of certain views of the human organism;
also specific views dictate what the crucial components of the psychological universe will be. When
the human is considered to be part of the natural
universe and another type of animal, psychological
reality usually is modeled after and continuous with
physical reality. When consciousness, or self-
awareness, is assumed to be a human's defining characteristic, psychological reality tends to take on
the trappings of a theological reality. Whether the
human is primarily conceived as an epistemological,
experiencing, irrational, or action oriented organism can determine the focus of a given psychological
system. Most recently, the realization that the female is not just a surrogate or less powerful male
has altered psychological reality (Nicholson, 1984).

The nature of the human being is considered as

a philosophical issue and is related to the dominant
classical and contemporary systems of psychology in
Chapter 6.

THE MIND-BODY PROBLEM The mind-body problem
bears a unique relationship to psychology. It
serves as both an impetus and a hindrance to the
construction of a psychological reality. Psychology's two fundamental, metaphysical categories--ex-
perience and behavior--derive from the mind-body dichotomy. The mind-body problem presumably even can
be resolved in the context of psychology, while it
cannot be at a strictly philosophical level. Many
contemporary psychologists (see Marx and Hillix,
1979) claim that they "do psychology" without reference at all to the mind-body issue; however, this
is only true in the superficial sense that the mind
is no longer conceived as a strange, mysterious,
noncorporeal entity diffused throughout the body.

The mind-body issue and its relevance for psychology are treated in Chapters 6 and 7.

GOAL OR PURPOSE The goal or purpose of a psychological system is an amorphous, but vital, notion. Rarely does a psychologist have a specific
goal in mind when postulating a system of psychology, beyond that of intellectual edification or con-
solidation (Robinson, 1979). But the fact remains
that there is a mutual, two-way relationship between the goal and content of a system. A predetermined goal can determine content; a specific content
affords only certain goals.

A thorough analysis of the possible goals of a
psychological system is beyond the bounds of our
analysis, but the goals of the dominant classical

and contemporary systems are implicitly covered in
Chapters 4 and 5.

CONTENT OF OBSERVATION For our purposes, this
is the most crucial of the eight decisions that have
to be made when constructing a model of psychological reality. This is the case for three reasons:
(1) it is related to or determines the type of orientation that a psychologist uses for constructing
psychological reality, (2) it is used as a critical
classificatory dimension in Chapter 3 to formally
derive the dominant classical schools and contemporary systems of psychology, and (3) it is employed in
both Chapters 4 and 5 as a convenient dimension for
comparing the various classical schools and contemporary systems.

The content of observation is the primary factor determining the nature of the psychological universe for a professional psychologist. It determines whether the psychological world is objective
(universal) or subjective (unique), physical or nonphysical, reducible or emergent, conscious or unconscious, given or derived, dialectical or nondialectical, and so forth. A credible analysis of the
task of constructing a model of psychological reality even could be conducted by using this feature a-
lone.

The notion of a content of observation derives
from the fact that psychology is one way of conceptualizing and organizing an organism's conscious experience, as discussed in Chapter 1. Psychological
reality must be imposed on the content of certain
observations that an organism makes and the inferences that can be made from these observations.

The content of observation is assumed to involve a two-term relationship; namely, that between
(1) basic object of study and (2) locus of psychological causation. The concept of a model as an
all-or-none package, discussed in Chapter 1, established the fact that the object of study and locus
of causation are not independent existential entities. The creator of a psychological system does
not rationally select a given object of study and
then separately select its most appropriate locus of
causation. This situation is formalized in our a-
nalysis by making them indivisible components of a
content of observation.

In many systems, such as descriptive behaviorism (Watson, 1913; Skinner, 1938, 1953), the content
of observation entails an input-output relation,
where the output is the phenomena of immediate interest, usually overt behavior, and the input is its
cause, usually assumed to be some physical, environmental event. In those systems where the locus of
causation and object of study do not constitute a
traditional input-output relation, either the locus
of causation is inferred from the object of study
(as in humanism {Rogers, 1951} where the organism's
psychological world is inferred from its conscious
experience) or the locus of causation is the basic
object of study (as in cognitive behaviorism {Solso,
1979} where the focus is on the mental determinants
of overt behavior).

The content of observation serves the same
function in our analysis as units of analysis do in
other analyses. But the phrase "units of analysis"
does not connote the experiential source of psycho-

logical phenomena and only is relevant for objective, experimental systems: its use is artificial in
the context of a subjective, phenomenologically
based psychology.

Our use of a content of observation also absorbs the traditional concept of object of study.
The phrase "object of study" simply is not precise
enough once one goes beyond the gross distinction
between conscious experience and behavior. A content of observation includes both direct objects of
study (behavior) and indirect objects of study (mental processes, cognitive events, and the like).

To illustrate the fact that the choice of a
specific content of observation has tremendous ram-
ifications for other aspects of a system, we can
appeal to (1) the free will-determinism issue and
(2) methodology.

1. Selecting an input-output relation as the
content of observation requires the adoption of
some form of determinism; selecting a person's psychological world, as revealed by the content of conscious experience, as the content of observation requires a belief in free will or at least in the possibility of self-generated changes in behavior.

2. The matter of permissible methodology merely
is a conceptual/logical extension of that of content
of observation: observations and inferences must be
made under certain conditions and only under certain conditions.

METHODOLOGY Methodology subsumes the proper
route to psychological truth. The creator of a system must proclaim, defend, and use specific methodology. Wundt (1883) advocated direct, critical in-

trospection. Gestaltists (Wertheimer, 1922; Koffka,
1935, 1963; Köhler, 1929, 1947) favored a freewheeling phenomenology. Watson (1916) raised the classical conditioning technique to hallowed status.
Skinner (1938) considers the Skinner box to be the
only valid psychological environment. Freud (1900)
used free association and dream analysis.

Historically, methodology contributed to the
pluralistic state of psychology as much as any other
factor. It was a critical metaphysical battleground
during the classical school era. Psychologists simply refused to accept as valid psychological truth
any "facts" generated by the techniques used by other systems of psychology. Methodology is less critical an issue today, but only because it has evolved
into its own subspecialty: psychologists exist whose
expertise is not in a given subarea of content psychology, such as learning or perception, but resides
in experimental design and statistical analysis.

Methodology functions as a microcosm of the
macrocosm because it is the context in which all the
other aspects of a system coalesce. Any situation
in which data is generated, such as an experiment,
is a miniature representation of the totality of a
given system. It is the specific arena in which a
psychologist is "doing psychology" in the procedural
sense of the term.

Chapters 4 and 5 will implicitly cover the specific methodologies associated with the models of
psychological reality derived in Chapter 3.

EXPLANATION Explanation specifies the ultimate
source of the psychological phenomena of interest
for a given system and usually amounts to the at-

tempt to resolve the nature of a psychological event
by reference to some higher order level of analysis.
The most prevalent form of explanation in psychology
is that of theory (Robert Brown, 1970). Any system
of psychology subsumes theory, but the theory is
distinct from the system itself. Rarely does a model of psychological reality dictate a specific theory; it merely establishes criteria for acceptable
theory. The theoretical level of any system is crucial because it is the specific aspect of the system
that attempts to represent the internal dynamics of
the psychological reality postulated by the system.
This is particularly true when a psychologist redefines psychological reality for the explicit purpose
of designing better theory.

     As we shall see in Chapter 8, the notion of ex-
planation is developed most fully in those systems
that regard psychology to be a science, because such
systems make no distinction between physical reality
and psychological reality.

     KEY PSYCHOLOGICAL PROCESSES OR MECHANISMS   The
total number of psychological processes or mechanisms is potentially infinite. At a conceptual level, this is no problem. It merely reflects the infinite domain of the psychological universe and testifies to the psychologist's high level of creativity in designing various psychological systems. At
a pragmatic level, however, infinity is a problem.
No psychologist can give equal weight to every possible psychological process or mechanism. Every
system of psychology emphasizes certain processes/
mechanisms to the exclusion of others. The emphasized ones constitute the primary entities respon-

sible for psychological adjustment and change in the
system.

Each system of psychology possesses a distinctive "psychological flavor" or psychodynamics. The
descriptive behaviorist Skinner (1969) reduces everything to reinforcement contingencies. Personality theorists, such as Allport (1955, 1966), emphasize structural traits. Freudian depth psychologists (see Munroe, 1955) resolve behavior in terms
of an internal psychic world seething with instinctual strivings and culturally based prohibitions. A
humanist, such as Maslow (1971) or Rogers (1961),
advocates the flowering of the individual psyche
(self) in the absence of as many externally sourced
psychological constraints as possible.

Psychological relativism with respect to key
processes or mechanisms naturally breeds psychological pluralism. Key processes get wedded to goals,
methodology, and preferred explanatory entities and
become inextricable components of the system. The
psychodynamics associated with a system become part
of the conceptual sunglasses through which an advocate of the system views the world. It colors and
gives "substantive content" to the characteristic
content of observation used by the system. All that
a Skinnerian can "see" are environmental contingencies; all that a Freudian can "see" are unconscious
conflicts and strivings.

The psychodynamics of a system cannot be altered without running the risk of system destruction
because it essentially constitutes the psychological
substance of the system. This is especially true
for nonexperimental systems, such as depth psycholo-

gy and humanistic or phenomenological psychology, in
which no pretense is made with respect to independent, external validation of psychological truth.
Refocusing of the critical psychological mechanisms
in depth psychology amounts to heresy, while refocusing in a version of experimentally oriented behaviorism merely constitutes a refinement.

It is primarily at the level of psychodynamics
that the various systems of psychology cannot be in-
terpenetrated; that is, judged by a truly impartial,
external, evaluative criterion. Psychodynamics is
judged in terms of insular goals, which in turn are
implicitly evaluated by social and cultural atti-
tudes, which are philosophically analyzed in turn in
a never ending cycle. Various approaches to psychodynamics wax and wane as ineluctable components of
an ever changing cultural milieu. They do not un-
fold on a linearly accumulating route to absolute
truth. For instance, cognitive psychology is "in,"
then "out," then "in" again; certain skills are
treated as educable, not educable, then educable
again; the nativistic and empiristic approaches to
perception alternate in degree of acceptability;
consciousness is alternately regarded as causative
and epiphenomenal in a never ending cycle.

Chapters 4 and 5 will tap the psychodynamic aspects of psychological reality in a reasonable a-
mount of depth.

PROTOTYPICAL PSYCHOLOGICAL SITUATION/ACTIVITY
One of the most frustrating aspects of constructing
a model of psychological reality is the fact that
the resulting system must focus on only one potential element of the psychological universe. Liter-

ally an infinite number of psychological situations
or activities exist. One of them must be chosen as
the prototypical, or most representative, case. This
in turn is used to model the rest of the population
of situations/activities.

     The choice of a prototypical situation/activity
is related more to the goal of a system than to any
other aspect of the system. The operant situation
slowly evolved in Skinner's (1956) hands because he
prized behavioral control. The notion of a standard
psychoanalytic therapy session developed because
Freud was engaged in helping hysterical patients
(Breuer and Freud, 1895). The Gestaltists (Wertheimer, 1912; Koffka, 1922; Köhler, 1920) focused on
the phi phenomenon and other perceptual phenomena
demonstrating immanent organization because they reacted in a phenomenal fashion to the structuralist
program of analysis and synthesis (Wundt, 1896;
Titchener, 1898). Humanism (see Keen, 1975) focuses
on individual self-awareness because it attempts to
recapture the uniqueness and inviolability of the
individual. When mathematical modeling was applied
to psychology in a meaningful way for the first
time, in the early 1950s, learning (especially probability learning and paired-associate learning) constituted the prototypical situation simply because
these activities afforded stable, predictable, discretely probabilistic data (see Bush and Mosteller,
1951, 1955; Estes, 1950).

     Because the prototypical situation/activity
provides the basic reference point of every system,
it guarantees the continued pluralism of psychology.
No psychologist has ever attempted to design a sys-

tem accommodating all the individual reference points
used by other extant systems. The task would be impossible. What is possible in many cases is a transcription of the reference point of one system into
the terminology and concepts of another system. But
advocates of the original system do not accept the
transcription. For instance, Skinner (1957, 1974)
redefines self-awareness as tacting responses about
tacting responses; but no humanist accepts this.
Conversely, a Rogerian wants to translate Skinner's
concept of response-contingent positive reinforcement
into the noncontingent delivery of unconditional positive regard; but a Skinnerian regards this as folly
(Rogers, 1956). A dialectical psychologist, such as
Riegel (1978, 1979), attempts to combine behaviorism
and humanism by treating the subject-experimenter relationship as an emergent unit of analysis; but this
violates the sensibilities of both the humanist and
behaviorist.

There will be more about prototypical situa-
tions/activities in Chapters 4 and 5.

CONCEPTUAL SUMMARY Although the construction
of a model of psychological reality is relatable to
a series of decisions with respect to eight distinct
dimensions, the resulting system is an all-or-none
package with three inevitable properties that contribute to psychology's pluralistic state:

1. It is distinctly a human product, subject to
human limitations and idiosyncrasies.

2. It is a constrained, finite effort, sampling
only a small portion of the potential psychological
universe.

3. It is an insular epistemological and meta-

physical entity, impervious to impartial, external
validation.

THREE ADDITIONAL ASSUMPTIONS GERMANE TO OUR ANALYSIS

These assumptions relate to (1) the proper interpretation of the objective-subjective distinction, (2) the choice of appropriate entities for
comparing the models of psychological reality to be
derived in Chapter 3, and (3) how much importance
should be attached to the distinction between a classical school and a contemporary system.

OBJECTIVITY VERSUS SUBJECTIVITY Individual psychologists differ on many interpretive dimensions.
Perhaps the most basic one is overall orientation:
objective versus subjective. A descriptive behaviorist constitutes the prototypical example of an
objectively oriented psychologist, while a phenomenological or humanistic psychologist serves as the
purest realization of a subjectively oriented psychologist.

One of the fundamental assumptions of our approach to the analysis of the task of constructing
a model of psychological reality will be that objectivity and subjectivity merely constitute convenient
descriptive and classificatory labels, not absolute
categories of existence. In principle, descriptive
behaviorism is just as subjective as humanism; and
humanism can attain a level of objectivity that is
putatively only characteristic of behaviorism, once
the realistic limits of the resolvability of behaviorism are taken into account.

This assumption is in accord with current views
in the philosophy of knowledge and of science (Polyani, 1958). More importantly, it is an extension

of the fact that a given model of psychological reality constitutes an all-or-none package that not
only defines the nature of the psychological universe
but also specifies the methodological and explanatory
standards by which it is judged.

Our analysis presumes that the process of constructing a so-called objective system of psychology
or a so-called subjective system of psychology is
fundamentally the same. Both objectivity and subjectivity, as traditionally defined, are involved in the
different stages of model construction, regardless
of the nature of the model. One consequence of this
assumption is that no value judgment can be made a-
bout the appropriateness of a given model of psychological reality based on its traditional classification as an objective or subjective system. Scientific, experimental systems are not inherently preferable over humanistic systems, nor are phenomenological systems inherently preferable over mechanistic systems.

APPROPRIATE COMPARATIVE ENTITIES Chapters 4
and 5 will require some basic dimensions on which to
compare the various models of psychological reality
derived by our analysis. Since our primary aim is
to describe how psychology is constructed in the context of each of these schools/systems, the comparison can be most incisively accomplished by focusing
on (1) the content of observation, as a combination
of object of study and locus of psychological determination, and (2) some reference psychological situa-
tion/activity. Because the concept of content of
observation already has been discussed, only the notion of a reference psychological situation/activity

need be elaborated here.

REFERENCE PSYCHOLOGICAL SITUATION/ACTIVITY

Let us assume that the "act of doing something" constitutes a reasonable interpretation of the notion
of a reference psychological situation/activity.
Doing something entails all the commonplace, everyday activities people take for granted: going to the
movies, eating a meal, studying for an exam, writing
a poem, talking on the phone, planning a party, playing a game, building a house, making love, and the
like.

Do not confuse the reference psychological sit-
uation/activity with the notion of a prototypical
psychological situation/activity, as discussed previously in the chapter. As will become apparent
later, only in an action system, such as Watsonian
or Skinnerian behaviorism, does the reference activity correspond to the prototypical activity; that is,
the act of doing something serves as the prototypical psychological situation for modeling the rest of
the psychological universe (Hillner, 1984).

The substance of the reference act of doing
something cannot be stated in technical language that
is model-free. Doing something can be variously described as (1) a goal directed response (Tolman,
1932), (2) behavior under the control of some environmental contingency (Skinner, 1969), (3) an intentional act (Giorgi, 1970; Rychlak, 1977), (4) rule
governed behavior (Miller, Galanter, and Pribram,
1960), (5) stimulus directed behavior (Guthrie,
1935), (6) an adaptive act (Carr, 1925), (7) holistic, molar activity (Koffka, 1935, 1963), or (8) a
functional response with consequences (Skinner,

DOING PSYCHOLOGY   37

1938, 1953).

What is connoted by all these descriptions is
the fact that a transaction occurs between a person
and the environment (or another organism), whereby
the environment changes or the person obtains something. Doing something is an existential event that
possesses meaning for its performer and possibly also
for an observer of the event. What is explicitly excluded by all these descriptions is the notion of a
reflex: pure physiological activity that is accorded
behavioral status by some systems of psychology,
primarily behavioristic ones (Hillner, 1984).

THE CLASSICAL SCHOOL-CONTEMPORARY SYSTEM DIS-
TINCTION As a model of psychological reality, a
classical school and a contemporary system differ on
at least three significant dimensions.

1. The classical schools could be meaningfully
differentiated in terms of their respective object
of study specifications and permissible methodology
dicta: conscious experience and behavior constituted
distinct metaphysical categories, and methodology
served as a crucial metaphysical battleground. Contemporary systems cannot meaningfully be differentiated in terms of object of study or methodology: conscious experience and behavior merely are semantic
(linguistic) distinctions, and methodology is now a
technical subspecialty. Current systems of psychology are most meaningfully distinguished in terms of
their respective goals or purposes.

2. Theorization during the classical school era
was quite primitive according to contemporary standards and amounted to general philosophical orienting principles. Contemporary theories are virtual

blueprints of how a specific psychological phenomenon is produced.

3. The classical schools were definitively pre-
paradigmatic in nature. The status of contemporary
systems in Kuhn's (1970) model is currently unresolved.

How important are these differences for our
analysis of the task of constructing a model of psychological reality? Interpretive status in Kuhn's
(1970) model of science does not apply because of
the third boundary condition specified in Chapter 1.
The other two differences involve the status of four
of the decisions faced by the creator of a system:
content of observation (recall that object of study
is a component of the content of observation),
methodology, explanation, and goals. Because significant shifts have occurred in the relative importance of some of the factors involved in system construction, a consideration of the classical schools
certainly can contribute to an understanding of the
pluralism of contemporary psychology.

THE DIFFERENCES IN PERSPECTIVE Classical
schools and contemporary systems differ for two basic reasons: (1) the status of psychology in society
has changed, and (2) the focus of the creative energy of the discipline has changed.

1. The ultimate task of the classical schools
was to establish psychology as an accepted intellectual discipline with legitimate subject matter
and appropriate investigatory techniques. That is
why they fought so bitterly over object of study and
methodology. Contemporary systems no longer face
this task: the discipline of psychology has been ac-

cepted as a component of intellectual life. Contemporary psychology faces the problem of determining
what kind of model would be most useful for people
and society in an instrumental sense. That is why
contemporary systems fight over the possible uses of
psychology, the relevance of psychology to society,
and various professional problems--all derivative of
and reflected in the current importance of the goal
dimension.

2. Classical schools flourished during the "gee
whiz" days of psychology. Psychologists merely were
concerned with the initial staking out of the psychological universe: they were occupied with determining what could be observed, quantified, and studied as psychological phenomena. For instance, it
was perfectly acceptable activity on the part of a
psychologist simply to put a rat in a complex multi-
unit maze to see what would happen and perhaps even
to introspect about what was going on in the rat's
mind (see Small, 1901). In this kind of atmosphere,
creative energy was focused exclusively on system
construction and justification; it was much too
early to be concerned with detailed theories for
specific psychological phenomena.

Contemporary systems no longer are occupied
with staking out the psychological universe: they
are concerned with detailed mapping of the internal
dynamics of a given psychological reality. Creative
energy primarily is channeled into theory construction and validation. Simply exposing an organism to
a new kind of apparatus to see what would happen is
considered frivolous today. At best, a rat would be
placed in a very simple maze and then only if its

behavior were expected to reveal some detailed aspect of an underlying physiologically based or mathematically encoded psychological mechanism (see
Deutsch, 1971; Bower, 1959). Doing psychology is
still fun, but it is the fun of the cartographer or
codifier; it no longer is the fun of the explorer or
surveyor.

CHAPTER 3

POSSIBLE PSYCHOLOGICAL UNIVERSES

The purpose of this chapter is to derive the major classical and contemporary models of psychological reality by postulating the existence of a psychological space, consisting of the possible components of the psychological universe, on which the various systems can be mapped. Our aim is to demonstrate the plausibility of the conceptual plurality of contemporary psychology. In-depth analysis of the derived classical schools and contemporary systems will not occur until the next two chapters.

It should be stressed immediately that the specific approach taken to deriving these models represents only one of many possible approaches and is explicitly designed to generate only one aspect of a model: its content of observation. Recall from Chapter 2 that the notion of a content of observation is assumed to involve a two-term relationship: a combination of (1) basic object of study and (2) locus of psychological causation.

Our derivation of the major systems of psychology consists of two phases: (1) an initial sketch of the possible structural components of the psychological universe (a description of our psychological space), and (2) a mapping of the systems onto the psychological space (derivation of the various models

of psychological reality by dividing the psychological space into separate domains). In terms of the
structure of our overall analysis, the psychological
space constitutes input; and the derivational mapping of the systems amounts to output.

THE PSYCHOLOGICAL SPACE

     The psychological space is depicted in Figure
3-1 as a 2 × 2 table, with four separate quadrants,
and is based on two assumptions.

     ASSUMPTION ONE The psychological universe is
composed of only three possible real-time and real-
space entities: the self, one or more significant
other, and the physical environment. The self and
significant other appear as circles on the figure
and help carve out two separate regions of the psychological space: the area above the bisecting hor-
izontal line subsumes phenomena associated with the
self; the area below the line subsumes phenomena associated with the significant other.

     The environmental milieu in which both the self
and significant other exist is not conveniently rep-
resentable by the figure. The phrase "physical environment" does appear on the figure, in the lower
left quadrant; but this does not represent the physical environment as one of the three possible components of the psychological universe. The physical
environment could be construed as a third dimension
perpendicular to the self and significant other that
generates a sphere containing the self and significant other as internal points. Visualization of
such a sphere is left to the imagination of the
reader.

     ASSUMPTION TWO Psychological reality is im-

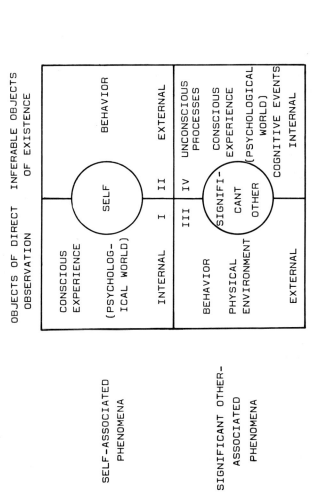

FIGURE 3-1 POSSIBLE STRUCTURAL COMPONENTS OF THE PSYCHOLOGICAL UNIVERSE

posed on the content of certain observations that an
organism makes and the inferences that can be made
from these observations. This assumption merely is
a linguistic extension of the fact that psychology
is one way of conceptualizing and organizing a human's conscious experience, as discussed in Chapter
1. The organism functioning as the observer and in-
ferrer in our psychological universe is the self,
not the significant other. These activities of the
self carve out two more regions of the psychological
space: the area on the left side of the vertical
line bisecting the self and significant other circles represents objects of direct observation; the
area on the right side of the line represents entities whose existence is only inferable from the objects of direct observation.

FOUR QUADRANTS The distinction between the
self and significant other and that between the
self's observing and inferring activities operate as
binary valued input dimensions. Orthogonal use of
these dimensions establishes a 2 x 2 table that div-
ides the psychological space into four separate
quadrants, as labeled on the figure by Roman numer-
als. The content of these four quadrants serves as
the potential contents of observation for the various models of psychological reality.

OBJECTS OF DIRECT OBSERVATION The descriptive
labels assigned to the objects of direct observation
in quadrants I and III is an arbitrary matter, but
one of great import. Psychologists traditionally
have been interested in two aspects of human experience: (1) conscious experience and (2) behavior
(Kendler, 1981). In other words, those aspects of

human experience that have been interpreted as being inherently psychological in nature usually are decoded as conscious experience and behavior. They constitute the fundamental metaphysical categories of psychology, and psychological reality must be constructed in terms of either or both of them.   It is reasonable to treat these two kinds of phenomena as the objects of direct observation, and the differential metaphysical properties of conscious experience and behavior are analyzed in Chapter 9.

Behavior and conscious experience bear differing relationships to the self as objects of direct observation. The self can directly observe the behavior of some significant other under normal circumstances. The self can only directly observe its own behavior under special circumstances: mirror, TV, film, and the like. Because of this, the self usually observes some ultimate product, or result, of its own behavior. The self can only directly observe its own conscious experience. Direct observation of the conscious experience of some significant other is impossible; at best it is a constructional entity inferred from the behavior of the significant other. These relationships are summarized in the figure by having conscious experience appear in quadrant I and behavior appear in quadrant III.

The physical environment also constitutes a potential object of direct observation for the self. Since this component of the psychological universe is not directly represented in the figure, the physical environment only appears as an object of direct observation in quadrant III.

INFERABLE OBJECTS The set of entities that

constitute inferable objects of existence in quadrants II and IV is indeterminate and open-ended.
Only some general examples need be given at this
point in our analysis. From the behavior of some
significant other, the existence of unconscious processes, conscious experience, or cognitive events
can be inferred. What is inferable from the content
of the conscious experience of the self constitutes
a problematical question. Somewhat arbitrarily, we
deem the self's current ongoing behavior, which is
not directly observable except under special circumstances, as an inferable object of existence.

INTERNALLY VERSUS EXTERNALLY RESOLVABLE PHENOM-
ENA. Note that the content of each quadrant is labeled internal or external in the figure. The content of quadrants I and IV is labeled internal. It
exists inside the self or significant other. Internal phenomena associated with the self are directly
observable; internal phenomena associated with the
significant other are only inferable. The content
of quadrants II and III is labeled external. It exists outside the self or significant other. External phenomena associated with the self usually are
only inferable; external phenomena associated with
the significant other are directly observable.

CRITICAL MAPPING ASSUMPTION So that the content of the four quadrants might serve as contents
of observation for various models of psychological
reality, a critical mapping assumption must be made
explicit. A model of psychological reality must refer to at least one of the objects of direct observation quadrants: I and III. A model can include
more than either of these quadrants, but the only

quadrants that can stand alone as the domains of
possible models are I and III.   This mapping assumption obviously derives from the fact that psychology
conceptualizes and organizes human experience.

DERIVATIONAL MAPPING

The major classical schools and contemporary
systems are easily represented by our psychological
space, if we use the notion of orientation as a mapping tool. Orientation refers to the specific manner in which a psychologist constructs psychological
reality. At least four types of orientation exist,
although only two of them have been emphasized in
the preceding chapters: (1) classic objective, (2)
classic subjective, (3) quasi-objective or mixed,
and (4) combined objective x subjective.

Each of these orientations specifies the domain
of psychology in terms of a different quadrant or
quadrant combination from our psychological space.
For each orientation, a different quadrant or quadrant combination exhausts psychological reality.
The content of a quadrant that is not used by an orientation still exists, but is not an aspect of psychology for that orientation. No orientation uses
all four quadrants to define the psychological universe, so no model of psychological reality can encompass all the possible components of our psychological space. Many different systems of psychology
are possible in the context of each type of orientation, enhancing the pluralism of contemporary psychology.

Each of the four types of orientation will be
briefly described in terms of its quadrant mapping,
content of observation, general features, and asso-

ciated psychological systems.

CLASSIC OBJECTIVE ORIENTATION Quadrant III exhausts the domain of psychology; psychological reality is defined solely in terms of the content of quadrant III. The content of observation is an input-
output relation, in which behavior of some significant other is the output and some physical, environmental event is the input. Both terms of the input-
output relation are objects of direct observation
and externally resolvable. The significant other
usually is called a subject. Since no inferences of
any kind are made, the subject can be an animal or
machine, as well as a human. The self, as observer,
is called an experimenter; but note that the self or
a self-surrogate is not a component of the psychological domain. The objective orientation seeks a
psychological reality independent of the consciousness of the self, as observer. Any sophisticated
measuring instrument can serve as a self-surrogate.
This approach to the construction of a psychological
reality mimics the way a physicist or chemist constructs a physical reality. Psychology is regarded
simply as another kind of science.

The classic objective orientation establishes
the notion of an action psychology, because the content of observation encompasses both overt behavior
and the presumed environmental events by which behavior is predicted and controlled. An action psychology is inherently practical and possesses indigenous social relevance. An action system often is
referred to as a descriptive system, because no reference is made to inferable, hypothetical entities.
The prototypical case of an action system is des-

criptive behaviorism, of which there are two primary
exemplars: (1) classical Watsonian behaviorism and
(2) contemporary Skinnerian behaviorism. Watson
(1913, 1925) formalized the objective approach to
psychology around 1912 in his "behaviorist manifesto." His brand of behaviorism dominated academic,
experimental psychology to approximately 1930.
Skinner (1938) inherited Watson's mantle during the
1930s, and the succeeding fifty years have seen his
radical behaviorism become the dominant form of
descriptive behaviorism. Skinner (1974) even considers his system to be a philosophy of the science
of behavior.

    CLASSIC SUBJECTIVE ORIENTATION Quadrant I ex-
hausts the domain of psychology; psychological reality is defined solely in terms of the content of quadrant I. The content of observation is some aspect
of the conscious experience or awareness of the
self, as observer, and the nature of the psychological world implicit in the self's verbal descriptions. Note that the notion of a psychological
world appears in parentheses in quadrant I. The
state of the self's consciousness and psychological
world is an internally resolvable event. Only the
self has direct access to it. This is the distinguishing feature of the subjective orientation. The
content of observation is not a publically observable, real-time and real-space event, subject to
external reliability and validity check. Ordinarily
this is no problem, because the reported psychological world need only have meaning for the observer.
This approach is empirical, as opposed to rationalistic; but it is not experimental in the usual sense

of the term.   The self is the subject, but is rarely
called such.   It is possible for a significant other,
or a significant other-surrogate, to operate as a recorder of the content of the self's observations;
but the significant other is not an experimenter or
an observer and is not a component of the psychological domain.   The self is the sole source and arbi-
ter of psychological reality in the subjective orientation.

        The classic subjective orientation has genera-
ted two types of psychology: (1) epistemological or
cognitive and (2) understanding or phenomenological.
The initial subjective systems were classical
schools of epistemological or cognitive psychology;
any contemporary subjective system is an understanding or phenomenological psychology.

        The classical schools encompassing this orien-
tation were Germanic in origin and included Wundt's
(1873-1874, 1896) and Titchener's (1898, 1901, 1905)
structuralism, Külpe's (1893) structuralism, Brentano's (1874) act psychology, and Wertheimer's
(1912), Koffka's (1935, 1963), and Köhler's (1929,
1947) Gestalt psychology (at least with respect to
perceptual consciousness).   Each of these systems
focused on the self's sensory and/or perceptual consciousness or the act of thinking.   These systems
are rarely classified as subjective in orientation,
because they all studied the universal mind; namely,
conscious processes that were supposed to be common
to all persons.   Structuralism even is regarded as
the first true exemplar of an experimental psychology.   But, in the context of our psychological space, they have to be classified as subjective because

the cognitive psychology inherent in the systems is
all based on self-report. The canonical methodological technique associated with each of these systems
was some form of introspection (see Boring, 1953).
Gestalt psychology is the only one of these systems
that possesses any significant contemporary residues.

The primary contemporary exemplar of the subjective orientation is the so-called third force
movement in psychology (Wertheimer, 1978): a loosely
formulated combination of humanism, existential psychology, and phenomenological psychology, begun under the aegis of Abraham Maslow (1962, 1968, 1971)
in the early 1960s. We can use the term humanistic
psychology to characterize the entire movement. Unlike the classical subjective systems, humanistic
psychology focuses on all aspects of the individual
human's experience. The human is treated as an e-
mergent phenomenon, discontinuous with other types
of organisms, and is regarded as a special type of
being. The humanist focuses on the individual organism's state of self-awareness and overall level
of adjustment to the environment. The basic aim of
humanistic psychology is the resolution of an organism's psychological being in terms of its view of
the world, and the only justification for activist
intervention is the increased psychological health
of the organism.

QUASI-OBJECTIVE OR MIXED ORIENTATION The combination of quadrants III and IV exhausts the domain
of psychology; psychological reality is defined solely in terms of the contents of quadrants III and IV.
The content of observation is the behavior of some
significant other and its presumed locus of causa-

tion. Behavior is externally resolvable and an object of direct observation; the locus of causation
is an inferred entity, whose existential reality level is internal. Interest in behavior is only incidental. It merely is a means for investigating the
true objects of concern, the internal psychological
determinants. Physical, environmental events are
still presumed to be causative; but they are subsidiary to the ultimate internal psychological determinants. The mixed orientation merely is an extension of the classic objective approach. Most of the
mixed systems are experimental in nature and differ
from descriptive behaviorism only in the willingness
to make inferences to unobservables. The self, as
observer, usually is an experimenter; the significant other usually is a subject; and the attempt is
made to construct a psychological reality independent of the consciousness of the observer.

The mixed orientation is the most popular approach to constructing a model of psychological reality and has given rise to a heterogeneous collection of systems:

1. contemporary epistemological or cognitive
psychology, such as cognitive behaviorism (based on
the computer analogy) (Lindsay and Norman, 1977) and
Piagetian or Chomskian epistemological psychology
(involving fixed developmental stages and various
logical capacities) (Piaget, 1953; Piaget and Inhelder, 1969; Chomsky, 1959, 1968);

2. the many versions of depth psychology, of
which Freudian psychoanalysis is the prototypical
case (Munroe, 1955; Freud, 1939, 1949);

3. the action oriented classical school of

functionalism that related behavior to the operations
of consciousness (Angell, 1904, 1907; Carr, 1925);

4. the many versions of action oriented logical
behaviorism (Mackenzie, 1977), such as the classical
learning psychologies of Hull (1943, 1951, 1952),
Guthrie (1935), and Tolman (1932).

Each of the above psychologies, except for the
Freudian approach, is indigenous to the academic environment. Freudian psychology originated in a context where the self, as observer, is a therapist and
the significant other is a patient. Freud constructed an elaborate psychodynamic system based on inductions from patients' physical and verbal activity exhibited during psychoanalytic sessions involving
free association.

It should be noted that both humanistic psychologists and Gestalt psychologists can operate in
the context of the mixed orientation. This occurs
for humanists when they induce the nature of the conscious awareness and psychological world _of_ _a_ _signi-
ficant_ _other_ from its overt behavior, including verbal description. Likewise for the Gestaltists when
they focus on the behavior _of_ _a_ _significant_ _other_
and induce the nature of the psychological environment in which it occurs.

COMBINED OBJECTIVE X SUBJECTIVE ORIENTATION
Quadrants I and III exhaust the domain of psychology; psychological reality is defined solely in terms
of the contents of quadrants I and III. In order to
map this orientation onto the psychological space,
one of our original assumptions must be modified.
No longer is it presumed that the self is the sole
observer, either of itself or the significant other.

Rather both the self and the significant other are assumed to be observers. The psychological domain consists of an interacting pair or dyad, each member of which is both a self and significant other concurrently. This approach is objective in the sense that it focuses on the externally resolvable behavior of a significant other; but it is also subjective because the observer of the significant other, the self, is a component of the psychological domain and can affect the contents of an observation. This approach also is subjective in another sense: either member of the dyad can engage in observation of its own conscious experience. The content of observation is behavior of the significant other as it occurs in an environmental milieu, tempered by the preconceptions of the self, as observer.

The closest approximation to the combined orientation in the context of contemporary psychology is Riegel's (1978, 1979) dialectical approach, which is a logical extension of Rubinstein's (Rubinshteyn) (1940) system. Rubinstein was a Russian psychologist who advocated various versions of dialectical psychology during his lifetime. Riegel presumably integrates the objective and subjective orientations by refusing to deal with the psychological subject (significant other) independently of the experimenter (self) and by refusing to deal with the environment (as a self-surrogate) independently of the psychological subject. Dialectical psychology presumes that a transactional relationship exists between the subject and experimenter in any psychological investigation, such that the subject and experimenter together constitute an irreducible, emergent unit of analysis. Psychological truth must be stated in terms of both parties to the transaction. The pro- totypical psychological situation for dialectical psychology is a dialogue between two organisms, either verbal or nonverbal; and the content of obser- vation is any meaningful description of the events occurring within the dialogue. Riegel's scheme am- ounts to a cognitively oriented developmental psy- chology, in which the individual organism is viewed as a point in a vast historical-cultural space. Both the individual organism and the historical-cul- tural milieu are assumed to mutually influence and change each other over time.

CONCEPTUAL SUMMARY By selective mapping of the psychological space, we have derived representations of the major historical and contemporary models of psychological reality. This process has generated one or more versions of various types of psychology: action, epistemological, understanding, depth, and dialectical.

Action psychology focuses on an organism's overt behavior and relates it to either environmen- tal or internal causes, or both. An action system must be objective or quasi-objective in orientation.

Epistemological psychology is a cognitive psy- chology, whereby the mind and mental processes con- stitute the primary psychological phenomena. Clas- sical epistemological systems were subjective in na- ture, but usually are not regarded as such; contem- porary cognitive psychology is quasi-objective in orientation.

Understanding psychology attempts to resolve the organism's feelings and awarenesses in terms of

its own view of the world. This approach is subjective when it focuses on the conscious experience of
the self and quasi-objective when it focuses on the
conscious experience of a significant other.

Depth psychology amounts to a closed system,
whereby the organism's psychological state is viewed
as a product of various internal psychodynamic
events. Depth psychology is quasi-objective in orientation.

Dialectical psychology focuses on the organism
as a point in a combined historical-cultural space
and treats the relationship between the organism and
the environment as an emergent entity. Dialectical
psychology combines the objective and subjective orientations.

CHAPTER 4

MAJOR CLASSICAL SCHOOLS

The purpose of this chapter is to analyze the four
major classical schools of psychology derived in
Chapter 3: (1) structuralism, a subjective epistemological system; (2) functionalism, a quasi-objective
action system; (3) Gestalt psychology, both a subjective and quasi-objective cognitive system; and (4)
classical Watsonian behaviorism, an objective action
system.

The historical importance of structuralism derives from the fact that it is now recognized as the
first institutionalized system of academic/experimen-
tal psychology: it serves as a case study for why the
initial academic/experimental system had to be an
epistemological, as opposed to action, psychology.
Functionalism indigenously evolved in a cultural
milieu that prized pragmatism and an action focus under the guide of consciousness. Gestalt psychology
shook the conceptual and philosophical foundations of
structuralism and fundamentally altered the focus of
epistemological psychology. Classical Watsonian behaviorism reacted negatively to both structuralism
and functionalism and promulgated the objective, action approach that was to dominate American experimental psychology for the first half of the twentieth

century.

        Recall that our basic aim is to describe how
psychology is constructed in the context of each of
these schools by focusing on (1) the content of observation, as a combination of object of study and
locus of psychological determination, and (2) the
reference psychological situation/activity, the act
of doing something.

STRUCTURALISM

        Structuralism was the first model of psycholog-
ical reality to be constructed by an individual self-
regarded as an experimental psychologist. Although
the system was not concerned with overt behavior or
the psychological nature of the human organism, it
was a perfectly predictable and legitimate component
of nineteenth century science, which reached its
greatest heights in Germany (Leary, 1978). Structuralism represented the culmination of the long-
standing interest of German science in epistemological aspects of the human mind. The content of structuralism was not new: it amounted to the three-way
synthesis of British mental philosophy, German experimental physiology, and German sensory psychophysics.
Significance resided in the fact that structuralism
encompassed the orienting assumptions, subject matter, and methodology of a new academic discipline.
In a sense, the fact that the first formal system of
experimental psychology was epistemological in nature represented a mere technical readjustment in
the boundaries of academic disciplines concerned
with the mind. Psychological research had been conducted by countless German scientists, such as Ernst
Weber (1846), Gustav Fechner (1860), and Hermann von

Helmholtz (1856-1866); but this activity was not
called psychological research and was not conducted
by self-conscious psychologists.

Structuralism became the first system of experimental psychology when Wilhelm Wundt arrived at
Leipzig in 1875 and was allowed to establish a Psychologische Institut for empirically studying aspects of conscious experience. Wundt had earned a
medical degree at Heidelberg in 1856 and remained
there for the next two decades in various teaching
and research positions in experimental physiology--
for six of these years he served as the laboratory
assistant of Helmholtz--before moving on to Zurich
and Leipzig, where he occupied full professorial
chairs in philosophy. The sociologists, Ben-David
and Collins (1966), argue that Wundt established the
role hybrid of experimental psychologist, as a melding of the roles of physiologist and philosopher,
under the impetus of certain social factors, such as
the necessity of retaining the prestige associated
with the scientific orientation and empirical methods of an experimental physiologist when conducting
research on traditional philosophical questions related to the nature of the mind. In effect, Wundt
and his students studied the mind experimentally,
not an activity traditionally associated with either
a physiologist or a philosopher, and were able to
have this formalized in the Germanic university system as a separate academic discipline.

The Psychologische Institut retained the latest
devices for making mental measurements and became a
model for other psychological laboratories. Eventually structuralism was caricatured by its detractors

as "brass instrument" psychology (see Keller, 1937).
The Institut served as a mecca for students from America and trained many first generation American
psychologists, most of whom later departed from
Wundt's rather constricted orientation and interests.
Structuralism was transported to the United States
by Edward Bradford Titchener, a native Englishman,
who set up a Leipzig laboratory in miniature at Cornell University.

Ironically, Wundt never used the term "structuralism" to denote his psychology. He preferred
the term "voluntarism," and his system generally was
known in Germany as existentialism (not to be confused with the contemporary denotation of the term).
Wundt focused on the existential, not intentional,
aspects of conscious experience. Titchener coined
the term "structuralism" to refer to his and Wundt's
brand of psychology in response to pressures from
American functionalistic psychology.

Although structuralism constitutes the ideal
physical realization of the abstract notion of a
classical school in many respects (Wundt, Titchener,
and Külpe were bona fide authority figures; both
subject matter and permissible methodology were
quite delimited and delineated clearly), today it is
recognized that the system was not as monolithic and
homogeneous as its historical image belies (Blumenthal, 1975; Evans, 1972). Significant differences
exist among the Wundtian, Titchenerian, and Külpean
versions of structuralism. In the discussion to
follow, we shall emphasize Titchener's version of
structuralism, because of its more ready accessibil-
ity to the American audience.

CONTENT OF OBSERVATION Structuralism focused
on the mind, not its dynamics or functioning, but
rather its content or structure. Structuralism
often is referred to as content psychology, in contrast to act psychology. The object of study for
structuralism was the content of conscious experience, and the goal of the structuralist program amounted to an analysis of conscious experience into
its elementary units. Structuralists, just as the
American functionally oriented philosopher William
James (1890), assumed that consciousness is a never
ending stream of different contents; but, unlike
James, they assumed it could be broken down into a
number of distinct mental elements. These elements
were supposed to be revealed by the systematic use
of direct, critical introspection. The fact that
the structuralists were constructing a psychological reality in an arbitrary manner is demonstrated
by two things: (1) their conception of conscious experience did not correspond to the general public's
implicit understanding of conscious experience, and
(2) only highly trained introspectors could serve as
the source of acceptable data on the content of consciousness.

The structuralist distinguished between immediate conscious experience and mediate conscious experience. Only the former served as the unique and
proper object of concern for psychology; the latter
could be the focus of any other science, such as
chemistry or physics. The structuralists' choice of
terminology is misleading, because what we immediately or directly are aware of is mediate experience;
we are only indirectly aware of immediate experience.

The distinction between immediate and mediate
conscious experience is metaphysical in nature and
difficult to characterize independently of an example. Suppose a structuralist places a bright red
apple in your line of sight and requests you to report on the content of your current awareness. You,
as observer, can do one of two things: (1) report on
the perceived presence of the apple itself or (2) report on the sensory experience of red and bright, as
presumably set up by the apple. The first kind of
report uses verbal categories referring to meaningful stimulus objects, presumably known to be external to the self. The second kind of report does not
use meaningful thing language, but merely characterizes the rudimentary sensations of which the self is
aware. The first kind of report entails mediate experience; the second kind of report is what is meant
by immediate experience. As a crude analogy, the
content of mediate experience is a matter of perception, while the content of immediate experience is a
matter of sensation. Because an observer's natural
reaction is to report on meaningful stimulus objects, the observer had to be trained to focus on
the characteristic sensory products associated with
such objects. Failure to report on the rudimentary
sensory qualities of experience was called the stimulus error, the most grievous sin that a trained in-
trospector could commit (Boring, 1921).
     The use of direct, critical introspection pre-
sumably isolated three kinds of elementary mental u-
nits: (1) sensations, (2) images, and (3) feelings
or affections. As is the case with the basic units
of analysis of any discipline, they really were meta-

physical in nature, as evidenced by the facts that
(1) the later structuralists reduced feeling to sensation and (2) Wundt and Titchener could not agree
on the number of dimensional attributes that were
associated with each kind of mental element.

1. Sensations (used for illustrative purposes
above) arise when an observer is stimulated by an
external object. Titchener postulated the existence
of seven kinds of sensations that corresponded to
the seven different sensory modalities known at the
time: visual, auditory, olfactory, gustatory, cutan-
eous, kinesthetic, and organic. A given sensory experience was assumed to possess certain attributes,
which simply were specific descriptive dimensions on
which a sensation could vary. Titchener distinguished among five such attributes: quality, intensity, duration, vividness, and extension. Wundt
only admitted the existence of quality and intensity.

2. Images occur in the absence of stimulation
by an external object. They are experienced after
the stimulus object is withdrawn and, as such, constitute residues of sensation. As conceptual extensions of sensations, seven kinds of images were
assumed to exist and were ratable in terms of two
(Wundt) or five (Titchener) dimensional attributes.
Since the observer cannot report on the content of
mediate experience without committing the stimulus
error, the observer does not know whether the content of current consciousness is a sensation or an
image. Only the experimenter has knowledge of when
the original stimulus event was withdrawn. The dif-
ferentiation between a sensation and an image could

<u>not</u> be made on the basis of the content of the im-
mediate experience itself.

3. Feelings are the affective components of
conscious experience. Stimulation of any one of the
seven sensory modalities gives rise to a subjective
feeling state, but the specific qualitative content
of the state is independent of the modality that is
stimulated. Titchener assumed that the qualitative
feeling state is unitary: it is either pleasant or
unpleasant. Wundt postulated that feelings <u>also</u>
have tension, relaxation components and excitement,
depression components.

The structuralists assumed that the elementary
sensations, images, and feelings combined associa-
tively to form the content of current awareness.
Consciousness at any moment in time consisted of a
combination of current perceptions, complex ideas,
and complex subjective feeling states. Current perception amounted to an associative combination of
elementary sensations. Complex ideas primarily amounted to an associative combination of elementary
images. Complex feeling states amounted to a synthesis of variously sourced elementary feeling
states.

The elementary mental units, as objects of
study, comprise only one aspect of the content of
observation. The locus of causation of these units
still remains to be considered. How did the structuralists conceive of the origin of conscious experience? The system did not postulate any formal locus of causation. Conscious experience was studied
as an island unto itself. Structuralists did not
relate the mental elements to external, physical

factors in a functional relationship context. They
did advocate a form of dualism known as psychophysical parallelism (see Chapter 6), in which mental e-
vents and bodily events are assumed to constitute
independent, but covarying, entities. Any facet of
conscious experience is correlated with some underlying physiological, neuronal, or brain event, although not every such event need have a representation in conscious experience.

The structuralist content of observation put a
premium on the age-old method of introspection. The
term "introspection" cannot be applied to one specific monolithic self-observational procedure; the
term merely is generic, covering a broad class of
self-observational procedures (Wundt, 1883; Titchener, 1912). The physical realization of introspection in terms of a given procedure varied from laboratory to laboratory: Wundt's Leipzig lab, Külpe's
Würzburg lab, and Titchener's Cornell lab. What the
different variants of introspection presumably had
in common was a stress on systemization and control,
but not every structuralist phenomenon was reproducible from lab to lab. The best example of this involved the so-called imageless thought controversy
(see Woodworth, 1906; Angell, 1911; Ogden, 1911).
Imageless thought existed for Külpe; it did not exist for Wundt or Titchener. Wundt also had some
battles with Carl Stumpf (1883-1890, 1898-1924) over
the existence of certain auditory phenomena.

Structuralist insistence on the use of highly
trained introspectors derived from many sources.
Only one will be mentioned here. Contrary to its
public image, structuralism is a subjective system:

only the self has direct access to its conscious experience. Conscious contents are not real-time or
real-space events, subject to external reliability
and/or validity check. The only way to generate uniform data exhibiting predictable regularities was
by fine tuning the measuring instrument, the intro-
spector. The structuralist controlled the psychological reality experienced by the subject by constricting the language and verbal categories the in-
trospector could use.

    The prototypical introspector was a psychology
graduate student, who was a highly motivated, intelligent, literate, verbally facile adult from the
normal population. Structuralist psychology effectively banned preverbal and nonverbal humans, chronic schizophrenics, mental retardates, animals, and
the like from the psychological universe.

    No other classical school was as wedded to its
methodology as structuralism. Structural psychology
can be termed introspective psychology, and the prototypical case of an introspective psychology is
structuralism. The mutually contingent relationship
of structuralism and introspection doomed them both.
Structural psychology, by arbitrarily focusing on
immediate experience as its exclusive object of
study, formally raised introspection to hallowed
status; but once immediate experience devolved to
merely an ancillary concern for the psychologist,
introspection became trivial. The introspection-
ists, by claiming exclusiveness and universality for
their methodology, legitimatized the structural program; but once it was demonstrated that introspec-

tion possessed only limited value, structuralism became viewed as a sterile, dead-end system.

REFERENCE SITUATION/ACTIVITY The structuralists limited the components of the psychological universe to those entities that appear in consciousness. Many significant events of psychological relevance to the individual simply do not occur in consciousness. The content of current awareness merely
is the tip of the iceberg of the individual's total
ongoing activities. Unconscious events, as emphasized by the Freudian psychoanalytic approach, various physiological and neuronal processes, and even
such cognitive activities as thinking, information
processing, and language or speech recognition do
not occur in consciousness and are not subject to
introspection.

Of related importance is the fact that structuralism could not relate conscious contents to ex-
tra-conscious events as possible explanatory mechanisms: they simply did not constitute parts of the
psychological universe. The act of breaking conscious contents down into fundamental sensations,
images, and feelings in and of itself is not a
worthless endeavor; but when such activity is presumed to exhaust psychological reality we have a
referenceless universe that exists only unto itself.

In the context of structuralism, the reference
activity of doing something is completely devoid of
psychological meaning. Doing something is behavior.
But the behavior exhibited by another organism is
not part of the structuralist psychological universe. We cannot legitimately observe the behavior
of another organism; that is, be aware of it in the

structuralist sense, because _it is a component of
mediate experience_. The epistemological focus of
structuralism is so pure that the content of consciousness cannot be related to anything: specific
stimulation on the input side or overt behavior on
the output side. It might appear that the reference
situation was preselected explicitly to show up
structuralism on this point; however, structuralism
will turn out to be the only system considered in
our analysis that has nothing substantive to say
about overt behavior. Contemporary epistemological
systems do relate the mind to behavior (see Chapter
5).

        The structuralist approach did touch bases with
overt behavior in one particular context: It conce-
ded that emotional feeling on the part of an organism sometimes possessed motor components and involved physical gestures.

        The structuralists exclusively focused on ex-
perience as an analytical category for various philosophical and historical reasons (see Boring, 1950).
Titchener explicitly argued that the problem of the
content of consciousness should be resolved before
tackling the issue of any possible use of consciousness, à la American functionalistic psychology. He
also attacked Watsonian behaviorism for being philosophically shallow and naive. In a sense a pure
psychology of consciousness is more sophisticated
than a pure psychology of objective acts. Titchener
believed to his dying days that American psychology
would eventually see the folly of its ways (obses-
sion with behavior and psychological adaptation) and
return to a strict concern for consciousness. But

such was not to be, primarily because a system of
psychology is more than an intellectual statement.
It is also a social, political, and cultural statement.   American culture would not tolerate an
elitist psychology with such a circumscribed psychological universe.   As we shall see later, the Watsonian and Skinnerian versions of the psychological
universe are equally circumscribed, but at least
they touch bases with the reference act of doing
something.

FUNCTIONALISM

Functionalism is the label attached to the numerous and varied quasi-objective, action oriented
models of psychological reality that seemed to
spring up spontaneously in America just before the
turn of the century.   These approaches had one fundamental tenet in common: the efficacy and utility
of consciousness.   Unlike structuralism, functionalism was not explicitly created as an intellectual
tool that allowed psychologists to compete with professionals of other disciplines.   Functionalistic
psychology primarily was a cultural statement that
was made long before most American institutions of
higher learning even had a formal psychology department.   It justified studying the organism as an active being adjusting to the environment.   The system served as an umbrella for the mental testing
movement and the psychology of individual differences and fostered educational, child, adolescent, and
developmental psychology in general.   It irrevocably
made the process of learning the primary source of
behavioral change in American psychology and implicitly functioned as America's first applied psychol-

ogy without making a big deal of doing so.

Although functionalism constituted the primary competitor of Titchenerian structuralism in the United States for at least two decades (approximately 1892-1912), its basic value for our analysis derives from the fact that it can be conceptualized as a transitional school between structuralism and classical Watsonian behaviorism (Hillner, 1984). Functionalistic psychology implicitly contains both structuralistic and behavioristic elements and acted as a necessary conceptual link between the Titchenerian and Watsonian brands of psychology. (Watson was trained as a functionalist {Murchison, 1936}. If he had begun as an indoctrinated structuralist, it is doubtful that he ever would have made the quantum leap to behaviorism.)

Functionalism is the most loosely formulated classical school of experimental psychology. It is more of a generalized attitude than a self-conscious, prescriptive system. Functionalism has no definitive founder, although it was influenced by the philosophical-psychological beliefs of both William James (1890, 1907) and John Dewey (1886, 1896). It has no rigid set of tenets that must be accepted by every professed functionalist. The school has no particular theoretical axe to grind. Functionalism is a low-key, tolerant approach to psychology. It is an open-ended and eclectic system in which practically any problem can be regarded as psychological in nature. It is inherently optimistic, in the sense that any psychological problem is assumed to admit of a final experimental resolution. Functionalism did not criticize structuralism at a concep-

tual level; rather it simply considered the structuralist program to be sterile. In many respects,
functionalism is a common-sense psychology and approximates the general public's conception of what
psychology is or should be. Functionalism still
possesses a certain charm: although its ultimate
goals have been absorbed by a more polemical behaviorism, contemporary experimental psychologists with
an "open mind" and working close to the data in a
parametric framework can call themselves functionalists (Hilgard and Bower, 1974).

The origin of functionalism can be related to
various nineteenth century intellectual developments
in England, such as the Darwinian evolutionary doctrine (Darwin, 1859, 1871) and Galton's work on individual differences and mental testing (Galton,
1869, 1879, 1889); however, functionalism basically
is indigenous to America where such philosopher-psy-
chologists as William James (1890) and John Dewey
(1886) fostered a pragmatic/utilitarian attitude
toward life and philosophy. Two universities stood
out as the primary centers of functionalistic
thought and research: (1) Chicago, under John Dewey
(1886), James Angell (1904), and Harvey Carr (1925),
and (2) Columbia, under James McKeen Cattell (1890,
1898), Robert Sessions Woodworth (1918, 1921), and
Edward L. Thorndike (1905, 1911). Clark University,
under G. Stanley Hall (1904, 1922), and Yale, under
George Ladd (1891, 1894) and Edward Scripture
(1897), also can be given honorable mention as hot-
beds of functionalism. Carr's (1925) version of
functionalism usually is assumed to be most representative of functionalism in its final form and

will be emphasized in our discussion.

CONTENT OF OBSERVATION   A discrepancy exists between functionalism's explicit and implicit object of study. Functionalism explicitly focused on the mind, but implicitly focused on overt behavior. Functionalism can be classified as either an epistemological or action system. This duality is easily resolvable in the context of the content of observation: behavior constituted the object of study; the workings of the mind served as the locus of causation. The system is action oriented if the object of study is emphasized; it is epistemological if the locus of causation is stressed. Functionalism is not an epistemological system in the same sense as structuralism. Functionalism is similar to contemporary cognitive behaviorism (see Chapter 5), in which cognitive processes are related to overt behavior. The basic difference between functionalism and cognitive behaviorism relates to the detailed mapping of the cognitive apparatus on the part of the latter (see Chapter 2).

Functionalism treated the mind as a dynamic, efficacious entity, not as a repository of passive contents. It focused on the operations and functions of consciousness. Consciousness was conceptualized as a causative, adaptive entity, not as a receptacle of phenomenal experience. The goal of the functionalist program amounted to an abstraction of the mind in terms of various mental activities. Mental activity refers to such processes as thinking, feeling, imagining, and perceiving. Each of these processes is a distinct category of mental activity of which the individual organism is aware and

which can serve as an object of introspective report. Like a structuralist, the functionalist focused on mental events; unlike a structuralist, the
functionalist observed what the mind was doing.

The functionalist was not interested in mental
activity as an end in itself. Mind was the primary
instrument responsible for the individual organism's
adaptation to the environment. The functionalist
fundamentally was interested in the actual working
of consciousness as it guides the individual organism in its adjustment to the environment. This focus on the instrumental, adaptive function of mind
made the functionalist an implicit behaviorist.
What is organismic adaptation or adjustment to the
environment, if not behavior? In effect, functionalism analyzed mental processes as the antecedent
conditions of overt behavior. Functionalism did not
study mind in an existential vacuum, as structuralism did. Mind was assumed to be causative and could
be related to explicit output, the organism's adaptive behavioral activity.

Note the reference to the term "environment" in
the preceding paragraph. The concept of an external
environment serves as another direct link to behaviorism. Another label for environment is stimulus
situation. Carr (1925) actually used the terms
"stimulus" and "response," the two fundamental units
of analysis of classical Watsonian behaviorism.
Functionalism basically was interested in the mind
as an intermediary between stimulus and response
events. Watson merely had to delete any reference
to this mental intermediary in order to create his
classical behavioristic approach.

Given functionalism's informal approach to its
basic object of study, it should not be surprising
that methodology did not constitute a problem for
the system. This does not mean that the functionalists were not methodologically oriented or did not
realize the limitations and disadvantages associated
with specific experimental techniques. Functionalists attempted to generate data on mental activities
and simply accepted the fact that there was no one
monolithic or ideal way to do this.

Carr (1925) made a fundamental distinction between the objective and subjective investigation of
mental activity. Objective investigation entails
the inference of the mental activities of an organism through the observation of its overt behavior.
Subjective investigation involves an organism reporting on its own mental activities. The former
procedure is analogous to physical experimentation;
the latter is equivalent to introspection. Carr realized that the content of introspective report was
beyond the bounds of a reliability and/or validity
assessment and that introspection was not applicable
to animals, children, members of the abnormal population, and the like. He also accepted all the criticisms that had been leveled at the structuralist
brand of introspection.

The ultimate source of a piece of data relating
to the existence of a mental event was irrelevant
for the functionalist. They accepted introspective
reports per se, introspective reports generated
while the subject performed some experimental task,
such as memorizing a list of words or reacting to a
stimulus (reaction time experiment), and data from

anthropological reports, literature, and art. They
even used ablation techniques to correlate mental
activity with underlying neurology and physiology
and photographs of eye movements to make inferences
about the mental activity underlying perception.

Implicit in the preceding discussion is the
fact that, in more cases than not, the functionalist
was observing and recording overt behavior (reaction
time, eye movements, verbal responses) or the products of overt behavior (art, literature). Watson
merely had to strip functionalistic data of their
mentalistic trappings in order to transform them into behavioristic data. The conceptual eyeglasses of
the functionalist made them "see" mental activities
or the results of mental activities; the conceptual
eyeglasses of the behaviorist made them "see" physical activity, devoid of any mental tag or any status as a mental event marker.

REFERENCE SITUATION/ACTIVITY Functionalistic
psychology's emphasis on organismic adaptation to
the environment amounts to an implicit focus on behavior, such that the system certainly subsumes the
act of doing something. The system even goes beyond
the content of observation related statement that
various mental activities guide overt behavior. Individual functionalists postulated specific mechanisms to account for adaptive behavior. An interesting feature of virtually all of these mechanisms is
that they are stated in nonmentalistic language:
they make no reference to mental activity. Most of
these mechanisms would have to be acceptable to any
but the most strict descriptive behaviorist. Five
of these mechanisms will be briefly discussed.

1. William James (1890), among his many slogan-
istic pronouncements, stated that "habit is the
enormous fly-wheel of society." This statement can
be translated to mean that the human being can ac-
quire relatively fixed behavioral patterns through
practice or learning. Once a specific activity becomes a habit, it is freed from conscious control.
This allows consciousness to focus on other things.
The general public still explains many behavioral
acts simply by labeling them "habits."

2. John Dewey (1896) wrote a classic paper on
the adaptive function of the reflex arc. Recall
from Chapter 2 that our notion of doing something
does not include simple reflexive responses that are
automatically elicited by specific stimuli and have
no effect on the environment. But Dewey assumes
that the response activity involved in a reflex arc
does have an effect on the environment: the response
alters the stimulus situation and provides the organism with positive feedback. Later activations of
the reflex occur in a changed environment or in a
stimulus situation that has a different meaning for
the organism.

3. Edward L. Thorndike (1927, 1932) was as much
an associationist or connectionist learning theorist
as he was a functionalist. His learning principles
circumscribed instrumental responding and its
strengthening or weakening through pleasurable or
aversive consequences. Many instances of doing
something can be conceptualized as instrumental responding under the control of its consequences. The
pervasiveness of Thorndikian psychology is demonstrated by the fact that many aspects of Skinner's

later descriptive behavioral system amount to mere
semantic extensions of his concepts (see Chapter 5).

4. Robert S. Woodworth (1918) postulated a
"mechanism become drive" concept, whereby a piece of
behavior takes on a life of its own after the original instigating motivational conditions have disappeared. A behavioral act that originally served as
a means to another end can become an end in itself.
It is certainly possible for some instances of doing
something to be explained by this concept.

5. Harvey Carr (1925) accounted for adaptive
behavior in terms of the notion of a motivational
sequence. This mechanism is quite similar to Clark
Hull's (1943, 1951) analytical description of instrumental response activity: stimulus situation--
drive--instrumental response activity--incentive--
consummatory activity--drive reduction. (Hull was a
logical behaviorist who dominated learning theory
from the late 1930s to the early 1950s.) The act of
doing something would correspond to the instrumental
response activity component of this sequence. The
notion of a motivational sequence still serves as
one of the primary explanatory mechanisms in the
psychology of motivation, especially in an animal
context. The notion also is implicitly preserved by
Skinner's concept of an operant conditioning contingency (see Chapter 5): deletion of any reference to
drive and drive reduction yields the event sequence
encompassed by operant conditioning.

Each of these possible explanations of doing
something, with the exception of the reflex arc, involves a learning and/or motivational mechanism.
Functionalism and later behaviorism used the instru-

mental responding situation with its associated consequences as the model for the rest of the psychological universe. The instrumental response is the
entity that is acquired in learning, and the associated consequences are motivational entities. Functionalistic psychology basically conceptualized
doing something as instrumental response activity
under the control of its consequences, which were
regarded as motivational in nature.

GESTALT PSYCHOLOGY

The Gestalt system can be approached from many
different perspectives:

1. It is an intellectual statement that originated in Germany, but ultimately influenced American psychology.

2. It is based on Kantian philosophy, rather
than British empiricism.

3. It is explicitly concerned with both conscious experience and overt behavior.

4. Its origin is traceable to a specific event,
discovery of the phi phenomenon.

5. It possesses a trio of founders: Wertheimer,
Koffka, and Köhler.

6. It revolutionized the psychology of perception.

7. It kept cognitive psychology alive during
the heyday of descriptive behaviorism.

8. It is an experimental system, whose substantive orientation is currently carried on by nonexperimental humanistic psychology.

9. It imported the field theory orientation of
physics into psychology.

This sampling of possible perspectives should

suggest the fact that Gestalt psychology is unique.
But the most striking feature of Gestalt psychology
is that it was constructed over a short twenty year
period by a set of erudite, civilized men who accepted psychological reality as given before it was
ruthlessly destroyed in its country of origin by a
set of the most ignorant, bigoted men ever spawned
who distorted reality for their own ends. Gestalt
psychology was both a product of German rationality
and intellectualism and a casuality of German irrationality and racism. The history of the Gestalt
movement should serve as an eternal reminder that
the discipline of psychology exists at the whim of
the governmental institution.

The Gestalt system basically was a perceptual
psychology, with learning, problem solving, and
motivational overtones. As a perceptual psychology,
it was concerned with conscious experience; as a
learning psychology, it was concerned with overt behavior. Based on Kantian philosophy (Kant, 1781),
it rebeled against the elementarism, molecularism,
analytical focus, and associationism of the structuralist and behaviorist systems that owe their intellectual heritage, in part, to British empiricism
(viz. Locke, 1690; Berkeley, 1710; Hume, 1748).
Gestalt psychologists derisively referred to structuralism and behaviorism as "bundle" or "brick and
mortar" psychologies (Keller, 1937).

The origin of Gestalt psychology can be traced
to the experimental investigation of the phi phenomenon by Max Wertheimer, Kurt Koffka, and Wolfgang
Köhler at Frankfurt between 1910 and 1912 (see Wertheimer, 1912). The phi phenomenon is an apparent

movement effect that cannot be reduced to a concatenation of sensations. It demonstrates the vacuous-
ness of the structuralist approach to conscious experience. Gestalt psychology supplanted structuralism in Germany, only to be persecuted ultimately by
the Third Reich. Its three founders immigrated to
the United States, where the system competed with
Watsonian and other variants of behaviorism during
the '30s and '40s, ultimately to be absorbed by cognitive behaviorism.

CONTENT OF OBSERVATION The German word Gestalt
roughly translates as shape, form, or configuration;
the plural form is Gestalten. The basic natural
phenomena of interest to Gestalt psychology typically possess an inherent structure or immanent organization; its basic objects of interest come in pre-
packaged forms or appear as meaningful wholes. This
statement presages the fact that the Gestaltists'
use of the terms "experience" and "behavior" is not
continuous with their use in structuralism and behaviorism respectively. The most neutral way to
characterize the content of observation of Gestalt
psychology is in terms of phenomenal experience as
related to underlying psychophysical processes or
fields. Phenomenal experience subsumes both the
content of conscious experience of some observer as
well as the overt activity of some experimental subject. Both conscious experience and behavior are
construed in a field orientation.

What the Gestalt psychologist essentially means
by conscious experience is perceptual experience:
the objects of our perceptual awareness. This is
the exact opposite of the structuralist conception

of conscious experience, conceptualized in terms of
rudimentary sensations, images, and feelings. Gestalt psychology focuses on the objects of mediate
experience and treats these as the natural givens of
consciousness. A Gestalt psychologist assumes that
an observer immediately and directly experiences objects, not the isolated, abstracted sensory attributes of the objects. The Gestalt approach to conscious experience corresponds to the public's view:
the content of consciousness is described in common-
sense, everyday, meaningful terms. We react to
stimuli as having an innate organization or as existing in a holistic pattern. This structured, organized experience must be accepted as such. It must
not be analyzed into subparts in a structuralist introspective sense. In the Gestalt approach, an observer need no special training in order to externalize the content of consciousness. The content of
perceptual awareness is given; one should not work
to artificialize it.

     While admitting the existence of simple reflex-
ive responses, Gestalt psychologists view instances
of behavior as possessing Gestalt-like properties.
By analogy to the perceptual situation, behavior is
a holistic, organized molar activity or pattern of
movement, having no parts. What is meant by parts
in this context is molecular, conditioned subres-
ponse units, as construed by the behaviorist. A legitimate piece of behavior is not reducible to a
linear string of componential conditioned response
units. An instance of behavior possesses an underlying hierarchically organized, intrinsic structure
and constitutes an emergent phenomenon, transcending

any simple physiological reality.

Both the experiential and behavioral aspects of
Gestalt psychology are held together by relating
them to the concept of an underlying psychophysical
field.   The notion of a psychophysical field is
strictly metaphysical in the context of Gestalt psychology and was borrowed from physics (see Planck,
1936).   Gestaltists assumed that a given perceptual
experience, or Gestalt, as well as a given instance
of molar activity, is a function of an underlying
field.   Gestalt psychologists speak of both psychological fields and physiological fields.   They amount to the same generic concept because it was presumed that a given psychological field is reducible
to a physiological field and possessed ultimate
physiological reality: thus, the notion of a psychophysical field.

A physiological field is basically neuronal in
nature and exists in the organism's brain; this kind
of field primarily is associated with perceptual experience or Gestalten.   Wertheimer and Köhler emphasized the neuronal fields underlying conscious experience.   The notion of a psychological field is
more general and can refer to the totality of causal
variables, or texture, affecting an organism at a
given moment in time: specific physical stimuli,
past experience, current motivational conditions,
the subject's immediate goals, and the like.   This
kind of field primarily is associated with overt molar activity and was stressed by Koffka.

The notion of a psychological field is largely
coextensive with that of behavioral environment,
which should be contrasted with the geographic en-

vironment. The geographic environment is the objective, physical environment in which a given behavior occurs. The behavioral environment is the subjective, psychological environment in which a given behavioral event occurs, the environment as perceived by the organism. These two environments need not correspond. The Gestalt psychologist assumed that a given instance of molar activity could not be understood unless the specific behavioral environment in which it occurred was known.

There is no substantive difference between an organism performing in a behavioral environment and an organism living and working in its own subjective world of private experience, the focus of interest of contemporary humanistic psychology (Giorgi, 1970). In both Gestalt and humanistic psychology, the organism only can be understood in terms of its own frame of reference.

The explanatory value of a field is described best in the context of a physiological field and its presumed relationship to perceptual experience. The ultimate source of the structural organization of a given Gestalt is assumed to be an underlying neuronal brain field. The Gestalt psychologist postulated that a perceived Gestalt and its underlying neuronal brain field existed in an isomorphic relationship: the structural organization of perceptual experience corresponds topologically to the structural organization of an underlying brain field. We perceive reality in meaningful wholes because neuronal fields exist in the brain that possess the same essential structural organization.

There is no direct physiological evidence that

these postulated neuronal brain fields actually exist, and attempts to verify their existence <u>indir-
ectly</u> through psychological experimentation have met
with mixed results (Hilgard and Bower, 1974). Critics of Gestalt psychology, such as Attneave (1954),
like to point out that the postulation of psychophysical fields and isomorphism amounts to a redes-
cription of the basic behavioral data at another
level of reality: they are merely circularly defined
concepts and amount to nominal explanations.

     In general, the Gestalt psychologist has no way
of identifying and giving substance to a particular
psychophysical field or behavioral environment independently of the report of conscious experience or
overt behavior. The psychophysical field and the
behavioral environment are response-defined or response-inferred constructs.

     The Gestalt psychologist did not make a fetish
of methodology. The system professed only one fundamental methodological prescription for each of its
objects of study: (1) The content of perceptual experience had to be accepted as given and not broken
down into subparts. (2) Behavior could only be
studied in a situation that allowed the subject to
be aware of the critical aspects of the psychophysical field determining its behavior. The first prescription leads to the use of phenomenology, the
phenomenal description of conscious experience. The
second prescription entails the use of low level
physical experimentation, amounting to virtual naturalistic observation.

     Both phenomenology and physical experimenta-
tion, as practiced by the Gestaltist, had the same

fundamental goal: the attainment of an experimentum crucis, which is a simple but convincing demonstration of some observed generality that can be interpreted by the Gestalt explanatory categories. Much of Gestalt research merely physically illustrates the general laws and precepts of the system. Phenomenological investigations are particularly convincing because they involve the immediate perceptual experience of the observer and the conclusions to be drawn from them are instantaneous. For instance, many of the Gestalt laws of perceptual organization achieve instant validity in the context of simple physical demonstrations, such as those involving figure-ground and perceptual grouping (Hochberg, 1974).

REFERENCE SITUATION/ACTIVITY The notion of phenomenal experience plays a dual role in Gestalt psychology: (1) In perceptual research, it is the output or content of perceptual awareness, as relatable to underlying neuronal brain fields. (2) It is the input, as the repository of the behavioral or phenomenal environment, to which molar activity is related in learning, problem solving, and motivational research.

For the Gestalt psychologist, the prototypical psychological situation or activity is the process of externalizing the phenomenal content of one's consciousness. The simplest, or most representative, instance of this occurs in perceptual research. The Gestalt psychologist views perception as the basic psychological process and uses the dynamics of perception to model the rest of the psychological universe.

Gestalt psychology derives the act of doing
something by assuming that molar activity occurs in
a phenomenal situation that possesses the same dynamics that a Gestalt does in a purely perceptual
situation: the behavioral environment or subjective
world of the organism produces its overt behavior.

For a Gestaltist, the prototypical experimental
situation for studying overt behavior is problem
solving, the primary example of which is Köhler's
(1917) classic study of banana procurement behavior
by apes. Apes confined in a cage either had to secure bananas located on the outside via the imaginative use of sticks or had to secure bananas sus-
pended from the ceiling via the imaginative use of
boxes. A problem solving situation is like a perceptual situation in that it possesses a certain
structural organization, such that the organism can
discover the correct response (solve the problem) by
the active cognitive restructuring of the elements
of the situation. Descriptively, this process is
usually labeled "the achievement of insight." The
problem solving situation allows the organism to be
aware of the critical aspects of the psychophysical
field that determines its behavior. Unlike the case
of the behaviorist's instrumental reward conditioning situation, the correct response need not be discovered adventitiously through blind trial-and-er-
ror responding.

The contemporary humanistic psychologist's resolution of doing something merely is an extension of
the Gestalt approach. The basic goal of humanistic
psychology is to make the organism aware of the reasons for its behavior, such that the organism be-

comes freer and only engages in behavior that it
wants (Rogers, 1961).

WATSONIAN BEHAVIORISM

John B. Watson (1913, 1914, 1916, 1919, 1925)
was the primary figure responsible for transforming
America's functionalistic, adaptation psychology into a behavioristic one. Trained as a functionalist
at the University of Chicago by James Angell (1904),
he eventually could not reconcile his interest in objective animal behavior with the dominant psychology
of human consciousness of the time. Watson's (1913)
"behaviorist manifesto" represented more of an evolutionary development than a revolutionary pro-
nouncement. Implicit trends toward objectivity in
psychology had existed for years: for instance, objective animal psychology, Russian objective psychology, and functionalism itself (Boring, 1964).
The startling aspect of his manifesto related to the
vigor and tenacity with which he attacked his mentalistic forebears.

Watson's basic aim was the establishment of psychology as an objective science, one comparable to
physics and chemistry. Consciousness, either in the
structuralist content sense or in the functionalist
utility sense, simply did not serve as a source of
public, verifiable data. Instead of blaming introspective observers for the irreplicability and un-
reliability of introspective report, he dismissed
the method of introspection from the realm of acceptable scientific methodology.

Watson's descriptive orientation is a natural
consequence of his desire to rid psychology of any
reference to mind and its trappings. Pure objectiv-

ity required relating behavior to external, environmental events and down playing any internal media-
tors of behavior. Watson banished mental events,
both as causal entities and as epiphenomenal output,
from psychology by fiat.

His position on the relevancy of physiology for
psychology is a logical extension of his approach to
mind. To Watson, the brain was a "mystery box," to
be avoided as a determinant of behavior. Watson focused on the peripheral nervous system and the muscles and glands. Any psychological phenomenon occurring within the skin, such as thought, was interpreted strictly in terms of peripheral mechanisms.
Psychologically relevant internal events were conceptualized by Watson in general as implicit, covert, peripherally based behaviors.

The positive aspect of Watson's descriptive orientation is his extreme environmentalism. The significant source of behavioral change is learning,
specifically classical conditioning. The classical-
ly conditioned response served as the unit of habit;
and any complex behavioral sequence, in principle,
could be broken down into subunits. Watson de-em-
phasized possible hereditary and nativistic sources
of behavior. Inherited capacities, talents, or tem-
peraments were illusory in his approach. Watson
found no need for a theory of motivation. He accepted the existence of some rudimentary reflexes and
of three basic forms of emotion at birth; but even
these became intertwined with learned habits, such
that emotional expression in adulthood primarily was
a matter of acquired components. His approach to
instincts evolved over the years, eventually reach-

ing the point where he denied their existence.

Watson's descriptivism made experimental psychology a truly self-contained and independent science by divorcing it from two of its three historical roots: philosophy and physiology. Denying both the substance and utility of consciousness and refraining from any appeal to mentalism severs psychology from its original philosophical base. Declaring that knowledge of internal physiology is irrelevant for the prediction/control of behavior prevents any ultimate reduction of psychology to biology. The third historical root, physics, was enhanced by the advent of behaviorism, since Watson sought the objectivity characteristic of that discipline (Hillner, 1984).

Although Watson vehemently attacked structuralism, his descriptive behaviorism amounts to a sensationistic, descriptive Titchenerian structuralism at a different level of analysis. Structuralism dealt with the analysis and synthesis of mental elements; Watsonian behaviorism dealt with the analysis and synthesis of reflexive units of behavior. His approach was just as molecular, atomistic, elementaristic, and associationistic as structuralism. That is why Gestalt psychology considered behaviorism as much an anathema as structuralism.

Any descriptive behaviorism implicitly is applied in orientation and serves as the basis of a social philosophy. Watson presaged Skinner (1948, 1962, 1971) with his "experimental ethics," in which behaviorism served as a "foundation for saner living" and encompassed a program of social control and betterment. Watson also focused on child develop-

ment, both as a subject of his own research program
and as a popular interest writing topic by which to
inform the general public of the benefits of an applied behaviorism. After Watson left academia in
1920, he made a career for himself in advertising,
the quintessence of an applied psychology.

Watson's objectification of psychology changed
the discipline's fundamental focus and set the stage
for the beginning of contemporary psychology. The
organism was no longer studied as an experiencing,
epistemological entity; it was now studied as an
acting being affecting the environment. Sensation
and perception were superseded as the canonical research areas by learning and conditioning. Behaviorism absorbed functionalism and Gestalt psychology, symbolizing the triumph of materialism or mechanism in psychology (Boring, 1964).

CONTENT OF OBSERVATION In any kind of behaviorism, psychological reality is assumed to be merely an aspect of physical reality (Mackenzie, 1977).
A physical scientist focuses on real-time and real-
space events, both at the input level of causation
and the output level of epiphenomena of interest.
Behaviorists consider psychological events to be
physical events, regard themselves as scientists,
and construct psychology in the same manner that
physical science is constructed. The specific aspect of physical reality that the behaviorist treats
as the unique domain of psychology is behavior and
its etiology.

Watson assumed that behavior was determined by
antecedent or concurrent environmental events. He
used the term "stimulus" for environmental causes

and the term "response" for behavior. In the context of this terminology, Watson described the goal
of behaviorism to be (1) given the stimulus, to predict the response and (2) given the response, to
predict the stimulus. Because the notions of stimulus and response are metaphysical entities, they
are resolvable at any level of reality that the psychologist considers convenient. Watson surprisingly
was very informal in his characterization of stimulus and response events.

Watson's program of translating mentalistic
terms into behavioristic language amounts to transforming them into stimulus and/or response terminology. A traditional mentalistic concept had to be
pushed into a stimulus or response category, primarily the latter. (The response category serves as
the critical metaphysical repository for most forms
of behaviorism {Churchland, 1984}). Watson gave a
behavioristic interpretation to sensation, image,
feeling, language, thought, emotion, and instinct.

In the context of Watsonian behaviorism, the
notion of stimulus merely amounts to a convenient
descriptive label. It was a functional substitute
for the notion of cause and possessed no real meaning above and beyond this. The term "stimulus" was
applied to whatever aspect of the environment was
discovered to be controlling the specific response
of current concern. Unlike later behaviorists, such
as Hull (1943) or Skinner (1953), Watson did not assign any function to stimuli other than that of pure
elicitation: stimuli did not possess reinforcing,
motivational, or discriminative functions.

Beyond giving the notion of stimulus a psycho-

logical reality, Watson did not have a formal conceptualization of stimulus events. He allowed both
external and internal stimulus events, the latter
primarily physicalized in terms of response produced
stimuli associated with peripheral response activity, for instance, kinesthetic stimulation produced
by muscle movement or organic stimulation produced
by visceral activity. Since behaviorism is not a
perceptual psychology and is not concerned with the
structure of conscious experience, Watson did not
require an elaborate theory of stimulus identification.

      Although Watson could avoid a formal character-
ization of a stimulus event at a conceptual level,
he could not avoid an operational problem common to
every type of behaviorism: how does one know whether
or not a given event X taken at random from the environment can serve as a stimulus? This is the
problem of stimulus specification, and it cannot be
resolved without appeal to the behavioral level of
reality. The only way to determine whether event X
is a stimulus is by assessing its effect on behavior: if event X elicits a response or comes to control response occurrence, it is a stimulus. The notion of a stimulus, as a unit of analysis, can only
be identified in terms of a response, the other unit
of analysis. Given a specific stimulus-response sequence, only one of the two terms is independent.
Most behaviorists accept this fact and assume that a
given stimulus-response pair amounts to only one independent existential event (see Hillner, 1978,
1979). Our analytical notion of content of observation takes cognizance of this fact by assuming that

object of study (response) and locus of causation
(stimulus) do not constitute independent units of
observation.

Watson distinguished among four types of responses: (1) explicit (external) learned, (2) implicit (internal) learned, (3) explicit unlearned (innate), and (4) implicit unlearned. The third and
fourth types assumed less and less significance as
his system evolved over the years. Any response occurrence, by definition, involves one or more of the
response effectors: the muscles and glands. The
striped or skeletal muscles were associated with external responses; the unstriped or smooth muscles
were associated with internal responses. The glands
generally entail internal responses, except for
those instances where the glandular secretion can be
externalized directly, as in the case of salivary
gland activity and the classical conditioning of
salivation in the dog.

At a more analytical level, Watson made a distinction between molecular and molar responses, by
which he attempted to have the best of two worlds.

The notion of a molecular response directly
corresponds to the conception of a response as effector activity: muscular movement or glandular secretion. Either of these, strictly speaking, is
physiological activity that is given straightway
psychological representation as a response event.
Molecular responses, as defined, are reflexive in
nature, elicitable by simple stimuli.

The concept of a molar response describes what
an organism is doing (Watson was fond of character-
izing behavior as doing) and involves the everyday

notion of a meaningful, intentional act. Quite often the content of a molar response is specified in
terms of its environmental effect or purpose. Watson's concept of molar response corresponds exactly
to our notion of the reference activity of doing
something. A molar response does involve physiological activity, i.e., response effector activation,
but this <u>cannot</u> be used to identify the response.
A given molar response can be physically realized in
any number of physiologically distinct ways. The
stimulus event associated with a molar response
tends to be complex and "recessed." The more complex the response, the more recessed the stimulus.
Watson could not operationally define molar responses without getting teleological. At a conceptual
level, he assumed that they amounted to a concatenation of molecular responses formed by conditioning.
Any complex molar response is reducible to molecular
muscular movements and/or glandular secretions, and
the basic combinatorial process involves molecular
S-R associations formed by classical conditioning.
(Later behaviorists, such as Skinner (1938), resolved molar response specification by using functional response definition: see Chapter 5.)

The behaviorist revolt, in large part, was
methodological in nature, although Watson originated
no new research techniques. His basic methodological contribution relates to the expressed goal of
increased objectivity that required an enhanced recognition of and higher standards for what constitutes an acceptable behavioral research technique.
In this context, he raised Pavlov's (1927) conditioned reflex method, classical conditioning, to

hallowed status and reconceptualized the method of
introspection as the method of verbal report.

Classical conditioning constituted an ideal
technique for Watson because it embodied explicit
stimulus-molecular response associations and was assumed to be the basis of all learning. The conditioned response (CR) was viewed as the unit of habit. Watson did not study classical conditioning as
a theoretical process or parametrically as a repository of certain variables. He merely used it as a
tool for demonstrating some of the abstract principles of his system, such as the fact that fears can
be learned and unlearned (Watson and Raynor, 1920;
Jones, 1924a, 1924b).

In the method of verbal report, a verbal response uttered by an organism is assumed equivalent
to a motor response or a pointer reading on a dial
and in no way reflects the contents of the organism's consciousness. In many experiments involving
adult humans, it simply is more convenient to accept
the subject's verbal expression as a physical discriminative response than to use a conditioned motor
response. Classical behaviorists did not go over-
board in their use of verbal report. They only allowed a restricted number of verbal report categories in order to maintain a high level of objectivity. Watson would find complete, unrestrained verbal
report, such as occurs in the descriptively elaborate responses given in the presence of a Rorschach
(1942) ink blot card, largely uninterpretable.
Classical behaviorists typically did not allow freewheeling phenomenological description in the Gestalt
sense.

REFERENCE SITUATION/ACTIVITY   Because Watsonian
behaviorism is an action system, the act of doing
something constitutes the prototypical psychological
situation.   Watson's conception of behavior as doing, physicalized in terms of molar responses, also
corresponds exactly to our reference situation.
Watson regarded both simple and complex adult behaviors to be a product of learning.   All learning gen-
erically was a form of conditioning, and what Watson
meant by conditioning was Pavlovian classical conditioning.   Any act of doing something was assumed reducible to a linear string of molecular responses
chained together by conditioning.

Because Watson was a descriptive behaviorist,
behavioral occurrence could only be related to overt
stimulus events.   The locus of psychological determination exclusively resided at the stimulus level.
Since Watson postulated only one stimulus function;
namely, elicitation, the presence of a stimulus sup-
plied the necessary and sufficient condition for
response occurrence.   In other words, stimuli were
viewed as automatic or indigenous response producing
entities.   This gave Watsonian behaviorism a bad
press, such that the organism was viewed as a prisoner of its environment.   A strict reading of Watson's principles (for instance, Chein, 1972) makes
the act of doing something an involuntary reflexive
response of some order of complexity.   Most inter-
preters of Watson neglect to point out that an organism's response repertoire is virtually infinitely
malleable through conditioning.   The content of an
organism's repertoire is less fixed under the assumption of exclusive environmental determination

than under the assumption of strict nativistic determinism.

The basic thrust of Watsonian psychology is to
make behavioral change, and the dynamics underlying
such change, real-space and real-time events in the
universe, open to observation and manipulation.
This is an improvement over functionalism, which
made behavioral change a function of consciousness,
and over Gestalt psychology, which made behavioral
change a mere external indicant of some underlying
subjective behavioral environment. A comparison of
Watson with Titchener (1898) on this point cannot be
done because the psychological universes of behaviorism and structuralism are not commensurate.

What Watson's system is explicitly lacking is
any means by which the individual organism, as a
psychological entity, can contribute to its own response output. Later forms of behaviorism corrected
this deficiency. Skinner's (1971, 1974) radical behaviorism presumes a bidirectional determinism, in
which it is assumed that both the environment and
the organism mutually affect each other. Contemporary cognitive behaviorism (Neisser, 1976) presumes
that an organism's cognitive information processing
system intervenes between physical input and ultimate response output, such that behavior is not a
strict linear function of stimulus input.

An action psychology must presume some form of
determinism at some level of analysis. Response
output does not occur in an existential vacuum. The
only choice to be made is with respect to how much
or in what way the individual organism contributes
to its response output. Those psychologists for

whom any form of determinism is an anathema (for instance, Rogers, 1961; Giorgi, 1970; Maslow, 1971) do
not construct action systems, but they face the
problem of accounting for the reference activity.

CHAPTER 5

MAJOR CONTEMPORARY SYSTEMS

The purpose of this chapter is to analyze at least
one major contemporary representative of each of the
five types of psychology derived in Chapter 3. We
shall focus on (1) Skinner's radical behaviorism (an
action system), (2) cognitive behaviorism or the information processing approach and Piagetian structural psychology (epistemological systems), (3)
Freudian psychoanalysis (the canonical depth psychology), (4) humanistic, existential, or phenomenological psychology (the understanding approach),
and (5) Riegel's dialectical system.

        Skinnerian behaviorism is the immediate intel-
lectual heir of Watsonian behaviorism. Cognitive
behaviorism represents a revival of interest in the
mind in America after a half century of neglect due
to the repressive effects of both descriptive behaviorism and peripherally oriented logical behaviorism. Piagetian psychology currently constitutes the
most well known and influential epistemological system of European origin. Freudian psychology is the
most inclusive system for resolving abnormal behavioral phenomena ever devised. Humanistic psychology
is a reaction to both descriptive behaviorism and
Freudian psychoanalysis. Riegel's dialectical sys-

tem is a conscious attempt to combine behaviorism
and humanism.

Our basic aim is to describe how psychology is
constructed in the context of each of these approaches by focusing on (1) the content of observation,
as a combination of object of study and locus of
psychological determination, and (2) the reference
psychological situation/activity, the act of doing
something.

SKINNER'S RADICAL BEHAVIORISM

Skinner (1976) began his psychological research
as a graduate student at Harvard University in the
early 1930s in relative obscurity. Building upon
the physicalistic tradition of both Pavlov (1927)
and Watson (1913), he refined the notions of stimulus, response, and the reflex. Early on he devised
experimental techniques whereby the organism is in
direct contact with the environment, such that there
is constant interplay between its behavior and the
specific experimental operation that is in effect.
Behavioral control through the use of inductively
validated techniques became the end goal of psychology, and the psychological universe was modeled after the reinforcement contingencies subsumed by operant conditioning. In Skinner's system, any meaningful piece of behavior must be under strict stimulus and/or reinforcement control.

Skinner (1974) explicitly construes his system
to be a philosophy of science with respect to the
subject matter and methodology of psychology. Although Skinner's behaviorism is descriptive in nature, his system is unique because it is neither (1)
nomothetic nor (2) unconcerned with mental events.

1. A nomothetic system attempts to resolve the behavior of a group of subjects or of some standard, statistical subject in terms of abstract psychological laws (see Watson, 1967). Skinner attempts to resolve the behavior of an _individual_ organism in terms of a set of presumed universally applicable psychological mechanisms. The denotation of individual organism is open-ended for Skinner. The individual organism is simply the lowest common denominator level at which psychological processes operate. The organism is regarded as a locus of interacting variables. Skinner historically has focused on the behavior of rats and pigeons, at least with respect to his basic research, and has assumed that what is true of either of these organisms also is straightway true of the human being. Skinner has been criticized for this extrapolation (for instance, see Wheeler, 1973); but Skinner never applies an experimental operation to a human subject that in principle could not be applied to a lower order organism. No one criticizes Skinner's system as an animal psychology or as a set of principles of animal behavioral control (within limits); the thrust of his critics concerns whether it is _also_ a viable human psychology. Skinner's system epitomizes the central feature of behaviorism: It focuses on behavior, regardless of who or what generates the behavior.

2. Skinner does not admit the existence of mental events inside the body and is particularly critical of appeals to various mentalisms as psychological determinants; however, he admits the organism's mental life into psychology by transforming it into

covert stimulus and response activities to which
only the organism has direct, but private, access.
Experiencing is behaving for Skinner. Skinner's
treatment of mental events as noncausative epiphenomena is what makes his system "radical." The individual's ability to externalize events occurring
within the body is an aspect of verbal behavior,
which specifically involves tacting, under the control of reinforcement contingencies that are a property of the surrounding linguistic community. When
other psychologists, especially Freudian and cognitively oriented ones, use phenomenologically based
mental events as explanations of overt behavior,
Skinner (1954, 1977) accuses them of employing circular explanations. Skinner prefers to have the
reacting organism in direct contact with the environment. Perceiving, thinking, and remembering are
not cognitive activities; they are simply forms of
behavior under some form of direct stimulus control.
Note that, whenever Skinner is investigating mental
events as private behavioral activity in his research, he must expand his psychological universe to
include quadrant I (see Chapter 3).

Over the years, Skinner's system has successfully competed with nondescriptive forms of behaviorism and has become the basic comparative reference point for virtually every other type of psychology. It has spawned psychopharmacology, behavior
modification and therapy, teaching machines, designs
for a Utopian society, and industrial incentive systems. It is the only academic psychology that comes
close to matching Freudian psychology in its impact
on everyday life. Now in his retirement years,

Skinner has become a virtual social philosopher and has seen his approach become an object of interest for analytic oriented philosophers (see Day, 1969).

CONTENT OF OBSERVATION As is the case with any descriptive form of behaviorism, stimuli and respon- ses constitute the two fundamental metaphysical cat- egories of psychological reality. Stimulus and res- ponse is merely technical jargon for environmental event and behavior respectively. Stimulus events constitute the input; response events constitute the output.

Unlike the case with nondescriptive behavior- ism, stimuli and responses are merely operational and observational entities. A stimulus is part of a physical operation under the control of the experi- menter or environment; a response is a physical act possessing different kinds of measurable properties. For Skinner, stimuli and responses do not constitute observable counterparts of unseen, underlying, hypo- thetical entities. The descriptive level of analy- sis is the only level of analysis. The structure of psychological knowledge can be expressed in terms of a series of significant stimulus-response correla- tions and relationships.

Skinner's descriptive approach sometimes is characterized as being atheoretical in nature (Hil- gard and Bower, 1974). No inductions are ever made to another level of reality from physical stimulus and response events as the immediate givens of ex- perience. But Skinner's system is theoretical. His theory is that we do not need theory. Skinner is a- theoretical only in the sense that he denies the relevancy of traditional learning theory, character-

istic of logical behaviorism (see Chapter 3: Hull,
Guthrie, Tolman). The observational process in
Skinner's system is just as theoretical as in any
other system of psychology. Skinner's assumptions
and preconceptions influence what he observes and
measures, as is the case with any other kind of psychologist. Skinner preselects his data, just as any
other psychologist does.

Skinner never observes stimulus and response
events in isolation of each other, and this fact is
formalized in his notion of a contingency. A contingency serves as the primary locus of psychological determination for Skinner. Skinner controls behavior in the laboratory by the use of some kind of
contingency, and he attempts to analyze the occurrence of a specific kind of behavior in the natural
environment by determining its controlling contingency. A contingency specifies the nature of the
relationship existing between the critical stimulus
and response events in a given situation.

There are many types of contingencies, the two
most basic ones being (1) reinforcement and (2)
stimulus control or stimulus discrimination. In a
reinforcement contingency, the delivery of the reinforcing stimulus depends on the prior occurrence of
the prespecified response of interest. In the stimulus control or stimulus discrimination contingency,
the occurrence of a response is reinforced in the
presence of a certain stimulus and is not reinforced
in the presence of another stimulus. Since the
specification of a contingency involves reference to
both a stimulus and response event, behavior and its
cause are co-observed and jointly determined.

Skinner identifies at least three kinds of
stimulus events, eliciting, reinforcing, and discriminative, and two kinds of response events, respondents and operants. To illustrate the fact that
the notions of a stimulus and a response are interdependent concepts that are circularly defined in
terms of each other, it can be noted that eliciting
stimuli are always associated with respondents and
reinforcing and discriminative stimuli are always
associated with operants.

Eliciting stimuli and respondents are involved
in Pavlovian classical conditioning, respondent conditioning in Skinnerian terminology. Conditioned
and unconditioned stimuli constitute eliciting stimuli; conditioned and unconditioned responses constitute respondents. The relationship between an eliciting stimulus and a respondent is assumed to be reflexive in nature, either physiological or learned.
Skinner does not consider respondent conditioning
to be a significant source of behavioral change.

For our purposes, the significant aspect of the
relationship between an elicitor and a respondent is
how an elicited response is operationally defined.
How do you determine when an instance of a given
respondent class actually occurs? Since a respondent is reflexive in nature, it is physiological activity or the byproduct of physiological activity.
For instance, the knee jerk and salivation amount to
muscular contraction and glandular secretion respectively. Most respondents can be measured as wave
forms, generated by the blip of a pen on a moving
piece of paper (Kimble, 1961).

The Skinnerian, or behavioristic, assumption

that a given instance of physiological activity can
be given straightway psychological representation as
a behavioral response often is criticized by nonbe-
haviorists. Physiological activity is given no psychological representation or only trivial psychological representation in many nonbehavioral systems,
such as the humanistic approach (Keen, 1975) and
depth psychology (Munroe, 1955). A respondent frequently constitutes the implicit reference when a
humanist complains that a behaviorist only deals
with "meaningless" behavior.

        Reinforcing stimuli, discriminative stimuli,
and operants are involved in Skinnerian free-respon-
ding, continuous-time, reward, instrumental learning, better known as operant conditioning. The concept of operant conditioning and its laboratory realization via the Skinner box slowly evolved during
the 1930s to eventually become America's dominant
form of conditioning and America's most well known
type of psychological apparatus. Skinnerians have
conditioned bar pressing in rats, key pecking in
pigeons, lever manipulation in monkeys, and button
pushing in humans. For Skinner, the most significant components of an organism's behavioral repertoire are operant responses; and operant conditioning constitutes the primary source of behavioral
change. The practical application relevance of
Skinnerian psychology derives directly from the concept of an operant and its control possibilities.
Behaviors in the natural environment are construed
as operants, subject to both reinforcement control
and stimulus control.

        Isolating a given operant from the stream of

ongoing behavioral activity requires exploitation of
the fact that an operant can have consequences, usually the procurement of a positive reinforcing stimulus, such as food. This allows a Skinnerian, or
any behaviorist, to engage in functional response
specification. Any given behavioral situation can
be subdivided into two functional responses: those
that lead to outcome X and those that lead to outcome Y. In a rat Skinner box, where X usually is
procurement of food and Y is not procurement of
food, only a bar press response (complete depression
of the bar manipulandum) is allowed to result in X;
any other response activity, such as climbing,
grooming, sleeping, or searching, results in Y. In
a typical operant conditioning experiment, only
those activities that activate the response manipulandum and result in reinforcement are ever recorded, usually in terms of sheer frequency counts of
all-or-none occurrence.

     REFERENCE SITUATION/ACTIVITY Since Skinnerian
psychology is an action system, the act of doing
something is used as the model situation (see Chapter 1) for the rest of psychology. The psychological universe is modeled after the events that are
assumed to underlie the act of doing something.

     Considering Skinner's objective and ultraposi-
tivistic orientation, the reference situation must
be externally resolved. An organism's activity must
be interpreted according to the observer's hopefully
unbiased external frame of reference. The canonical
assumption of Skinnerian psychology is that any instance of doing something must involve one or more
operants under the environmental control of some

kind of contingency, either stimulus control or reinforcement control or both. Skinner models the
psychological universe in terms of various operant
contingencies, such that operant conditioning constitutes the key psychological process.

Skinner's functional analysis of individual behavior in terms of interrelated operants and controlling discriminative and reinforcing stimuli is
quite powerful, possesses much intuitive validity,
and allows realistic practical application; however,
since it is descriptive, Skinner's interpretation of
the reference situation merely is semantic. Skinner's system merely entails a descriptive vocabulary
for labeling various psychological events. This can
be demonstrated by analyzing his two key notions of
reinforcement and stimulus discrimination.

Reinforcement is the primary mechanism of behavioral occurrence and change in Skinnerian psychology. Organisms ultimately emit behaviors that
are reinforced and refrain from activities that are
not reinforced. Doing something is not a purpose-
ful, intentional, or goal directed activity; it is
not a physical expression of an organism's conscious
mental state. A given instance of doing something
is reinforced, either by design or adventitiously;
and its frequency of occurrence is a function of
the organism's reinforcement history. The rat's bar
pressing behavior in a Skinner box serves as the
model for any and every organismic behavior.

Since Skinner's system is descriptive, a reinforcer cannot possess any special theoretical properties. Reinforcement merely is an operational notion. The only property that a reinforcer can pos-

sess is behavioral: a reinforcer strengthens behavior upon whose occurrence its delivery is contingent. The only reason that we know that a given
stimulus event can serve as a reinforcer is because
it conditions behavior. The possible reinforcing
power of a given stimulus event must be assessed in
the context of many different behaviors, exhibited
by many different organisms, and in many different
situations.

The capacity of a reinforcer to condition behavior usually is referred to as the descriptive law
of effect. This law serves as a critical control
principle in Skinnerian psychology. But this law is
not explanatory in any significant sense and is circular when it is applied to those responses that are
used to determine the possible reinforcing effects
of a given stimulus in the first place. For instance, if we find out that stimulus X is a reinforcer
for response Y in organism Z, we cannot explain the
conditioning of response Y by saying it was reinforced by stimulus X.

Although Skinner's descriptive law of effect
merely amounts to verbal labeling, it does avoid a
critical philosophical problem associated with many
theoretical conceptions of reinforcement; namely,
how does reinforcement act backwards in time (see
Hillner, 1978). Remember that response occurrence
precedes reinforcement delivery; in fact the reinforcer cannot be delivered unless the response occurs first. In Skinner's system, an operant response is assumed to be controlled by past reinforcement
history, not the currently delivered reinforcing
event. A given instance of reinforcement does not

affect the response that produced it; rather it affects future response occurrences.

As a real-space and real-time entity, reinforcement can be varied on many different dimensions, with attendant effects on behavior. The
quantity, quality, speed of delivery, and schedule
of delivery are all physical, manipulable aspects of
a reinforcer and can be observed to affect the rate,
intensity, and topography of responding. While subtle nuances in behavior are explained by reference
to numerous esoteric concepts such as will, desire,
impulse or drive in other systems of psychology
(Weiner, 1980), Skinner resolves the infinite variation in behavior strictly in terms of a corresponding infinity with respect to how reinforcement can
be delivered.

Since Skinner's system is inductively constructed, he need not worry about failures of reinforcement to control behavior. There are limits to the
viability of reinforcement as a principle of behavioral control (see Schwartz, 1978), but Skinner has
no way of specifying these ahead of time. The limits must be induced by empirical investigation.
Current critics of radical behaviorism (for instance, Herrnstein, 1977) focus on certain biological
limitations on reinforcement, opting to repress
those situations in which reinforcement has been
demonstrated to be highly successful.

In Skinner's system it is possible to bring behavior under stimulus control, in addition to reinforcement control. A given act can be reinforced in
the presence of some stimulus and not reinforced in
the absence of this stimulus or the presence of an-

other stimulus. For instance, a rat can be reinforced for bar pressing when a white light is on and
not reinforced for bar pressing when it is off.
Once the rat forms a stimulus discrimination between
"light on" and "light off," the presence and absence
of the light come to control responding and nonres-
ponding respectively. Stimulus discrimination functions as a powerful control technique in the natural
environment and allows Skinner to bypass many problems faced by perceptual, cognitive, and motivational psychologists.

It should be emphasized that a discriminative
stimulus is not an elicitor of responding or nonres-
ponding and in no way guarantees response occurrence
or nonoccurrence. It merely is an informational
event that sets the occasion for responding or non-
responding. A discriminative stimulus merely tells
the organism what specific contingency currently is
in effect and what consequences a specific response
will have. As in the case of reinforcement, there
are limits to stimulus control. It cannot be meaningfully applied or evaluated on a response by response basis, but only over a period of time in the
context of a series of response occurrences or non-
occurrences.

Skinner's strictly physicalistic and positivistic approach to the reference activity of doing
something often is misconstrued and negatively evaluated because it presumably makes the organism an
automaton (Wheeler, 1973). Such a conclusion is not
warranted for two reasons:

1. Although Skinner constructs psychological
reality in strictly physical terms, the everyday

psychological phenomena of interest to the general
public that are usually stated in mentalistic language, such as intelligence, love, faith, hope, respect, and persistence, are all derivable from Skinnerian concepts.

2. Skinner's determinism is bidirectional. Not
only does the environment influence the organism and
its behavior, but the organism and its activities
can also affect the environment. In fact, Skinner
believes that the best way to implement the change
imperative (see Chapter 1) is by intentionally designing benign physical and cultural environments
for the optimization of behavioral expression.
Skinner's conception of determinism will be analyzed
in greater detail in Chapter 8, as an aspect of descriptive explanation.

COGNITIVE BEHAVIORISM

Some form of epistemological psychology has always existed. The primary philosophical input into
psychology, as represented by the speculations of
Descartes (1650, 1662), Kant (1781), and the British
empiricists (viz. Locke, 1690; Berkeley, 1710; Hume,
1748), concerned the nature of the mind and mental
processes. The first recognized system of experimental psychology, Wundt's (1873-1874, 1896) and
Titchener's (1898, 1901, 1905) classical structuralist school, basically was cognitive in nature. American functionalism implicitly constituted a cognitive psychology, because it focused on the operations of consciousness (James, 1890). Germanic Gestalt psychology amounted to an epistemological system in which perception, or the construction of perceptual reality, constituted the canonical psycho-

logical activity (Koffka, 1935, 1963).

In classical cognitive psychology, the focus
was on mental events independent of their effect on
overt action. Many of the classical approaches to
cognition possessed no formal concept of behavior,
in the behaviorist's sense of the term. Study of
the organism's mental activities constituted an end
in itself, unconstrained by any necessity to account
for the organism as an actual response generator.
As a consequence of this, the practice of cognitive
psychology merely amounted to an effort to investigate the structure and dynamics of mentation.

The metaphysical neglect of behavior by classical cognitive psychology also led to a methodological neglect of behavior. Classical epistemological
psychology, particularly structuralism and functionalism, eventually was criticized and dismissed by
Watson (1913) as being unscientific. Investigation
of cognitive events via various forms of self-report, such as constrained introspection and unconstrained phenomenology, did not yield reliable data
subject to some kind of external validity check.
The rise of classical Watsonian descriptive behaviorism circa 1912 and its historical legacy in the
guise of many forms of neobehaviorism extending up
to the late 1950s effectively repressed epistemological psychology as a viable approach to constructing
psychological reality.

This fifty year eclipse of the epistemological
orientation in America came to an end in the early
1960s as a result of many factors that are too extensive and diverse to analyze in any depth. Suffice it to say that a new conceptual analogy and

methodological tool appeared on the psychological
scene that allowed latter-day behaviorists to relate
overt activity to internal, central processes: the
computer. Epistemological psychology was reborn in
the guise of a cognitive behaviorism, in which overt
behavior was neither conceptually nor methodologically neglected. Cognitive activities now constitute antecedents of behavior and can only be inves-
tigated through behavior. As established in Chapter
3, the classical approaches to cognition were subjective in orientation; contemporary cognitive psychology is quasi-objective in orientation.

Contemporary cognitive behaviorism is a rather
heterogeneous collection of diverse conceptual view-
points that possesses no one dominant spokesman (see
Neisser, 1976; Solso, 1979). This is an accident of
history, rather than a substantive feature of the
approach. By the time cognitive behaviorism appeared on the psychological scene, the monolithic,
closed shop atmosphere associated with the classical
schools was gone; and the practice of psychology had
become a social endeavor, with thousands, not hundreds, of investigators contributing to the construction of psychological reality. To list even a
few famous contemporary cognitive behaviorists would
slight the remaining ones and also constitute an idiosyncratic exercise; however, no one could complain
about mentioning the fact that Herbert Simon (Newell
and Simon, 1972) recently received the Nobel prize
in economics for his work on decision making and
problem solving in psychology.

Contemporary cognitive behaviorism is not the
only extant form of an epistemological psychology.

Many psychologists operate in the general tradition
of Jean Piaget (1953) and Noam Chomsky (1959, 1968)
who take a more rationalistic approach to cognition.
For want of better terminology, it can be called the
structural approach to cognition because of its emphasis on underlying fixed developmental cognitive
stages, structures, and abilities. We are not going
to be concerned with the structuralist approach to
cognition until the next section.

Two basic assumptions lie at the heart of cognitive behaviorism.

1. Any and every psychological process is implicitly cognitive in nature. This assumption is
best discussed historically. Prior to cognitive behaviorism, each of the dominant systems focused on a
particular psychological process and made it the
cornerstone of the psychological universe. An action system, such as Watsonian or Skinnerian behaviorism, is a learning and/or conditioning psychology. Classical Freudian psychoanalysis is a motivational, developmental, and/or personality psychology. Gestalt psychology in its pure form is a perceptual psychology. Humanism is a psychology of
self-adjustment. Cognitive behaviorism absorbs all
these processes--learning, memory, perception,
thinking, and the like--and makes them coequals,
such that they all constitute separate components of
the overall cognitive process. It is in this sense
that the statement "Psychology seems to be becoming
more cognitive these days," can be most meaningfully
interpreted.

2. The organism is an information processor
converting either physical or symbolic stimulus in-

put into appropriate response output or experiential
reality. This assumption is also best viewed historically. No system of psychology, not even descriptive behaviorism, denies the existence of cognitive events intervening between stimulus input and
response output. Watson (1913) banished them from
psychology because for him the brain was a great
mystery box and cognitive events were beyond the
then acceptable extant methodology. Skinner (1974)
denies that cognitive events are ever efficacious
and causal: they merely are epiphenomenal. Skinner
(1974) pushes cognitive events into the response
category; mental experience is simply another form
of behavior. Contemporary cognitive psychology exists because it is willing to regard cognition as a
causal source of behavior and current acceptable
methodology is capable of investigating such events.
The computer analogy serves as both the conceptual
and methodological basis of cognitive behaviorism.
The organism is treated as simply another kind of
information processor, à la the computer; and the
computer is used to evaluate numerous cognitive theories, models, and mechanisms via computer simulation and artificial intelligence techniques (see
Weizenbaum, 1976; Boden, 1977; Newell and Simon,
1981). Although the computer analogy holds less
fascination for the cognitive behaviorist than it
once did, it is still the general heuristic that
makes a contemporary epistemological psychology possible.

     CONTENT OF OBSERVATION Cognitive behaviorism
is a logical extension of descriptive behaviorism.
Stimuli and responses are still regarded as physi-

cal events, but their observation and manipulation
in a laboratory setting are incidental to the primary goal of inferring the nature of the organism's
cognitive apparatus. Cognitive behaviorism also is
a conceptual extension of logical behaviorism. The
attempt is still made to relate overt behavior to
internal processes; but they are central, as opposed
to peripheral, in nature.

     Construction of the internal cognitive appara-
tus intervening between input and output is a complex process, involving many theoretical assumptions. The series of events involved in information
processing is potentially infinite in number, such
that the cognitive behaviorist finds it convenient
to assume that a limited number of information processing stages exist and that they are organized in
some hierarchical fashion. The content of the stages corresponds to the more-or-less traditional psychological processes: stimulus or sensory decoding,
pattern recognition or perception, memory formation
and retrieval, concept formation, decision making,
problem solving, thinking, and the like. In the
context of the human being, the language function
constitutes a cognitive domain unto itself and also
influences the traditional processes. A given experiment usually focuses on only one stage or substage, such as pattern recognition, iconic memory,
short term memory, long term memory, or decision making. It still is an unresolved experimental question whether processing occurs in a sequential or
simultaneous manner in the context of a given stage
or substage (Kendler, 1981). The cognitive psychologist is discovering what the functionally oriented

verbal learning specialist (see Underwood and
Schulz, 1960; Jung, 1968) has known for decades: the
organism can credibly perform in a wide variety of
cognitive tasks, with each one admitting of virtually infinite parametric variation.

   A hypothetical cognitive model amounts to a
theory and usually is tested via computer simulation
(Simon, 1974). The model is stated in mathematical
or computer program form and is "run" on a computer.
The computer's performance is compared to that of
the human, and the degree of correspondence between
the two performances is used to infer the viability
of the model. Three logical outcomes are possible:

   1. The performances essentially match. This is
a successful simulation, and it is assumed that the
cognitive model represents what the human is doing.

   2. The performance of the human exceeds that of
the computer. This is an unsuccessful simulation,
because too little is imputed to the human. The
cognitive model underestimates the human's information processing capacity.

   3. The performance of the computer exceeds that
of the human. This is an unsuccessful simulation,
because too much is imputed to the human. The cognitive model overestimates the human's information
processing capability. This outcome is conceptually
tricky, because in many cognitive tasks it is possible to program a computer to act more intelligent-
ly than a human. This situation is provided for in
the technical literature by the investigation of artificial intelligence, in which machine or computer
intelligence is focused on independently of the human being as a comparative reference point (Dennett,

1978a).

REFERENCE SITUATION/ACTIVITY   Doing something
for the cognitive psychologist is the product of
some kind of internal significating structure, such
as an expectation, belief, hypothesis, value, or
rule.   Instrumental activity need not be rationalistic or optimal in the context of some mathematical
decision making model in order for it to be cognitively determined.   The basic thesis of cognitive
behaviorism is simply that overt behavior is not an
automatic or mere linear function of the stimulus
input.   Each person's cognitive apparatus processes
the input and determines the nature of the output.

Cognitive psychologists are fond of exposing
subjects with different expectations or beliefs to
the same ostensible objective physical stimulus situation and demonstrating that the exhibited behavior
is a function of the differential cognitions.   For
instance, it has been shown (1) that verbal conditioning only occurs if the subject is aware of the
specific operant contingency involved (see Dulany,
1962), (2) that instrumental learning is demonstrated only if the subject possesses the expectation
that the exhibition of the learned behavior leads to
the procurement of some valuable stimulus object
(Tolman, 1932; Phares, 1976), and (3) that many
problem solving behaviors are guided by hypotheses,
instead of being random (Krechevsky, 1932; Restle,
1962).

Much, if not all, of the cognitive activity
that determines overt behavior is implicit and beyond the conscious awareness of the reacting organism: people simply are not aware of deciding to do

something. The ultimate source of overt behavior
for the cognitivist is the same as that for the descriptive behaviorist: past experience. But it is
stated in different language in the two approaches.
In Skinnerian behaviorism, past experience is codified in terms of specific reinforcement history. In
cognitive behaviorism, past experience is codified
in terms of the content of internal, mediating significating structures. Significating structures are
not innate, do not exist in a vacuum, and are not
immutable entities. They change over time, and the
organism's behaviors change over time as a result of
exposure to differential experience.

The cognitive account of doing something possesses much more face validity than a purely descriptive behavioristic account because it mimics the
everyday use of verbal jargon on the part of the
general public. We are wont to say "I think," "I
believe," or "I expect." We never say "I am reinforced for ......," or "The controlling stimulus
is ...."

The cognitive account of doing something is not
necessarily teleological at a technical level; however, the everyday verbalisms characteristic of cognitive language often contain reference to future
goals and intentions. For instance, a college student might say "I am going to school in order to
earn a degree and get a good job in the future."
This statement omits reference to the causal conditions that Skinnerians like to emphasize; namely,
the specific reinforcement history and controlling
stimuli that maintain current, ongoing college behavior. A Skinnerian argues that mentalistic langu-

age always is reducible to physical thing language. The cognitive behaviorist argues that cognitive processes are emergent in nature and thus not reducible to physical thing language.

Cognition is not assumed to be unique to the human organism. A cognitive interpretation can be given to an animal's instrumental behavior, although it is recognized that animal cognition is not as symbolically rich as that of the human (Restle, 1975). This is why contemporary humanistic psychology (Rychlak, 1977; Wertheimer, 1978) does not consider cognitive behaviorism to be an appreciable advance over Skinnerian psychology. Cognitive behaviorism does not treat the human being as a unique form of life and does not regard doing something as a unique form of human behavior. Cognitive behaviorism might put the mind back in psychology, but it does not put the human back in psychology.

PIAGETIAN STRUCTURAL PSYCHOLOGY

Many people (for instance, Flanagan, 1984) consider Jean Piaget (1953, 1954, 1970, 1977) to be the greatest European psychologist, if not the pre-eminent psychologist, of the twentieth century, although he has virtually nothing in common with the overall American behavioristic, experimental tradition. Piaget is similar to both Pavlov (1927) and Freud (1939, 1949) in the sense that his thought serves as a standard by which other systems are judged, such that the basic tenets of his system remain unchallenged in the face of contradictory empirical evidence. Piaget often is compared to Skinner (1974): both men have had tremendous philosophical and operational influence on the thrust and directionality

of twentieth century psychology. Actually, Piaget
is quite similar to Wundt (1896): both men basically
were mental/cognitive philosophers who found it
pragmatic to generate empirical data on one or more
aspect of conscious awareness.

Piaget died in 1980, at the age of eighty-four,
having spent over half a century focusing on the
epistemological aspects of human development. A native Swiss who preferred speaking and writing in
French, Piaget was a recognized expert on mollusks
as a teenager and earned a doctorate in zoology at
Neuchâtel by the time he was twenty-two years old.
His initial work of a purely psychological nature
involved his standardization of some of Cyril Burt's
(1921, 1958) reasoning tests at Simon's (with Binet,
1913) pedagogical laboratory located in a Paris
grade school. Piaget went beyond the mere psychometric, or calibrational, aspects of IQ testing by
investigating why a child was correct or incorrect
on a specific item. The act of interviewing children as to why they were wrong on an item served as
the model for his future research activities.

Piaget became research director of the J. J.
Rousseau Institute in Geneva in 1921, and this post
developed into a lifetime position. His voluminous
writings were not translated into English until the
1960s; to the best of my knowledge, Piaget never
visited the United States. Various colleagues, such
as Bärbel Inhelder (with Piaget, 1958), have spread
Piaget's message to America. Piaget's thought currently is part of the contextual milieu in which
contemporary cognitive behaviorism operates.

Piaget's system can be described from many dif-

ferent perspectives. We are going to stress (1) his
Kantian (1781) heritage and (2) his structural, as
opposed to functional, orientation.

CONTENT OF OBSERVATION   Piagetian psychology
amounts to a structural, genetic-epistemological
system. Epistemological essentially means cognitive; genetic denotes a focus on development; structural refers to Piaget's preferred mode of explanation. Piaget's system encompasses the evolution of
the overall reasoning or thinking abilities of the
human being from birth to adolescence, in an interpretive framework emphasizing structural changes in
underlying biologically based mental capacities.
The psychological reality that Piaget created is one
that exists inside a child's brain. Unlike Freud,
Piaget's system strictly focuses on rational or logical aspects of the child's world, not on emotional
or motivational aspects.

Piaget is not interested in information processing in the cognitive behavioristic (Anderson, 1980)
sense of the term. He commenced his research program long before the computer became the conceptual
and methodological model for cognition. Piaget does
not conceive of cognition as a series of interrelated recognition, learning, and memory tasks that can
be studied in the laboratory. Piaget focuses on abstract laws of thought, or logical reality construction, and the underlying biological capacities that
make them possible.

Just as Wundt can be construed as bringing British empiricism into the laboratory, Piaget can be
viewed as subjecting some basic Kantian notions to
empirical analysis. Piaget focuses on a child's

conception of space, time, causality, logic, self,
and object, most of which constitute the substance
of Kantian a priori categories. Piaget is Kantian
in an additional respect: his system presupposes
that a child's cognitive apparatus actively constructs these entities; they are not passive products of mere accidental or associational experience,
à la the British empiricists. Piaget's system does
assume some degree of nativism or preformationism
(see Flanagan, 1984), although it is not committed
to a strict preformationism in an all-or-none sense.
The mind is not a blank slate at birth. There is
some initial structure, but its evolutionary development is a product of the child's continual interaction with the surrounding physical and social environment.

Piaget is probably most well known for his abstraction of cognitive development in terms of four
monolithic, or absolutistic, stages: (1) sensory-motor, (2) preoperational, (3) concrete operational,
and (4) formal operational. A stage merely is a
specific constellation of mental structures and capacities. It is shorthand notation for the specific
potentialities that the organism's cognitive apparatus possesses at a given moment in time. The fundamental features of Piaget's developmental theory revolve around the assumption that each successive
stage is quantitatively more complex than and qualitatively different from the immediately prior stage.
Transition from one stage to another entails the capability of constructing a vastly different psychological reality.

1. The sensory-motor stage encompasses the

first two years of life. The child developes a general sense of things through sensory stimulation and
motor contact with the world. The child learns
about its own body and differentiates it from external objects. This stage does not involve cognition,
or thinking, in the traditional sense of the term.

2. The preoperational stage characterizes children between two and seven years of age. The world
and the self are now represented by words and mental
images: the child is now capable of some basic cognitive activity; however, it is primitive by adult
standards. Thought at this stage is characterized
by egocentrism, anthropomorphism, and random serial-
ization.

3. The concrete operational stage extends from
the age of seven to eleven. The child manipulates
the words and mental images representing reality in
a meaningful way for the first time. The child is
capable of quasi-adult thinking in specific concrete
situations: it displays most of the traditional con-
servations, such as quantity, number, and substance;
it engages in rudimentary concept formation and
classification; and it displays a primitive capacity for measurement.

4. The formal operational stage commences at
eleven and continues throughout adulthood. The
child now can manipulate representations of representations: it indulges in abstract adult thinking
and reasoning. No longer is thinking egocentric or
stimulus-bound. The individual is in possession of
a set of abstract rules or logical operations that
transcend specific circumstances and seem to have
analytic truth value.

Piaget's stage conception of cognitive development has five identifying features that distinguish
it from other approaches to epistemological development:

1. The stages are universal in two respects.
They are characteristic of all cultures and every
normal person within a culture. Every child with
standard biological equipment and stimulation can be
expected to attain the formal operational adult
stage.

2. The sequencing of the stages is fixed, with
no exceptions, although the ages of stage transi-
tions only are approximate. Each child must progress through the same standard sequence with some
variation in age of stage transition.

3. Progression through the stages is irrever-
sible. No regression to a prior stage is possible.
Degeneration of cognitive capacity does not even occur for the elderly.

4. Each stage amounts to an integration or logical development of the prior stage and, therefore,
of all prior stages. Although each stage affords
the construction of a radically different psychological reality, it emerges from and builds onto the
foundation established by the prior stage(s).

5. Each successive stage affords a closer approximation to actual physical reality. Each successive stage is epistemologically more adequate
than the prior stage. This is a normative, as opposed to descriptive, aspect of Piaget's psychology,
with the formal operational stage representing the
highest degree of cognitive development.

Piaget's genetic epistemology is structural be-

cause he conceives of the stages as explanatory entities. (Remember a stage merely is a constellation
of specific biologically sourced mental capacities.)
Many American psychologists (see Flavell, 1963;
Brainerd, 1978) consider the stage notion to be descriptive at best and circular at worst. It is descriptive because it merely relabels the behavioral
phenomena at another level of analysis. Its circularity is evident once the age constraints on a
stage are removed. The only difference between a
specific Piagetian mental structure--the one underlying conservation of number for instance--and the
more general notion of a mental faculty or power--
derivative of eighteenth and nineteenth century
Scottish philosophy (Hillner, 1984)--is the age
specification (see Chapter 8 on circular explanation).

     Piaget does attempt to explain stage transi-
tions. In other words, he attempts to account for
the stages as explanatory entities. His dynamics
involve the complementary processes of assimilation
and accommodation. New information from the external world must be assimilated, and the cognitive apparatus must change to accommodate the new information. In this manner a state of overall cognitive
equilibrium or equilibration is maintained. The
overall process can be viewed as a self-regulating,
cybernetic feedback system involving the interaction
of constitutional and experiential components. Un-
fortunately, Piaget's dynamics does not sufficiently
explain the accretive or constructivist aspect of
cognitive development: why is cognitive development
teleologically aimed at a more perfect representa-

tion (construction) of the world; or why is each
successive stage an improvement over the prior
stage?   The push toward accretive or constructivist
equilibration requires a firm commitment to the notion of biological prewiring, much in the Chomskian
(1968) sense with respect to the language facility
(see Fodor, 1979).

At a methodological level, the components of
Piaget's content of observation are continuous with
those of American functionalism or cognitive behaviorism.   The object of direct observation is behavior; the locus of causation is an inferred cognitive
entity or operation.   Piaget both observed the behavior of children in naturalistic and experimentally constrained contexts and accepted their self-report, or introspections, in various cognitive contexts.   But the similarity between Piaget's research
endeavors and those of functionally oriented American cognitive psychologists ends at the componential
level of the content of observation.   Piaget viola-
ted virtually every tenet of experimental psychology.   For instance:

1. He ran no control groups.

2. He did not systematically use or vary independent variables.

3. He did not engage in statistical analysis.

4. He did not conceive of subjects as points in
a more comprehensive subject space (subject specification and sampling).

5. He was completely oblivious to the physical
form or format of his experiments and how these
could interact with the object of study (mental processes).   He did not realize that his research was

domain or task specific.

   6. He did not engage in elaborate operational
definition.

   Piaget has inspired a vast amount of American
research (see Donaldson, 1978; Gelman, 1978), seeking to replicate his basic conclusions, the results
of which are not entirely unexpected: Piaget's basic
conception of cognitive development has not been de-
throned, but merely fine tuned. American psychologists sympathetic to Piaget merely have leavened his
tenets to accommodate the operational, domain or
task specific, and cultural aspects of cognition.

   Piaget's structural approach and contemporary
cognitive behaviorism complement each other in many
respects. Piaget focuses on structure; cognitive
behaviorists focus on function or dynamics. Piaget
attempted an overall macro analysis; information
processing psychology seeks a micro analysis. Piaget's approach is more philosophically oriented or
pure; computer oriented psychologists are more operationally or practically oriented.

   REFERENCE SITUATION/ACTIVITY Piaget's approach
to the act of doing something is conditioned by the
fact that he created an epistemological system.
Such a system is not compellingly concerned with
overt behavior as an end in itself. Prediction and
control of overt behavior in the Skinnerian (1974)
descriptive behavioristic sense is foreign to Piaget. Yet, like cognitive behaviorists (Anderson,
1980) and logical behaviorists (see Chapter 3), Piaget realizes that the organism is not a simple stimulus input-response output machine. Overt behavior
is the expression or extension of bona fide cogni-

tive events intervening between input and output.

Piaget's unique contribution to the history of
psychology is his explicit attempt to construct the
purely epistemological, or reasoning, aspect of this
intervening system. In effect, he only attempts to
specify the structural/cognitive constraints on behavioral functioning. For Piaget, the human organism merely is a semantic machine or logic device.
Piaget's system is mute with respect to motivation,
emotion, and personality. In this respect, Piaget's
psychology is analogous to the Freudian (1939, 1949)
depth psychology approach, except that he focuses on
the rational, cognitive antecedents of behavior, not
the irrational, unconscious, conative antecedents of
behavior. Piaget is a Freud of rationality, while
Freud is a Piaget of irrationality. Even their respective methodologies correspond, in the sense that
they are unorthodox by behavioristic standards.

Piaget's approach to overt behavior lies somewhere between Wundt's (1896) epistemological system
and those of American functionalism (Carr, 1925) and
cognitive behaviorism (Solso, 1979). Unlike Wundt,
Piaget realizes behavior exists. Like American cognitivists, Piaget's interest in overt behavior is
only incidental. Like Wundt, Piaget locates the
primary psychological reality within the skin. Unlike American cognitivists, Piaget embeds behavior
in a truly structural framework reminiscent of erstwhile faculty psychology (Hillner, 1984). Unlike
Wundt, Piaget's thought does have practical application consequences, especially with respect to education, although he has left the implementation of
these to others. Like American epistemological psy-

chology, his system is not divorced from pragmatic
considerations and does not exist in a behavioral
vacuum. Like Wundt, Piaget's psychology is an extension of his interest in epistemological philosophy. Unlike American cognitive psychology, Piaget's
system is not a reaction to a historical neglect of
cognition occasioned by the overweaning influence of
descriptive behaviorism.

Certainly, Piaget's temperament and values are
closer to those of Wundt, but his goals and objec-
tives correspond more closely to those of functionalism and cognitive behaviorism. In Piaget we have
a figure who does not want to divorce behavior from
conscious activity, or intelligence. For Piaget,
human behavior is epistemologically orchestrated behavior or the behavior of an intellectually viable
organism. In a sense, Piaget is a humanist (à la
Maslow, 1971), but one strictly concerned with our
intellectual life.

Piaget is neither a strict nativist nor a
strict environmentalist. He embeds the human organism in a naturalistic context such that mentation
and overt behavior are both a function of and constrained by structures and mechanisms, sometimes
called schemata, that are the joint product of neural wiring and interaction with the environment. Because Piaget basically is an "experimental epistem-
ologist," his life work is propaedeutic to the creation of a "meaningful" action psychology.

In Piaget's system, behavioral expression would
have to be strictly stage dependent. Behavior during the sensory-motor stage would be indistinguishable from that exhibited by an animal, especially

one with no known appreciable cognitive facility.
(This is the level at which a descriptive behaviorist prefers to interpret all behavior.) Behavior
produced in the succeeding tripartite operational
stages would have to reflect the organism's current
conception of psychological reality as constructed
by the then extant rules and operations permitted by
its cognitive apparatus.

　　　To demonstrate that Piaget's approach is gener-
alizable beyond mere epistemology, we can refer to
Kohlberg's (1981) work on moral development. He
uses Piaget's developmental theory as a model for
his own moral system, in which the organism is construed as progressing through a series of more differentiated and enlightened moral stages. Kohlberg's research does suffer from one essential draw-
back: successive stages cannot be evaluated with
respect to adequacy because there is no universally
agreed upon ethical reality. Ethical injunctions
possess a vastly different epistemological status
than empirical facts about the so-called real world
(see Chapter 12).

FREUDIAN PSYCHOANALYSIS

　　　The Freudian psychoanalytic approach is perhaps
the world's best known attempt to construct a psychological reality, although Freud himself was a
trained physician/neurologist who only dealt with
certain members of the abnormal population. Psychoanalysis transcends psychology and constitutes a
significant component of our intellectual history
and cultural development. Freud ranks with Christ,
Copernicus, Newton, and Darwin as individuals who
profoundly affected humanity's view of itself and

the universe.

Psychoanalysis is a depth psychology, which basically is a philosophy of human nature, as opposed
to a scientific account of the organism as a real-
space and real-time entity (Fancher, 1973). Freud
focuses on the individual's inner psychic life; and
he views the human being as a battleground of numerous inner forces, many of which are unconscious and
in conflict. In depth psychology, both overt behavior and its internal psychodynamic determinants constitute a self-contained, closed system, such that
the significant components of the psychological universe are located within the skin of the organism.

Freudian psychology legitimatized the study of
abnormal behavior and established abnormality as a
psychogenic entity (Menninger and Holzman, 1973).
It was psychoanalysis, not the academic, experimental systems, that fostered the notion that the human
organism possesses a unique psychological being that
cannot be accounted for by any other professional
discipline. The prototypical psychological query
for the general public is "What makes a person
tick?" The specific approach to psychology and conception of the human being implied by this question
is indigenous to Freudian psychoanalysis. Psychoanalysis exhausts psychology for the average person.

No other system of psychology is as personal as
psychoanalysis or has been as closely tied to the
personality, background, and aspirations of its creator. Elaborate psychoanalytic interpretations have
been made of the origin of psychoanalysis (for instance, Jones, 1953, 1957, 1961; Rieff, 1959; Schur,
1972; Roazen, 1975). When was the last time a be-

havioristic interpretation was given to the origin
of classical Watsonian behaviorism?

No other system of psychology possesses as much
intuitive validity as psychoanalysis. This derives
from the fact that Freud (1965) focuses on psychological phenomena that are of inherent interest to
the general public: neurotic symptoms, dreams and
dream symbolism, slips of the tongue, sex, unconscious desires and motivation, religion, and primitive instincts.

Freud's approach to the construction of a psychological universe is so all-encompassing and pervasive that many a phenomenon in the natural environment frequently is explained simply by saying that
"It is Freudian." Psychoanalysis presumably explains everything from an erection to the ressurec-
tion. You never hear an analogous statement such as
"It is Skinnerian."

Freudian psychoanalysis is different from other
brands of psychology, amounting to virtual dogma requiring "true believer" status on the part of its
adherents (Robinson, 1979). Since Freudian psychology possesses many of the characteristics of a religion, dissidents (i.e., heretics) are forced to
leave the movement and create different versions of
depth psychology, Jung (1916, 1953) and Adler (1959)
constituting the two primary cases. Experimental
psychologists (for instance, Skinner, 1954) are wont
to deride the internecine warfare among the different versions of depth psychology. Yet, the Freudian
approach is the only view of psychological reality
to endure for an entire century and shows no sign of
imminent demise.

CONTENT OF OBSERVATION   Freud constructed his psychological universe from observations of a patient's self-report during a psychoanalytic therapy session. The self-report is usually that of an adult, upper-class female, suffering some kind of neurosis and attempting to recall various childhood experiences. Inducing the nature of psychological reality from the content of self-report is not unique to psychoanalysis. It is done in any phenomenologically based psychology, such as structuralism, Gestalt psychology, and humanism. Like structuralism and Gestalt psychology, Freud sought nomothetic truth, in his case a universally applicable psychodynamic system. Unlike humanism, Freud did not seek idiographic truth: a person's own private view of the world. This means that Freud faced problems of reliability and validity that were not resolved satisfactorily because he denied the applicability of any external empirical check on the content of his inductions. Freud merely subscribed to intuitive validity and internal self-consistency as appropriate criteria for judging the relevancy of his inductions (see Chapter 8).

Although Freud's system is personalistic in the sense that another therapist faced with the same type of self-report need not induce the same underlying psychodynamics, criticism of Freud on this point is not appropriate. Freud had received philosophical, scientific, and medical training (Jones, 1953). He was not a naive observer and inducer. The concept of psychoanalysis (1) as a type of therapy and (2) as a world view evolved concurrently. Not only were the content of Freud's inductions nov-

el, but the situation giving rise to the inductions
was also novel. The primary components of psychoanalytic therapy, free association and dream interpretation, had diagnostic value for Freud. It was not
incumbent on Freud to demonstrate that they also
served as unbiased sources of universally applicable
psychological truth. Any system of psychology possesses a preferred data base. It had to be the psychoanalytic therapy session for Freud; it had to be
a rat in a Skinner box for Skinner. Remember that
Freud legitimatized the psychogenic interpretation
of abnormality, specifically the neuroses; and he
very cautiously constructed his revolutionary view
of the psychological universe. He did not accept
the necessity of postulating the existence of unconscious processes or the role of sex without distress. In retrospect, it is unfortunate that
Freud's inductive activities are evaluated almost
exclusively in terms of his own personality, desires, and aspirations (for instance, Rieff, 1959).

Freud can be criticized for his refusal to accept the validity of any other psychoanalyst's interpretation of "depth reality" and his failure to
realize the limitations of his very restricted patient population. Freud contributed to social and
cultural history, but he did not realize that his
system is also the product of a given social and
cultural environment. Contemporary neo-Freudians
are more tolerant in this respect and seek an integration of psychoanalytically derived truth and general social science knowledge (Horney, 1939, 1950;
Fromm, 1947; Sullivan, 1953).

REFERENCE SITUATION/ACTIVITY Freud is not com-

pellingly concerned with the everyday, mundane act
of doing something. He has no formal concept of behavior. It is not really a real-space and real-time
event for him. Behavioral occurrence is incidental.
It is merely the external representation of the
seething psychological reality existing inside the
organism. Psychoanalysis basically is a motivational, developmental, and/or personality psychology;
and it is only the motivational aspect that is of
any direct relevance to individual behavioral occurrences. Developmental and personality psychology
primarily focus on long term capacities and traits
characteristic of a given organism.

Psychoanalysis can explain doing something; but
this is not the primary goal of a depth psychology,
as it is for most experimentally derived systems of
psychology. Psychoanalysis focuses on the state of
an organism's psychodynamic system and the organism's overall level of psychological adjustment.
Both the observation and explanation of overt behavior merely serve as a means to this end.

Freud's (1939, 1949) psychodynamic system consists of (1) two basic motivational constructs--the
life instinct or libido and the death instinct; (2)
three levels of awareness--conscious, preconscious,
and unconscious; (3) three systems of personality--
id, ego, and superego; (4) five psychosexual stages
of development--oral, anal, phallic, latency, and
genital; and (5) numerous defense mechanisms, such
as projection, displacement, repression, and regression.

Freud's system overdetermines individual behavioral occurrence and only affords after-the-fact, or

post hoc, explanation (Cummins, 1983). Overdetermination means that a given instance of doing something can occur for more than one psychodynamically
related reason. Post hoc explanation occurs after
the behavioral occurrence of interest happens.
Freudian psychoanalysis only allows postdiction, not
prediction. Overdetermination and postdiction of behavioral occurrence by Freudian psychodynamics are
two of the reasons why experimental systems, such as
behaviorism, do not take psychoanalysis seriously
(Skinner, 1954).

        Freud does not focus on activities that are
done in a normal way. For instance, the act of
walking or washing one's hands does not interest
Freud. But when an activity is done in an abnormal
way, Freudian psychodynamics enters the picture.
When a person walks so as to avoid the cracks and
lines in a sidewalk or when a person compulsively
engages in hand washing every five minutes, psychoanalysis is relevant and has a ready explanation.
Because Freud was a member of the helping profession
(contemporary terminology here), he was more interested in those cases where the underlying psychodynamic system malfunctions or breaks down than in
those instances where the system is working smoothly
and the organism experiences no psychological distress.

        The resolving capacity of the Freudian system
is unquestioned by the general public (Marx and Hillix, 1979). It is fascinated by sex; aggression;
involuntary, unconsciously motivated, often antisoc-
ial behavior; convoluted defense mechanism derived
behaviors; dreams and dream symbolism; neurotic

symptoms; and minor aberrations, such as fetishes, slips of the tongue, and manipulatory accidents. In this context, Freud's crowning achievement was the demonstration that many everyday, mundane activities are complexly determined by forces beyond the organism's awareness. The existence of unconscious motivation makes everyone suspect; the existence of defense mechanisms makes everyone irrational; the existence of psychic determination makes everyone simply another impulsive animal. Psychoanalysis may take the purity, idealism, and rationality out of life; but it makes life far more interesting.

HUMANISTIC PSYCHOLOGY

Humanistic psychology is an aspect of the third force movement in America that also includes elements of existentialism and phenomenology. Third force psychology is a protest movement, membership in which by and large is by self-acclamation (Robinson, 1979). The humanistic approach is quite eclectic and diverse; however, its basic tenet is clear: the objective, natural science orientation is irrelevant for a proper psychological understanding of the individual organism. Physical materialism or mechanism, physiological reductionism, and analysis by synthesis are decried by the humanistic psychologist. Experimental psychology removes the humanness, humaneness, or humanity from the individual.

Human is a technical term in the humanistic approach. We are special, unique, and emergent; we transcend the natural universe. Human experience must be resolved on its own terms. Humanism assumes that there is some unique residual component of an individual over and above any model contingent enti-

ties characteristic of the other systems of psychology, such as information processing, conditioning
mechanisms, primitive instincts, or irrational forces.   In humanism, the model of an individual is the
revealed nature of that individual.   The basic reference point is people as they know themselves.   As
a consequence of this, it could be argued that much
of the derivative content of humanistic psychology
is circular.

The humanistic system is a reaction against
both behaviorism, especially descriptive, and classical depth psychology, especially Freudian psychoanalysis (Maslow, 1971).   It decries the environmental determinism, reflexology, blind conditioning,
and animal as model aspects of behaviorism.   It decries the psychic determinism, irrational forces,
and focus on abnormality characteristics of psychoanalysis.   Humanistic psychology actually is an intellectual extension of depth psychology and could
be regarded as a latter-day depth formulation (Hillner, 1984).   Humanism emphasizes the positive, not
negative, aspects of people; stresses the benign inner determination of behavior, making people responsible for their own destiny; and focuses on the
characteristics of well-adjusted and self-fulfilled
individuals.

The humanistic approach strictly is idiographic, focusing on the consciousness, awareness, feelings, and overall state of psychological well being
of the individual person, as revealed by the content
of self-report.   It is assumed that each organism
lives in its own subjective world, and the notion of
psychological reality only has meaning on an indi-

vidual basis. The ultimate goal of humanism is the
understanding of the individual organism in terms of
its own view of the world. The only possible justification for active psychological, or psychiatric,
intervention is the enhancement of an organism's adjustment to life. This makes humanism a clinical,
as opposed to an experimental, psychology; and humanism only overlaps with traditional experimental
psychology in such areas as personality, development, therapy, counseling, motivation, and emotion.
The abstract psychological processes, such as perception, conditioning, and memory, are bypassed by
humanistic psychologists. They are only concerned
with the ultimate end product of these processes:
experience.

       A naive reading of the humanistic literature
would lead to the conclusion that a humanist is a
super Christian. The humanist stresses love, trust,
faith, values, concern, happiness, commitment, self-
awareness, an authentic or validated self, and the
like. Humanism is not religious in its orientation,
but its 180° turn from behaviorism and its use of
immanently anthropomorphic terminology make it appear as an applied Christianity. The humanistic
literature is particularly frustrating to the hard-
core behaviorist because of its exhortatory tone and
its confounding of means and ends, or mechanisms and
goals. To the behaviorist (for instance, Skinner,
1974), humanistic dogma exists in a vacuum; and the
mere willing of a set of desirable goals is not sufficient for their realistic attainment.

       The third force movement coalesced in America
in the early 1960s under the tutelage of Abraham

Maslow (1962, 1968, 1970, 1971). Since his death in
1970, humanism has been carried on under the aegis
of Carl Rogers (1942, 1951, 1961). Maslow, a con-
verted behaviorist in the Harlow (1949) tradition,
is best known for his concept of self-actualization
and his hierarchical theory of motivation. Rogers,
the father of client-centered therapy, is the most
well known and accepted American phenomenologically
oriented psychologist. Other prominent contemporary
humanistic psychologists in the United States include Theodore Rychlak (1976, 1977), Amadeo Giorgi
(1970), and Adrian van Kaam (1965, 1966).

CONTENT OF OBSERVATION Humanistic psychology
demonstrates better than any other system that the
distinction between conscious experience and overt
behavior merely is semantic in nature. The basic
subject matter of humanism can be characterized by
either labeling: the organism's feeling state and
level of awareness or the organism's holistic, adaptive activity. The main thing is that the humanist's approach to conscious experience is discontinuous with that of structuralism and its conception
of behavior is radically different from that of behaviorism. Humanism really is an expanded form of
Gestalt psychology, which focused on both the content of perceptual experience and holistic, organized motor acts (Hillner, 1984).

Psychological reality is the exclusive property
of the feeling, experiencing, self-aware organism in
humanism. There is no external psychological reality independent of the consciousness of the individual organism. The humanistic psychologist infers
the existence and content of this reality by accep-

ting a person's self-report or observing the person's behavior. But note that the humanist is not
allowed to bring any external interpretive criterion
to an observation situation. All interpretation
must be done in the context of the person's own view
of the world. Strictly speaking, humanistic psychology has no reliability and/or validity problems.
No generalization is made beyond the individual case
to some underlying, transcendental psychological universe.

Humanism has no monolithic methodology beyond
some prescriptive negatives (Weiner, 1980):

1. The relevance of a given research project
should be judged solely on its ability to reveal the
psychological nature of the individual organism, not
on methodological purity or convenience.

2. Animal subjects are irrelevant for a psychological understanding of the human being.

3. Only healthy, wholesome, well-adjusted individuals constitute proper objects of concern.

4. Frequency counts of behavioral occurrences
are meaningless unless the behavior possesses meaning for the organism.

5. Traditional experimental operations and independent variables are artificial and destroy the
humanity of the subject in most laboratory contexts.

Much of the humanist's phenomenological analysis occurs in a therapeutic situation, as opposed to
a strictly experimental situation focusing on one or
more of the abstract psychological processes (Rogers, 1951). Humanistic psychology deals almost exclusively with response-derived and response-inferred constructs--the kind of information that comes

from projective personality tests, surveys, self-
analysis inventories, and the like. The structure
of humanistic knowledge basically involves response-
response laws and relationships, as opposed to behavioristic knowledge that involves stimulus-response laws and relationships.

REFERENCE SITUATION/ACTIVITY Since humanism is
a form of latter-day depth psychology, doing something is not a real-space and real-time event.
Overt activity, in itself, is incidental and merely
serves as a reflection of the organism's inner psychological state. Accounting for everyday, mundane
acts in terms of physicalistic mechanisms is an anathema for the humanist. The humanistic approach
simply is not interested in the lower level, or
physiologically dependent, maintenance activities
exhibited by the human organism.

Humanistic psychology disregards all forms of
overt behavior that are common to both humans and
animals. Humanism focuses on our unique aspects.
In this context, the fundamental human property is
self-awareness or self-consciousness. This is mani-
fested in the exhibition of intentional behavior
that attempts to fulfill goals which are distinctly
human in nature. In the humanistic view, the primary goal of the individual is self-fulfillment,
self-actualization, or self-realization (Maslow,
1970; Rogers, 1961). Humanism only deals with
"meaningful" behavior that reflects an organism's
uniqueness, goals, and humanity. In Skinnerian descriptive behaviorism, only controlled behavior is
true behavior. In humanism, only behavior interpre-
table in the context of the individual's subjective

view of psychological reality is true behavior.

The humanistic approach to overt behavior is
prescriptive, as opposed to descriptive. It takes
doing something for granted at a descriptive level
and only deals with doing something at an evaluational level. The humanist judges whether a piece
of behavior is meaningful in the context of an organism's conception of psychological reality. Non-
meaningful behavior is refractory and must be corrected; meaningful behavior is congruent and must be
encouraged.

Humanists stress personal growth and like to
use a flowering analogy. The humanist's role is
similar to that of a gardner tending plants and fa-
cilitating growth. Much of humanistic explanation
tends to be teleological in nature, because current
behavior is resolved in terms of future goals. To
say that a person is going to college to earn a degree and secure a good job; that is, for self-realization purposes, is perfectly legitimate for the humanist.

Because humanistic psychology is so evaluative,
it is more readily exploitable than the hard-core
experimental systems. It is somewhat fortuitous
that the value system of the typical contemporary
humanist is so benign and overlaps so highly with
Christian ideals. On the reverse side of the coin,
it should be remembered that humanism is a component
of the general tradition of understanding psychology that was exploited by various European racist,
totalitarian regimes in the 1930s and 1940s (Dilthey, 1924; Spranger, 1925, 1928).

Humanism's exclusive focus on meaningful, self-

validating behavior is certainly a worthy goal; however, one wonders about such organisms as children,
retardates, and chronic schizophrenics, essentially
preverbals or nonverbals, who cannot express their
feelings and goals in any coherent fashion, even if
they possess them. By definition, humanistic psychology is not applicable to them. By divorcing itself from the objective, scientific tradition and
the kinds of psychological phenomena that are indigenous to this framework, humanism makes psychology
the private domain of a restricted sample of normal,
educated, verbal adults. In the long run, humanism
may devolve to a rationalization psychology, possessing no effective mechanisms of psychological
change, that will merely justify the status quo.
The humanist must accept received psychological reality as the only psychological reality, and what
constitutes meaningful behavior may always be a random function of unknown variables.

DIALECTICAL PSYCHOLOGY

Dialectical psychology began as a self-conscious system in America in the early 1970s under
the intellectual guidance and public relations efforts of the late Klaus Riegel (1975, 1978, 1979),
a native German who eventually became associated
with the University of Michigan. Dialectical psychology represents an explicit attempt to bridge the
gap that exists between objective psychological systems, or behaviorism, and subjective psychological
systems, or humanism. It does this by assuming that
the transaction between a subject and experimenter
constitutes an irreducible whole, such that both the
subject and experimenter mutually influence and

change each other.   The dialectical approach is the
psychology of both the subject and the experimenter
in an emergent relationship.

Two concepts are fundamental to an understanding of dialectical psychology: (1) change and (2)
dialectics. Every aspect of the psychological universe is assumed to be in a state of constant flux:
the subject and experimenter, the independent and
dependent variable, behavior and conscious experience, the organism and environment, and social factors and biological factors. Also, a valid psychological event is dialectical in nature; that is, it
involves some kind of mutually efficacious interaction between two or more subevents.

Riegelian psychology primarily focuses on dialectically induced changes, of which there are two
basic types: (1) long term, developmental, or structural and (2) short term, situational, or episodic.
Long term changes correspond to the kinds of changes
that are studied by traditional developmental psychologists (for instance, Erikson, 1963; Piaget,
1954). But in Riegel's approach the organism is assumed to be simultaneously affected by four dialectical progressions that both extend through and
change over time: inner biological, individual psychological, cultural sociological, and outer physical. Short term changes correspond to those behavioral and experiential alterations that occur in a
one-shot laboratory study or a temporary social interaction situation. But in Riegel's approach they
are assumed to be the result of dialectical interaction between the subject and experimenter or between
the members of a social group.

   Riegel claims to be studying the real or concrete human being: the individual organism and its
thoughts, ideas, and activities, especially those
the individual deems to be important--in a historical, cultural, developmental framework. The notion
of the real or concrete human being by and large is
synonymous with the everyday conception of a person
as a thinking, feeling, loving, and doing being.
Riegel criticizes the traditional predialectical
systems for analyzing the organism in terms of a set
of absolutistic, static entities, such as abilities,
traits, and statistical norms. For Riegel, the organism is a confluence of numerous dialectical interactions, of most of which the organism is currently aware.

   Dialectical psychology is not really revolutionary. It merely expands both behaviorism and humanism concurrently by attempting to be descriptively exhaustive. Traditional predialectic psychology
focuses on only one component of the postulated psychological universe at a time, observes it change,
and assumes that all the other components are static. Dialectical psychology presumably focuses on
all components at once and assumes that they all
change, or observes them all change, concurrently.
Traditional psychology is a freeze-frame or stop-ac-
tion approach; dialectical psychology treats the
psychological universe as a system in continuous
motion, whose elements are in a state of constant
change.

   The Riegelian perspective certainly is lauda-
tory. It focuses on the kinds of behavior that are
of interest to the general public and relates them

to psychological determinants that have face validity, as revealed through phenomenological investigation. It attempts to capture both the creative and
reactive aspects of the individual. It treats the
organism as a unique, conscious, cognitive entity
existing in a combined historical (developmental)-
cultural (social environmental) milieu. But it is
physically impossible to express the psychological
truths obtained in such an approach in a <u>continuous
time</u>, <u>dialectical</u> <u>manner</u>. Because of this, Riegel
must use numerous analogies that transform time
based, dialectical concepts to timeless, static concepts, stated in terms of the eternal present.

CONTENT OF OBSERVATION Since the interactive
relationship between a subject and experimenter constitutes the basic unit of observation in dialectical psychology, Riegel uses both the structure and
dynamics of the <u>dialogue</u> as the model psychological
situation. The dialogue specifically serves as the
optimal situation for investigating short term dialectically induced changes.

The term <u>dialogue</u> is applied to any social interaction situation in which at least two persons,
<u>A</u> and <u>B</u>, speak in an alternating fashion, such that
the content of the Nth verbal statement uttered by
<u>A or B</u> is related to the content of at least the im-
mediately prior statements uttered by both <u>A and B</u>.
In a dialogue two people are engaged in an extended
conversation with each other, the constituent verbal
expressions of which are emergent in nature: they
derive from the mutual interaction between the two
talkers. Each speaker <u>A</u> and <u>B</u> influences the other
and is influenced by the other, such that they con-

stitute both change agents and changed objects concurrently. Any sequence of three successive statements emitted by the members of the dialogue, A-B-A
or B-A-B, exists in a thesis-antithesis-synthesis
relationship. The first statement by A or B expresses a thesis; the response by the other member constitutes an antithesis; and the rejoinder by B or A
amounts to a synthesis. The individual A and B responses in a dialogue need not be verbal events. Any
alternating sequence of responses emitted by organisms A and B that are mutually contingent on each
other constitutes a dialogue. Riegel's prototypical
example of a dialogue is the kind of interaction
that occurs between mother and child. He also conceptualizes the psychotherapeutic situation as a dialogue, in which both diagnosis and therapeutic effects occur concurrently, such that both the patient
and the therapist are constantly changing.

The basic content of observation in Riegelian
dialectical psychology is anything that occurs in a
dialogue or dialogue-like situation. It is irrelevant whether it is conceptualized as overt behavior
or self-report of conscious experience. The main
thing is that each observed psychological event is
both an object of study and a locus of psychological
determination concurrently. Each isolatable psychological event is an object of study emitted by A or
B and a locus of determination for B or A. Using
more behavioristic terminology, the response of A or
B is the stimulus for B or A, ad infinitum.

In the context of the Riegelian dialogue analogue, traditional behavioristic methodology is unidirectional. The experimenter is not supposed to

affect the subject; the experimenter is merely supposed to be an unbiased observer or measuring device (see Chapter 3). Likewise, traditional humanistic phenomenalizing is unidirectional. The subject is not supposed to affect the experimenter or
recorder of the self-report; the subject is merely
supposed to be an epiphenomenal generator of self-
report (see Chapter 3).

A dialogue does not serve as the model for long
term dialectically induced changes, although a long
term change can be the ultimate result of an exposure to a series of dialogic type interactions. Long
term changes are ideally studied in multisession developmental experiments. In this context, Riegel
advocates the use of a combination cross-sectional,
longitudinal, time-lag research design, so that the
influence of both the individual organismic developmental sequence, or self, and the historical cultural milieu, or social environment, on the long term
change can be quantified. The technical specifications and requirements of this kind of design are
beyond the purview of our analysis. Suffice it to
note that in this methodology only the object of
study is directly observed and the possible loci of
determination result from statistical abstraction of
the obtained data.

REFERENCE SITUATION/ACTIVITY Although dialectical psychology probably was not explicitly designed to explain the reference activity of doing
something, it can be very easily mapped into the
framework of the dialectical system. Doing something involves a transaction between an organism and
the environment or another organism, such that both

the organism and the environment or both organisms
mutually affect and change each other. Doing something is semantically equivalent to either a short
term dialectically induced change or a long term dialectically induced change. As such, doing something can be viewed from two perspectives:

1. An individual instance of doing something
can be conceptualized dynamically as a one-unit dialogue, A-B-A, where A is the behavior of the organism, B is the environmental change or response of
the other organism, and A is the acknowledgment behavior of the organism after B occurs or the resul-
tant behavior of the organism that the occurrence of
B allows.

2. An individual instance of doing something
can be conceptualized structurally as a point event
in a combined biological, psychological, sociological, and physical space. The specific act is the
result of causal input from each of these dimensions: it has physiological, descriptive psychological, cultural, and environmental components.

The dialectical interpretation of doing something quite nicely illustrates the fact that Riegel's (1978) approach basically is descriptive, just
as Skinner's (1974) is. Although Riegel expands the
acceptable domain of descriptive variables beyond
Skinner's, he postulates no higher order explanatory
entities. Doing something dynamically is analyzed
strictly in terms of the overt events involved;
doing something structurally is resolved strictly in
terms of a classification system for the significant
components of the psychological universe.

Dialectics also is supposed to tap the inner

nature of an organism and its relationship to the environment, just as the concept of self-realization does in humanistic psychology (Rogers, 1961). Dialectical interaction is supposed to possess appreciable psychological authenticity for a person and be an object of awareness in the person's psychological world.

CHAPTER 6

TWO PHILOSOPHICAL ISSUES

The process of constructing a model of the psychological universe involves many philosophical assumptions. The two most relevant philosophical issues
for the psychologist are (1) the mind-body problem
and (2) the nature of the human being. The fact
that these two issues have not been resolved at a
philosophical level helps explain the current pluralistic state of psychology. Every system of psychology must take a position on each of these issues
and then proceed accordingly.

The mind-body problem has both epistemological
and metaphysical aspects; the nature of the human
being basically is a metaphysical issue. Epistemology concerns the ultimate nature and source of
truth; metaphysics involves the nature of reality
and the kinds of substances out of which it is composed. Each of the major classical schools and contemporary systems discussed in Chapters 4 and 5 is
to some degree committed to empiricism at the epistemological level, so we shall be concerned primarily with the metaphysical aspects of these two philosophical issues.

The mind-body problem will be considered first,
followed by a discussion of the nature of the human

being. This is the most appropriate order of presentation because the latter question is more inclusive than the former. A position with respect to
the nature of the human being presupposes a position
with respect to the mind-body problem, while the con-
verse of this statement is not necessarily the case.
The classic philosophical approaches to each issue
will be described, as well as put in cultural and
psychological perspective.

THE MIND-BODY PROBLEM

The mind-body problem in a psychological context reduces to the question of the relationship existing between consciousness and behavior. Four
broad classes of philosophical resolutions apply:
(1) dualism, (2) monism, (3) epiphenomenalism, and
(4) double aspectism. In only one approach, dualism, are both consciousness and behavior presumed to
exist and function as coequal entities. In monism,
either consciousness or behavior, but not both, is
presumed to exist; the nonexistent entity is illusory. Epiphenomenalism can be construed as a variant
of monism, in which the illusory entity is regarded
as a nonefficacious derivative of the existing entity. In double aspectism, consciousness and behavior merely are complementary linguistic descriptions. A given psychological entity can be reacted
to either as mental in nature, an aspect of consciousness, or as physical in nature, an aspect of
behavior.

PHILOSOPHICAL APPROACHES TO THE MIND-BODY
PROBLEM

VARIANTS OF DUALISM Since both consciousness (mind) and behavior (body) exist in dualism,

the critical issue concerns the nature of the relationship that exists between a person's mental activity and physical activity. Do mind and body interact? Does consciousness (ideas, mental events) determine behavior? Or, are mind and body merely parallel entities? Are mental and physical events
merely parallel processes? Does conscious experience and behavior merely exist in a relationship of
pre-established harmony? The first set of questions
entails the variant of dualism known as interaction-
ism; the second set of questions entails the variant
of dualism known as parallelism.

      INTERACTIONISM In this variant of
dualism, the mind and body are assumed to interact.
Ideas and mental processes do determine behavior and
bodily processes. Since this is the classic philosophical position of René Descartes (1650, 1662),
the seventeenth century French rationalist, it frequently is called Cartesian dualism. Descartes even
went so far as to postulate the exact physiological
locus of mind-body interaction--the pineal gland--
primarily because to his knowledge it was the only
unduplicated structure in the brain. Cartesian dualism generates another philosophical problem. How
can an unextended, noncorporeal, indivisible substance such as mind interact with an extended, cor-
poreal, divisible substance such as matter? It is
inconceivable for many philosophers (see Bunge,
1980) that two substances with such diametrically opposed properties can interact operationally. Thus
the genesis of parallelism.

      PARALLELISM In this variant of dual-
ism, the mind and body are not assumed to interact.

Mental activities and bodily activities merely are
correlated and exist in a state of pre-established
harmony. Conscious experience and behavior merely
are covarying, parallel events. Classical parallel-
ists liked to use a clock analogy. Mind and body
correspond to two different clocks that are wound up
and set off together, but subsequently operate independently. For every mental state, there is a corresponding physical state; for every physical state,
there is a corresponding mental state. Parallelism
often is referred to in the psychological literature
as psychophysical parallelism (viz. Lundin, 1979).
Leibnitz (1704, 1714), a classical German philosopher, held the parallelism view. Occasionalism is a
subset of parallelism, in which it is assumed that
the original establishment of the pre-established
harmony between mind and body explicitly was due to
God's intervention. The seventeenth century French
philosopher, Malebranche (1674), was an occasional-
ist.

          VARIANTS OF MONISM Since only conscious-
ness (mind) or behavior (body), but not both, exist
in monism, this approach also serves as a solution
to the problem of Cartesian dualism. Two pure forms
of monism exist: (1) materialism and (2) idealism.

          MATERIALISM In material monism, only
body, behavior, and physiological processes exist.
Mind and mental phenomena do not exist. Behavior is
strictly due to physical processes. Conscious experience or mental activity is mere appearance or
illusion. LaMettrie (1748) took this position and
was fond of conceptualizing the human organism essentially as a machine or a purely mechanistic enti-

ty.

IDEALISM   Idealism is the opposite of
materialism.   In idealistic monism, only mental
events, ideas, and conscious contents exist.   Mind
is the only reality.   The objects of direct experience are mental in nature, and these are all that
can be presumed to exist.   Body, behavior, physiological processes never are experienced directly and
cannot be presumed to exist.   Idealism has the problem of accounting for the source of conscious experience and mental events.   Bishop Berkeley (1710), a
British empiricist, assumed that God was the source
and functioned as the metaphysical glue holding together the universe of ideas.   David Hume (1748),
another British empiricist, refused to make this assumption and presumed that each individual is only
conscious of the self and its own ideas, a view that
technically is called solipsism.

VARIANTS OF EPIPHENOMENALISM   Two forms of
epiphenomenalism exist, as extensions of the two
types of monism: (1) mental epiphenomenalism and (2)
physical or material epiphenomenalism.

MENTAL EPIPHENOMENALISM   This ap-
proach is an extension of material monism, in which
it is assumed that mind, mental events, and conscious experience are derivative phenomena.   They
merely are the epiphenomenal effect of having a
body.   Consciousness merely is the byproduct of bodily processes.   In no sense is consciousness efficacious.   Thomas Hobbes (1650, 1651), a British empiricist, advocated this view.

PHYSICAL OR MATERIAL EPIPHENOMENALISM
This approach is the opposite of mental epiphenomen-

alism and an extension of idealistic monism, in
which it is assumed that body, physical events, and
behavior are derivative phenomena. They merely are
the epiphenomenal effect of having a mind. Behavior
and physiological processes merely are the byproduct
of consciousness and mental activity. In no sense
are bodily processes efficacious. I have been unable to locate a classical philosopher who explicitly espoused this position.

DOUBLE ASPECTISM In double aspectism,
both conscious experience and behavior merely are
linguistic attributes of the same ultimate reality
that in and of itself is unlabeled. The mind-body
problem devolves to a linguistic issue. The distinction between conscious experience and behavior
merely is a matter of semantic labeling. Psychologists legitimately can use either label, contingent
on the nature of their current theorizing and research activity. The classical Dutch philosopher,
Spinoza (1677), was a double aspectionist and so was
Bertrand Russell (1927, 1945), the pre-eminent twentieth century English philosopher and mathematician.

DIAGRAMMATIC SUMMARY Since the various
philosophical approaches to the mind-body problem
are quite abstract and consist of similar subvari-
ants, it would be instructive to represent each of
the eight variants pictorially, as in Figures 6-1A
and 6-1B. M symbolizes mind or consciousness, and
B symbolizes body or behavior in the figures. Other
aspects of the diagrams are self-explanatory.

PHILOSOPHICAL APPROACHES IN PERSPECTIVE The
purpose of this section is to put the mind-body
problem in cultural and psychological perspective

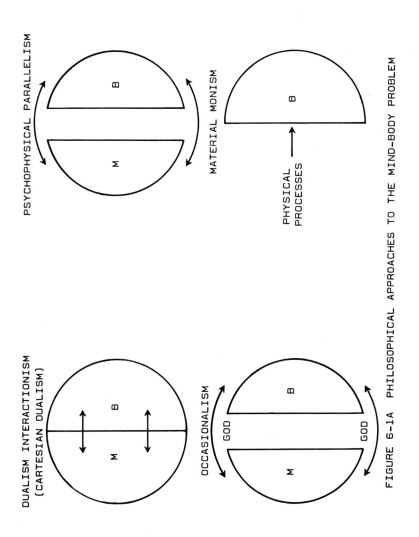

FIGURE 6-1A PHILOSOPHICAL APPROACHES TO THE MIND-BODY PROBLEM

by relating the various philosophical approaches to
(1) significant components of society and (2) the
classical schools and contemporary systems derived
in Chapter 3.

CULTURAL PERSPECTIVE Cartesian dualism is
the variant that possesses the greatest degree of
cultural validity (Churchland, 1984). Society, in
general, and the average person, in particular, are
not even cognizant of the existence of the competing
views. This approach even is implicit in our choice
of vocabulary when we attempt to make a low level
psychological statement about somebody's everyday
behavior. The Christian formally accepts Cartesian
dualism because of the mind-soul synonymity, such
that the soul implicitly operates as a viable psychological concept for the average person.

Double aspectism probably is the most accepted
variant in the context of contemporary positivistic
philosophy, analytic philosophy, and natural language philosophy (Bunge, 1980). Idealistic monism and
material or physical epiphenomenalism are implicit
in contemporary existential philosophy (Kaufman,
1956). Monism of either the material or mental epiphenomenal variety is the approach favored by the
physical science establishment (Bunge, 1980). Science presumes a totally mechanistic or naturalistic
universe. The objects of study of physics and chemistry consist of matter in motion, and mind is not a
part of the naturally occurring universe.

DERIVED PSYCHOLOGICAL SYSTEMS Each of the
conceptual approaches to psychology derived in Chapter 3 must take a position with respect to the mind-
body problem, and they will be presented in loose

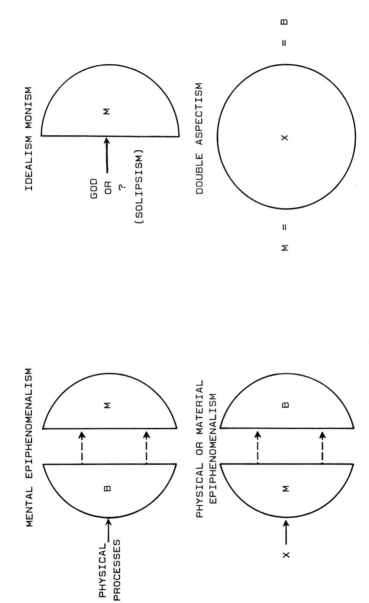

FIGURE 6-1B PHILOSOPHICAL APPROACHES TO THE MIND-BODY PROBLEM

historical order.

1. Structuralism: This system explicitly assumed the psychophysical parallelism approach.
Structuralists focused on the content of conscious
experience and presumed that an underlying physical
or physiological state corresponded to each conscious mental state.

2. Functionalism: Although the views of individual functionalists varied to some degree, the
system, as a whole, can be characterized as being
Cartesian dualistic in orientation. Functionalism
focused on how the dynamics of consciousness guided
the individual organism's adaptation to the environment.

3. Gestalt psychology: It is very difficult to
categorize the Gestalt approach to the mind-body
problem. Some psychologists (for instance, Lundin,
1979) argue that the system advocated a modified
psychophysical parallelism; other psychologists
(viz. Marx and Hillix, 1979) argue that the system
advocated a strict double aspectism interpretation.

4. Classical Watsonian behaviorism: As part of
the behaviorist's revolt against any psychological
system concerned with consciousness in either the
content or function sense, monism became the only
acceptable resolution of the mind-body problem.
Watson (1913, 1925, 1930) vacillated between the
material monism and mental epiphenomenalism interpretations in his writings. Each variant is associated with a different kind of behaviorism. Material
monism generates so-called metaphysical or dogmatic
behaviorism: mind simply does not exist. Mental
epiphenomenalism generates so-called methodological

or empirical behaviorism: mind is a derivative, nonefficacious entity irrelevant for explaining behavioral occurrence.

5. Freudian psychoanalytic approach: Although
Freud (1939, 1949) postulated an elaborate mental
apparatus that directly affects overt behavior, in
which context unconscious determinants are stressed
over conscious determinants, the current dominant
interpretation (Flanagan, 1984) is that his system
is not dualistic. Rather, Freud's psychic determinism is resolved in a modified material monistic orientation in which mental events are conceived as
nonreductive physical or physiological entities. As
we shall see in Chapter 7, another name for this is
functionalism (not to be confused with the classical
school of the same name).

6. Skinnerian radical behaviorism: This system
is mental epiphenomenal in orientation. Mental
events exist, but in no way are efficacious. Private mental events simply are covert responses, subject to the same set of reinforcement contingencies
that overt responses are.

7. Contemporary cognitive behaviorism: Contemporary cognitively oriented behaviorists, associated
with the information processing approach, are modified material monists. They investigate mental processes; but these are regarded as physical events,
emergent in nature and irreducible to more basic
physiological or conditioning processes. Cognitive
behaviorists study the mind, but mind is simply a
linguistic euphemism for emergent physical cognitive
processes. Chapter 7 considers contemporary conceptions of mind that are compatible with cognitive be-

haviorism.

8. Piagetian structural psychology: Piaget's
(1953, 1954) genetic-epistemological system is best
conceived as a material monistic one in which mentation basically is a biological or physical process.

9. Humanistic, existential, phenomenological
psychology: Although not every humanist is an exis-
tentialist, this approach, as a whole, focuses on
phenomenal experience and feeling. It must be classified as monistic in orientation, but of the idealistic or material or physical epiphenomenal variety.

10. Dialectical psychology: This system advocates a double aspectism resolution of the mind-body
problem. In Riegel's (1978, 1979) melding of the
objective and subjective orientations, consciousness
and behavior are interpenetrating, dialectically determined phenomena, the distinction between which is
solely semantic in nature.

THE NATURE OF THE HUMAN BEING

Psychological systems, in part, are attempts to
resolve the nature of the human being. The creation
of a psychological reality can be modeled after the
creation of a theological reality or after the creation of a physical reality (Royce, 1961). Theological systems relate humans to God or some kind of su-
preme being; specifically, human consciousness is
related to that of a higher level being. Physical
systems merely resolve the nature of the physical
world (the material world without which life as we
know it would be impossible); specifically, they
place humans in the physical world and model them as
a component thereof.

The theological approach considers the human

being to be transcendental or supranatural; the physical approach regards the human being as nontranscendental or natural (Wertheimer, 1972).   The transcendental view will be considered first, simply because it is the older of the two interpretations.

TRANSCENDENTAL, SUPRANATURAL VIEW   This interpretation considers the human being to be beyond the
bounds of the natural universe.   Humans transcend
nature and are supranatural.   The human is located
above the animal, but below the angel, in the overall order of things.   Refer to Figure 6-2 for a diagrammatic representation of this view.

TWO PRIMARY CHARACTERISTICS   There are two
primary consequences of this view: (1) free will or
nondeterminism and (2) vitalism.

1. Since humans transcend the natural universe,
the physical laws that govern inanimate objects and
nonhuman animate beings (animals) do not apply to
them.   Human beings essentially possess free will;
their behavior is not determined.   As a consequence,
they cannot be treated meaningfully as an object of
scientific analysis.

2. Since humans transcend the natural universe,
they must be more than the mere sum of their bodily
parts or physiological functioning.   The human being
is an emergent creature that is more than the sum
total of evolutionary inputs.   Vitalism essentially
means that our inner essence cannot be described in
strict physical-chemical terms.

SUBSIDIARY, DERIVATIVE CHARACTERISTICS
The two primary characteristics of the transcendental view lead to a number of derivative consequences.   These subsidiary characteristics are not

necessarily independent of each other. In some cases, they merely amount to semantic generalizations
of the principle of nondeterminism, vitalism, or
transcendentalism itself. A representative set of
six derivative characteristics will be presented.

1. Humans are morally responsible for their
deeds and are worthy of praise or censure, depending
upon the moral evaluation of their acts according to
an objective external criterion. This condition is
a direct consequence of the assumption of free will.
Since we are self-determined and have control of our
behavior, we freely perform good or evil and freely
can be rewarded or punished.

2. The human being is not an animal or, more
technically, another type of animal. A fundamental
discontinuity exists between them. The label "human" is a technical term in the transcendental approach. It implies a unique form of life. Certain
aspects of our existence are unique to the state of
being human.

3. The second derivative characteristic frequently is extended to include the human as possessing an immortal soul and as being a creature of God.
The basic reference point for interpreting our inner essence is the outer ring, not the innermost
circle, of the transcendental diagram in Figure
6-2. This extension has all sorts of implications
for saving the soul, serving God, and earning one's
way into Heaven.

4. Mind, mentalism, or mental life is an efficacious property of humanity. Mind exists and is a
component of our being. Translated into terminology associated with the mind-body problem, our trans-

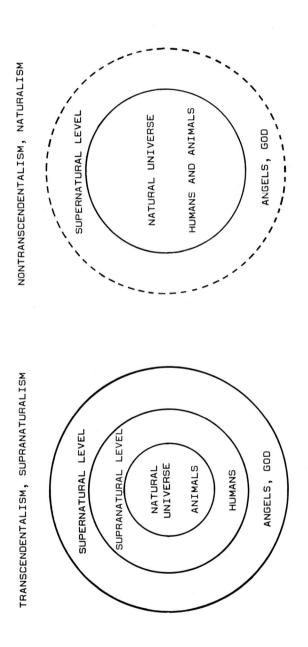

FIGURE 6-2 TWO INTERPRETATIONS OF THE NATURE OF THE HUMAN BEING

cendence implies either a dualistic, idealistic monistic, or material epiphenomenal conception of reality.

5. Humans possess special status in the universe. The universe was created for us, for our development, for fulfilling our destiny. The universe
exists because we exist. The notion of humanity is
logically prior to that of the universe. Consequently, it is possible to argue that human life has inherent meaning in the context of the transcendental
approach.

6. The human being is an open-ended, incom-
plete, ever changing entity. Humanity is a potentiality, as opposed to a finality. What we are now
is not what we necessarily shall be in the future.
As such, the transcendental view tends to be optimistic about our future.

NONTRANSCENDENTAL, NATURAL VIEW Although the
nontranscendental interpretation is virtually the
mirror image of the supranatural approach, there is
a sufficient number of subtle differences between
the two to justify a complete discussion of the nontranscendental approach. This interpretation considers the human to be part and parcel of the natural universe. We do not transcend and constitute a
natural phenomenon. We simply are another kind of
animal life, bound by the material conditions of existence. Refer to Figure 6-2, for a diagrammatic
representation of this view. Note that the supranatural level has been deleted and the human has devolved to the innermost circle of the diagram. The
postulation of a possible supernatural level of existence strictly is optional in this approach, so it

is represented in the diagram by a dotted line ring.

One of the arguments against the assumption of a supernatural level in the context of the natural view is the belief that different forms of life must leave traces. Traces of animal life in the primitive wilderness state are obvious and cannot be mentioned in polite company; traces of human life are more variegated and serve as objects of analysis for anthropologists. Do traces of supernatural beings exist; and, if so, what are they?

TWO PRIMARY CHARACTERISTICS   There are two primary consequences of this view: (1) determinism and (2) mechanism.

1. Since humans are part and parcel of the natural universe, the physical laws that govern inanimate objects and animals also apply to them. We are not free and do not exist in an existential vacuum; our behavior is determined. We constitute an appropriate object of scientific analysis, and our nature can be resolved in a scientific framework.

2. Since humans are part and parcel of the natural universe, they are the mere sum of their bodily parts or physiological functioning. The human is a material entity, a real-space and real-time event in the universe. No _deus_ _ex_ _machina_ is possible in the natural view. The human being is not an emergent creature that is more than the sum total of evolutionary inputs. Mechanism essentially means that our inner essence is describable in strict physical-chemical terms.

SUBSIDIARY, DERIVATIVE CHARACTERISTICS The two primary characteristics of the nontranscendental view lead to a number of derivative conse-

quences that are not necessarily independent of each
other and in some cases merely amount to semantic
generalizations of the principle of determinism,
mechanism, or nontranscendentalism itself. A corresponding set of six derivative characteristics
will be considered.

    1. Humans are not morally responsible for their
deeds. This statement is a direct consequence of
the assumption of determinism. Our behavior is determined, and we do not freely perform good or evil.
It does not follow from this assumption that we cannot be rewarded or punished. Reward and punishment
are inherent components of the causal texture of
which behavior is a function. In the naturalistic
approach, reward and punishment are morally neutral
events and are not dispensed according to an external evaluative criterion. Psychological systems
that assume the naturalistic view merely treat reward and punishment as techniques of behavioral control and not as morally earned or deserved consequences.

    2. The human being is an animal or, more tech-
nically, another type of animal. No fundamental
discontinuity exists between the human being and the
animal. There is no aspect of our existence that is
unique to the human condition. The term "human"
merely connotes the highest form of animal life.
This statement is a bit presumptuous. Humans usually are regarded as the highest form of animal life
because they presumably are self-conscious, have an
active symbolic life or the speech function, and
possess superior intelligence. On the basis of other criteria, the insect is the highest form of life:

for instance, lack of pollution, sheer adaptability
to the environment, efficiency of morphologic design, and enormous physical strength to weight ra-
tio.

    3. Our continuity with the animal often is ex-
tended to the machine. Many naturalistically oriented philosophers (see Russell, 1945) regard the human being as simply another kind of machine. What
is meant by machine in this context is the properties encompassed by a machine at a conceptual level,
not an actual physical embodiment of a machine. The
contemporary conception of the human organism as a
computer, or simply another kind of computer, is a
subset of the traditional man-machine analogy.

    4. Mind, mentalism, and ideas are not regarded
as significant aspects of humanity. Either mind
does not exist, or it merely is epiphenomenal. The
naturally occurring universe solely is material in
nature. In the nontranscendental view, you would
never account for behavior by an appeal to mind and
mentalistic notions. Translated into terminology
associated with the mind-body problem, our nontranscendence implies either a material monistic or a
mental epiphenomenal conception of reality.

    5. Humans possess no special status in the uni-
verse. We are a mere accident in the overall evolutionary development of the universe. The universe
was not created for us, for our development, for
fulfilling our destiny. We exist because the universe exists. The notion of humanity is not logically prior to that of the universe. More than
likely we shall disappear from the universe long before the universe ends. Consequently, it is possi-

ble to argue that human life has no inherent meaning
in the context of the nontranscendental approach.

6. The human being is a closed system. This
statement does not mean that we can never change.
We can change if the texture of the causal system to
which we belong changes. Nontranscendentalism merely prohibits self-generated changes or changes in
isolation of the physical system to which we belong.
As such, the nontranscendental view is not necessarily pessimistic about our future.

TWO VIEWS IN PERSPECTIVE The purpose of this
section is to put the nature of the human being in
cultural and psychological perspective by relating
the two views to (1) significant components of society and (2) the classical schools and contemporary
systems derived in Chapter 3.

CULTURAL PERSPECTIVE Transcendentalism is
the view that possesses the greatest degree of cultural validity. Society, in general, and the average person, in particular, are not even cognizant of
naturalism. Transcendentalism is implicit in Christian theology, and in many respects transcendentalism is indistinguishable from the Christian conception of humanity. Transcendentalism also is the
view held by the legal establishment, whose major
functions revolve around moral condemnation and ret-
ribution. Naturalism is espoused by only one significant component of society, the scientific establishment. Physical, biological, and social scientists assume the principles of determinism and mechanism and treat the human as an appropriate object
of scientific analysis.

DERIVED PSYCHOLOGICAL SYSTEMS Each of the

conceptual approaches to psychology derived in Chapter 3 must take a position with respect to the nature of the human being and can be assigned to one
of three classes: (1) explicitly transcendental, (2)
explicitly nontranscendental, and (3) implicitly nontranscendental.

1. Humanistic psychology, in general, and existential and phenomenological psychology, in particular, are explicitly transcendental. The understanding approach to psychology uses human being as a
technical term, presumes free will, abhors treating
the human being as an object of scientific or symbolic analysis, emphasizes becoming or striving, encourages self-generated changes, and the like.

2. Any variant of behaviorism is explicitly
nontranscendental. The behavioristic approach to
psychology views the human simply as another animal
or machine, presumes some form of determinism, advocates changes through environmental manipulation and
external inducement, treats humans as amenable to
scientific analysis, and the like.

3. Structuralism, functionalism, Gestalt psychology, the psychoanalytic approach, genetic-epistemological psychology, and dialectical psychology
are implicitly nontranscendental. Each of these approaches either is scientifically oriented or presumes determinism and accepts the basic tenets of
the overall naturalistic orientation with one glaring exception: the nonexistence or inefficacy of
mind, mental phenomena, or mental apparati in general. This exception goes a long way toward explaining the immediate past history of academic/experi-
mental psychology. Behaviorism attempted to purge

the dualism inherent in structuralism, functionalism, and Gestalt psychology from academic/experimen-
tal psychology. The _apparent_ dualism of the psychoanalytic approach and genetic-epistemological psychology prevents them from being absorbed by contemporary mainstream academic psychology. The dualism
implicit in dialectical psychology is merely semantic in nature, and only time will tell whether this
approach has a significant impact on academic/exper-
imental psychology.

             CONCEPTUAL NOTE   The distinction be-
tween explicitly nontranscendental and implicitly
nontranscendental corresponds _in part_ to Flanagan's
(1984) materialism-naturalism dichotomy.

     Both materialism and naturalism are subvariants
of physicalism, whereby real-space and real-time
events--those possessing the denotative properties
of matter in the Cartesian sense of the term--ex-
haust the universe. In physicalism, mental events
in the Cartesian sense of the term do not exist: a
so-called mental event is simply another kind of
physical event.

     In materialism, a mental event is assumed redu-
cible to or expressible as a simple physical event.
Mentation is mechanical, possessing no special properties uncharacteristic of other physical events.

     In naturalism, mental events--although physical
in nature--constitute a special class of emergent
events, not reducible to simple physical mechanisms.
Mental events comprise an autonomous system with its
own characteristic laws and properties.

     In the context of Flanagan's dichotomy, any
descriptive or logical behaviorism, with the possi-

ble exception of Tolman's (1932) approach, is a materialistic system; Freudian psychoanalysis and Piagetian structural psychology are naturalistic systems; contemporary cognitive behaviorism, the information processing approach, can be interpreted as
either kind of system.

The materialism-naturalism dichotomy is pursued
in greater depth in the next chapter in the context
of discussing contemporary physicalistic conceptions
of mind.

CHAPTER 7

CONTEMPORARY CONCEPTIONS OF MIND

The prior chapter delineated the classic positions
with respect to the mind-body problem and related
them to the classical schools and contemporary systems discussed in Chapters 4 and 5. Mental events,
or mentation, are part and parcel of every psychologist's conception of the psychological universe, although some psychologists either reduce them to physical events, or assume they merely are epiphenomenal in nature, or both.

The nature and status of mental events constitute a continuing problem for psychology in two different respects: (1) as output or direct object of
study and (2) as input or indirect object of study.
Mental events can occupy either slot of the content
of observation: phenomena of interest or locus of
causation. In the first focus, mental events are
synonymous with the content of consciousness: conscious experience. In the second focus, mental
events are construed as processes that determine
other psychological events of interest, such as
overt behavior. Mind can be viewed as (1) content
or structure or (2) function or dynamics. The first
focus will be treated in detail in Chapter 9, where
it will be compared with psychology's other classic

concern: behavior. This chapter analyzes mental activity as a possible locus of psychological causation. We are particularly going to be concerned
with contemporary philosophical conceptions of the
mind as they relate to cognitive behaviorism.

Mentation, as an active, causal construct, is a
residual of the days when virtually every phenomenon
was explained by an appeal to some kind of animistic
entity (Owens, 1959). Animistic entities, such as
souls, spirits, or "mind," were all-or-none agents
with no subparts that inhabited both inanimate and
animate objects and accounted for their physical motion and activity. Animism disappeared from the inanimate, or physical, context centuries ago with the
rise of modern science. Animism did not disappear
from the animate, or psychological, context, but
merely became more refined--with Cartesian dualism
serving as the prototypical conception from which
all contemporary remnants of animism derived. It is
interesting to note that contemporary conceptions of
the mind are not necessarily conceptual advances
over classical interactionist dualism. For instance, Descartes (1650, 1662) limited mentation to
the human organism; some contemporary conceptions of
the mind find it impossible to deny mental states to
animals, machines, disembodied brains, and even ex-
tra-terrestrial creatures (see Block, 1978; Fodor,
1981).

The mentation involved in cognitive behaviorism
can be subsumed by two distinct philosophical approaches to the mind: (1) material or physical monism, called materialism or physicalism in this chapter, and (2) functionalism (not to be confused with

the classical school of the same name). We shall
initially focus on how each approach gives substance
to the notion of a mental event and then attempt a
relational comparison among them. Also some older
variants of materialism, from which the more contemporary versions of physicalism and functionalism
(applicable to cognitive behaviorism) derived, are
presented to provide some historical perspective.

MATERIALISM

The fundamental assumption underlying every
version of materialism is that a mental event or
state is a physical event or state (Churchland,
1984). Physical, in this context, is an attribu-
tional property of body or matter in the Cartesian
sense of the term. Unlike dualists, materialists do
not assume that mental events are a property of a
substance called mind. Mental events merely constitute another kind of physical event; namely, those
physical events responsible for thought, imagination, feeling, desire, belief, and the like.

Four versions of materialism will be analyzed:
(1) eliminative materialism or descriptive behaviorism; (2) reductive materialism or logical behaviorism; (3) central state identity theory, of which
there are two subkinds--type and token; and (4)
emergentist materialism. The term "behaviorism" in
this context refers to a philosophical approach to
the mind and should not be construed as necessarily
identifying any of the behavioristic schools/systems
of psychology. The order in which these four materialistic positions are listed is not arbitrary: (1)
It loosely corresponds to their order of historical
appearance, and (2) it encompasses a basic evolu-

tionary trend from elimination or reduction of mental events to nonreductive reification of mental
events. As we shall discover, only the last two approaches are compatible with contemporary cognitive
behaviorism.

ELIMINATIVE MATERIALISM; DESCRIPTIVE BEHAVIOR-
ISM Recall that for a descriptive behaviorist
strict S-R causal laws exhaust psychological reality. Mental events can exist as physical entities,
but are regarded as irrelevant for predicting or
controlling behavior. Traditional mentation devolves to merely a response property and is eliminated
as a possible source of behavior.

In Watson's (1913, 1925) system, mentalistic
notions are translated into response terminology:
for instance, thinking is an implicit, covert, sub-
vocal speech habit. In Skinner's (1957, 1974) system, mental activity is simply another kind of behavior, internal covert responding to which only the
individual organism has direct access. In eliminative materialism, mental events constitute physical
output, not input. Neither Watson's nor Skinner's
approach to mentation supports an epistemological
cognitive psychology.

Philosophers (for instance, Armstrong, 1980;
Fodor, 1981) criticize eliminative materialism on
two bases: (1) It contradicts the intuition (virtually a technical term in philosophy) that mental
events are causative, regardless of whether mental
events are in addition assumed to be physical
events. (2) Since mentation now merely is a response property, it is impossible for an organism to
be in a certain mental state unless it is directly

reflected in overt behavior. There is no active
mentation divorced from overt behavioral activity.
For instance, an organism cannot be in a state of
anger, independent of the act of exhibiting hostile
responses.

  REDUCTIVE MATERIALISM; LOGICAL BEHAVIORISM
Logical behaviorists, such as Carl Hempel (1969a,
1972) and Gilbert Ryle (1949), respond to the second
criticism of descriptive behaviorism by defining
mental states in such a way that they can exist independently of overt behavior. They assume that
physicalistic mental entities occur between stimulus
input and response output, but still in such a way
as to be noncausative. A mental state has the status of a behavioral disposition.

  A behavioral disposition is a tendency to perform response outcome Y in the context of stimulus
input X. For instance, thirst is a behavioral disposition. A thirsty organism in the face of some
kind of acceptable liquid is liable, or disposed, to
drink. A behavioral disposition merely encompasses
an if-then hypothetical and in no way guarantees behavioral occurrence. It is possible for an organism
to be disposed to drink in a certain situation, but
still not drink.

  A behavioral disposition is analogous to the
notion of a physical disposition. For instance,
fragility is a physical disposition characteristic
of glass. When struck by some object, glass is disposed to break. But fragility is not the cause of
the breaking of the glass. Fragility merely is a
relational state specifying what the glass is likely
to do in the context of a certain input.

Logical behaviorism exists in at least two different versions: (1) a strict or strong form, originally advocated by Hempel (1972) in the 1930s and
1940s, and (2) a liberal or weak form, promulgated
by Hempel (1969a) beginning in the 1960s.

1. The strong form is derivative of logical
positivism (the Vienna Circle), wherein any mental
entity has to be reducible to a physicalistic or behavioral term in order to meet the conditions of existence and be empirically meaningful (Carnap, 1934,
1959, 1967). This form assumes that behavioral
translations of mental terms are very easy to make
and that the resulting translation uniquely characterizes the mental event or exists in a one-to-one
correspondence with it, such that the reduction is
analytically true. This form of logical behaviorism
presumes that psychology can be ultimately reduced
to physics, the prototypical case of a science exclusively expressed in physicalistic language, and
views such reduction as an inherently worthy goal.

2. The weak form derives from the realization
that behavioral translation is not easy and does not
result in analytic truth (Hempel, 1969b). Quite often, no one-to-one mapping of a mental event and a
behavioral indicator is possible: a specific mental
event can be translated in an infinite number of
ways by an open-ended set. A specific translation
is viewed as a tentative hypothesis subject to empirical validation. In this form, logical behaviorism is merely a matter of principle, as opposed to a
systematic philosophical program.

Neither the strong nor weak version of logical
behaviorism is conducive to the development of a

cognitive psychology. Logical behaviorism is subject to a number of nonmutually exclusive criticisms, five of which will be discussed here (see
Block, 1980; Block and Fodor, 1972; Putnam, 1967).

1. Although logical behaviorism entails a relationship between a behavioral disposition and overt
behavior, it makes no provision for relationships
among two or more behavioral dispositions. For instance, frustration and anger are behavioral dispositions, and each individually can be related to behavior; but logical behaviorism cannot handle the
case where frustration leads to anger and then anger
in turn leads to some overt response.

2. Only rarely is a specific behavioral occurrence associated with only one behavioral disposition. Behavior is multisourced: for instance, drinking behavior is associated not only with a state of
thirst, but also with a belief in the beneficial results of drinking, and the like.

3. The existence and/or content of a specific
behavioral disposition can only be inferred from behavior Y in context X. But such inferences can be
arbitrary and capricious. For instance, a man hit-
ting his wife can be interpreted as being in a state
of anger; but he might be drunk, temporarily insane,
or a sadist.

4. The goal of logical behaviorism--the reduction of mental events to physicalistic, behavioral
entities--is not achievable, because the specification of a behavioral disposition requires implicit
reference to one or more other mental states that do
not get translated and reduced. Even if such translations were actually done, the process would result

in an infinite regress of reductions.

    5. The one-to-one correspondence, or even a less strict correspondence, between a given behavioral disposition and a specific behavioral manifestation is vitiated by the so-called perfect actor criticism. A perfect actor can mimic the behavior of a person in a certain mental state <u>without</u> being in such a state, as well as refrain from exhibiting the behaviors symptomatic of a certain state <u>while</u> being in such a state. The possession of a certain behavioral disposition is neither a sufficient nor necessary condition for behavioral expression.

    CENTRAL STATE IDENTITY THEORY In many respects, central state identity theory constitutes the prototypical form of materialism (Churchland, 1984; Fodor, 1981). The physical state subsumed by a mental state is assumed identical with (exists in one-to-one correspondence to) some neurophysiological entity, such as a brain state. The identity (or correspondence) is not one of semantic equivalence, as is the case in the strong form of logical behaviorism; rather it is an empirical proposition subject to test.

    The mental state-brain state identity hypothesis is an improvement over logical behaviorism in two respects (Fodor, 1981): (1) brain states can be causative (a source of behavior), and (2) brain states can interact or influence each other (causation at a purely mental level is possible). In central state identity theory, mentation possesses all the properties assigned to it by a dualist; however, mentation is not some strange, mysterious process occurring in a vacuum: it is physical activity subsumed and bounded by an organism's physiology.

Many philosophers, such as Jerry Fodor (1981), distinguish between two versions of central state identity theory: (1) type and (2) token. Type theory is constructed in terms of universals or universal properties; token theory is stated in terms of individual instances or particulars. For instance, type theory specifies that pain in general, as a class of phenomena, possesses a neurophysiological representation; token theory merely specifies that a particular instance of pain need possess neurophysiological representation. An interesting consequence of this difference is the fact that the type doctrine precludes any entity other than a standard biological creature from possessing mental states, while the token approach allows machines and disembodied brains to possess mental states.

In type theory, a mental state is solely defined compositionally in terms of its constituent physiological components. For instance, pain is C-fiber firing. This either (1) <u>can</u> or (2) <u>cannot</u> be a problem, depending on one's perspective.

1. If one attempts to specify some common denominator physiological process or entity characteristic of each physical realization of a mental state, none can be proferred (Putnam, 1967). The question of what it is by virtue of which a specific mental state is such (i.e., what makes pain a pain) is unresolvable in the context of type theory. This criticism of type theory serves as the primary impetus to the functionalistic approach to mental events.

2. If one accepts the fact that species-specif-

ic differences in physiological or brain states can
exist, such that the characteristic content of an
identically labeled mental state (say pain) can differ, there is no problem with type theory (Lewis,
1969; Kim, 1972). Specifying a mental state in
terms of a physiological/brain state does not guarantee a uniform representation common to every type
of biological creature: a human's pain need not correspond to a dog's pain, although both pains involve
brain states.

Central state identity theory is compatible
with contemporary cognitive behaviorism because mentation has a causative role in behavioral production
and also is given a representation in terms of physical properties and processes.

EMERGENTIST MATERIALISM This version of materialism amounts to a conceptual extension of central
state identity theory, especially the type variety.
Although the type doctrine identifies mentation with
physical processes, specifically activity of some
central nervous system, in no way does it characterize these physical processes as being unique. Neuronal activity, brain activity, biochemical events,
and the like are simply more complex at a quantita-
tive level than the activity associated with other
physical systems; such activity is not qualitatively
distinct from that occurring in other physical systems. As such, mentation is ultimately describable
by physical laws of the same genre as physics.

Many philosophers, as exemplified by Mario
Bunge (1980), prefer to emphasize that the physiological events underlying mentation are not continuous with other physical events. The human being's

brain and central nervous system are viewed as an emergent biological system, both quantitatively and qualitatively distinct from other systems, such that the physico-chemical events underlying mentation are not reducible to lower level physical events. Bunge specifically identifies mental events with the biological activity of plastic subsystems of the central nervous system, explainable only by the use of biological laws containing predicates not found in any other science. By "plastic" Bunge essentially means "adaptable" or "changeable." Plastic neuronal systems mediate learning and adjustment to the environment.

Bunge presumably solves the compositional dilemna of the central state identity theorist by identifying mentation with highly selective and refined neuronal subsystems characteristic of only a small portion of animal life; however, he is operating as an implicit functionalist because plastic nervous systems themselves are not defined compositionally, but by their functional roles and properties.

Emergentist materialism is particularly relevant for cognitive behaviorism because it can be used to justify the view that human cognitive processes are emergent in nature, not reducible to purely associational or conditioning mechanisms.

CONCEPTUAL SUMMARY Although materialism provides a physicalistic interpretation of mentation, the nature and status of a mental event varies across different versions of the materialist doctrine.

1. In eliminative materialism or descriptive behaviorism, mental events are reduced to properties of response output and cannot serve as possible

sources of behavior.

2. In reductive materialism or logical behaviorism, mental events are conceptualized as behavioral dispositions that merely prescribe what is
likely to happen when an organism is faced with certain stimulus input.

3. In central state identity theory, a mental
event is given a physical representation as some
kind of physiological entity (neural process, brain
state, biochemical event) and possesses all the
causative properties characteristic of Cartesian
dualism.

4. In emergentist materialism, a mental event
has the same physical realization that it does in
identity theory, with the additional stipulation
that this realization involves some emergent biological subsystem.

FUNCTIONALISM

Functionalism is regarded as the dominant contemporary approach to the philosophy of mind by consensus (Block, 1978, 1980; Fodor, 1981; Block and
Fodor, 1972). It is a rather heterogeneous collection of separate subapproaches to mentation, all of
which hold only one tenet in common: mental states
must be defined functionally; that is, in terms of
causal role, rather than by compositional specification.

The relationship of functionalism to both behaviorism and central state identity theory is both
arbitrary and ambiguous (Block, 1980). On some accounts, functionalism can be construed as a form of
behaviorism; however, most functionalists currently
would claim that such a construal is misleading and

noncognizant of the conceptual advances accomplished by functionalism. Likewise, functionalism can be construed as both compatible with and justifying the mental state-brain state identity approach; but again such a construal minimizes the unique nature and distinct contributions of functionalism. According to Ned Block (1978), behaviorism is too _liberal_ in comparison with functionalism, because it ascribes mental states in certain contexts where functionalism denies them; central state identity theory is too _chauvinistic_ in comparison with functionalism, because it denies mental states in certain contexts where functionalism ascribes them.

The basic conceptual impetus to the creation of functionalism is physicalism's problem of specifying a standard physico-chemical state for each mental state (Putnam, 1967). Species-specific physiological differences and changes in physiology within the human organism over time preclude any simplistic mental state-physiological state identities. More generally, physicalism is not definitive enough about the range and content of the mental properties that have to be comprehended by the thesis of psychophysical correspondence; that is, those mental properties for which neural correlates must be found, in order to make the thesis valid.

Functionalism bypasses the compositional problem by the "topic neutral" strategy of defining mental states as functional entities that play a causal role in an organism's mentation process (Fodor, 1981). Specifically, an entity is a mental state if it can be meaningfully related to stimulus input, response output, and _other_ mental states. For in-

stance, pain is a mental state because it is caused
by aversive stimulation, results in withdrawal responses, and conceivably is related to the belief
that pain is harmful. A functionally defined mental
state intervenes between stimulus input and response
output, just as a behavioral disposition or a physiologically specified brain state does; but it is this
very relational configuration that specifies a mental event in functionalism.

    Since functional specification is composition-
free, any kind of system (biological or nonbiologi-
cal, animate or inanimate, human or nonhuman, machine or nonmachine, physical or nonphysical) that
possesses functionally specifiable entities can be
regarded as exhibiting mental states. Whether or
not a relationally defined entity, interpreted as a
mental state, has a possible physical realization is
irrelevant in functionalism. Functionalism can be
viewed as a kind of nonreductive materialism or non-
realizable materialism (Fodor, 1981).

    Functionalism provides philosophical justifica-
tion for empirical analysis of the mind: specifically, it justifies treating the organism as an information processing or computational entity, admissable to scientific investigation. Mentation is activity that must be modeled after physical processes. Physical systems, such as the computer, with
functionally specifiable internal states serve as
the natural model for human cognition. Contemporary
cognitive behaviorism, in effect, concerns mental
representation and the interfacing of mental representation and functionalism.

    To simplify the analysis, we are going to as-

sume that two general classes of functionalistic approaches to mentation exist: (1) the functional
specification version, characteristic of Smart
(1959), Lewis (1971), and Armstrong (1980); and (2)
the functional state identity version, advocated by
Fodor (1981), Block (1978), and Putnam (1967). It
also will be instructive to consider the specific
criteria functionalism uses to specify a mental
state, primarily because it will serve as a natural
transition to the analysis of phenomenal experience
in Chapter 9.

     FUNCTIONAL SPECIFICATION APPROACH In this ap-
proach, a mental state is identified with an abstract causal property tied to the real world only
via its relations, direct and indirect, to inputs
and outputs (Block, 1978, 1980). This kind of functionalism is a logical, semantic endeavor in the
sense that common-sense psychology, or folk psychology, serves as the source of the possible mental
states. The functional specificist operates within
the framework of the general public's conception of
mentation. The input and output must be common-
sense, nonconceptual entities and are limited to external stimuli and responses in the behaviorist
sense of the terms. The functional specification
approach must draw the line between the inside and
the outside of the organism at the skin.

     Advocates of this approach like to argue that
the viability of functionalism demonstrates that
physicalism is probably true. Functional specifi-
cists assume that a functionally defined mental
state also has a physical representation: a mental
state involves some physical structure or is an ac-

tual physical thing.

Since this approach to functionalism is so informal, it is characterized by at least four basic
weaknesses (Block, 1978, 1980):

1. It is possible for an entity to have a causal property tied to the real world via its relations
to stimulus input and response output and still <u>not</u>
be a mental state.

2. Common-sense, folk psychology is a notoriously unreliable source for possible mental states.

3. The functional specificist is prone to defining mental states circularly. The content of a
mental state is merely or exactly what is necessary
at a deeper level of analysis to account for the
current, ongoing behavior. This is B. F. Skinner's
(1977) basic objection to any kind of epistemological philosophy or psychology.

4. The use of external stimuli and responses as
common-sense inputs and outputs precludes a nonstan-
dard or deficient organism from possessing mental
states: for instance, a paralytic (with no functional motor system) or a disembodied brain (with no
functional sensory and motor systems).

The functional specification approach is not
that much of a conceptual advance over the central
state identity theory, except for its short-circuit-
ing of the compositional problem. This fact helps
explain the development of the functional state
identity approach.

FUNCTIONAL STATE IDENTITY APPROACH In this approach, specification of a mental state in terms of
causal role related to input and output is deemed
insufficient (Block, 1978, 1980; Block and Fodor,

1972).   The functionally characterized entity must
also be identifiable as or correspond to a specific
state of some independent, external system that is
usually physically realized in terms of a Turing
(1964) machine.   A Turing machine is a computational
device--a restricted class of possible computers--
characterized by certain input, output, and transition states (Fodor, 1981).   Such a machine can be
used to define both deterministic and probabilistic
automata.   The basic point is that a functionally
characterized entity must be realizable as a machine
table state of some Turing machine in order to be a
mental state.   This machine version of functionalism
directly addresses the first and third weaknesses of
the functional specification approach.

        (Note: A Turing machine is not an _actual_ compu-
tational device.   It merely is a conceptual system
with prespecified properties that is used as an
evaluational device in many academic disciplines,
such as mathematics, philosophy, logic, psychology,
and automata theory, to either state conceptual
problems more clearly or solve conceptual problems
operationally.   A Turing machine can be physicalized
by any one of a number of different hardware devices
or software programs.)

        The functional state identity approach is an
empirical endeavor in the sense that the technical
psychological literature serves as the source of the
possible mental states.   Problems associated with
the use of folk psychology are bypassed.   The input
and output need not be specified in common-sense
terms.   They can be specified in terms of any conceptual entities that are meaningful in the context

of psychology. The functional state identity theorist can draw the line between the inside and outside
of the organism at any point that is necessary to
avoid undesirable conceptual consequences. For instance, specification of output in terms of stimulation of motor neurons solves the problem of the paralytic; specification of input and output in terms
of neuronal communication between different subparts
of the brain solves the problem of the disembodied
brain.

Advocates of this approach like to argue that
the viability of functionalism demonstrates that
physicalism, specifically the type variety, is def-
initely false. (Functionalism ostensibly is compatible with token physicalism.) The machine version
of functionalism enhances the compositional problem:
if a machine table can be formulated for an organism, it would be absurd to identify any of the machine table states with a type of brain state, because presumably all manner of brainless machines
could be described by the table as well. A mental
state cannot be a physical state, structure, or
thing. A mental state merely is a property by which
a relational, causal role gets performed.

The functional state identity approach is subject to at least six nonmutually exclusive criticisms, the majority of which derive from the inclu-
sion of a technical machine table state specification (see Block and Fodor, 1972).

1. Functional state identity theory cannot distinguish between dispositional states, such as beliefs and desires, and occurrent states, such as
sensations, thoughts, and feelings.

2. Functional state identity theory is independent of qualia, the characteristic phenomenal content of an occurrent state. Qualia are not used to
define a state or to specify its function.

   The initial two criticisms collectively defer
to the contentual or structural aspect of mind: phenomenal experience. No version of functionalism is
designed to handle qualia or aspects of qualia. (No
version of behaviorism or central state identity
theory is either.) Contemporary conceptions of the
mind merely model its functional, dynamic aspects.
The consequence of this for functionalism will be
specified later in the chapter.

   3. Functional state identity theory can handle
behavior that is the result of a series of mental
states occurring in temporal succession. Only one
mental state (machine state) occurs at a time, and
the organism can progress through a series of mental
states (machine states) in a stepwise fashion. On
the other hand, this approach cannot handle behavior
that is the result of multiple mental states occurring simultaneously. A Turing machine cannot be in
more than one machine state at a time, and it cannot
represent the situation of being in two or more mental states concurrently.

   4. The individual machine states of a Turing
machine can be uniquely defined and type identified.
The individual mental states of an organism cannot
be uniquely defined and type identified. The constraints on type-identity conditions on mental states in functional state identity theory are insuf-
ficiently abstract (as is the case with logical behaviorism and central state identity theory). In

other words, the methods used to identify machine
states cannot be used to identify mental states.

    5. The mental states of an organism cannot be
placed in one-to-one correspondence with machine
table states. Machine table states are finite in
number and can be descriptively listed. Mental states are productive and potentially infinite in number, precluding descriptive enumeration.

    6. The machine version of functionalism does
not provide for the structural, or logical, relationship that can exist between certain mental states. A Turing machine, for all practical purposes,
has no internal structural configuration beyond
specification of the possible stepwise change in
states. For instance, the machine version has no
way of representing the fact that a belief in $\underline{P}$ is
more related to a belief in $\underline{P} \cap \underline{Q}$ than to a belief in
$\underline{Q}$.

    Although machine version functionalism is an ap-
preciable advance over nonmachine version functionalism, its physical realization via a Turing machine
still results in an overall conceptualization that
is too primitive for human mentation.

    TECHNICAL SPECIFICATION OF A MENTAL EVENT Be-
cause many versions of functionalism exist, it is
necessary to consider the set of criteria for a mental event associated with a specific functional theorist. Jerry Fodor (1981), a machine version, functional state identity theorist, postulates three
conditions for classifying an entity as a mental
event:

    1. The entity must be amenable to a relational,
causal role definition.

2. The entity must be realizable as a machine table state in some Turing machine.

3. The entity must possess qualitative or intentional content.

The first two conditions constitute review in this context and need not be considered further. The content criterion already has been partially considered with respect to its qualia component, but will be analyzed in depth.

QUALITATIVE CONTENT COMPONENT As previously indicated, no version of functionalism is designed to handle the qualia associated with occurrent states. For instance, functionalism cannot explain the phenomenal experience of red or redness when an organism perceives a ripe apple. Since functionalism models the dynamic aspect of mind; that is, information processing and its effect on behavior, it might seem that qualia are irrelevant for functionalism. But if qualia are arbitrarily banished from the domain of functionalism by fiat, the functionalistic approach to mentation runs the risk of being accused of not being able to handle the characteristic nature and content of consciousness. In fact, many philosophers (see Shoemaker, 1975) do argue that functionalism's inability to handle qualitative consciousness invalidates the entire approach.

The severity of functionalism's quandry can be illustrated by the following fact. Functionalism accounts for information processing via the concatenation of a series of substates or symbolic computations. These can occur in a human being or any nonhuman conceptual system, such as a computer, mechanical calculator, or animal. But qualia are

a property of the entire intact human organism per
se.   (Who knows if a machine, computer, or animal
experiences qualia!) Qualia do not automatically or
implicitly arise from a concatenation of a series of
computational states (Dennett, 1978b).

    Functionalism's neglect of qualia leads to
three interrelated conceptual problems, over and
above its possible immediate invalidation (Shoemaker, 1975): (1) inverted spectra, (2) absent qualia,
and (3) differential qualia.

    1. The inverted spectrum problem can best be
introduced by an example. Suppose person X's green
is person Y's red, and vice versa. Since the content of phenomenal experience is subjective, consistent occurrences of inverted spectra do not affect
overt behavior--in fact, they might not even be diagnosed during a person's lifetime. But, at a conceptual level, X's green and Y's red have the same
causal role, although they are qualitatively distinct mental events. Inverted spectra vitiate functionalism if qualitative content is taken to be one
of the criteria of a mental event.

    2. The absent qualia problem arises in the fol-
lowing context. Person X is in mental state C and
experiences qualia; person Y is in the same mental
state C, but does not experience qualia. Again, we
have a situation in which two people are in the same
mental state according to causal role criteria, but
are not in the same mental state according to the
qualia criterion.

    3. The differential qualia problem can be con-
ceptualized as a subset of either the inverted spectrum or absent qualia problem. Suppose person X is

in mental state $\underline{C}$ and experiences qualia $\underline{P}$ and that
person $\underline{Y}$ is in mental state $\underline{C}$ and experiences qualia
$\underline{Q}$. Again, we have a situation in which two people
are in the same mental state according to causal
role criteria, but are not in the same mental state
according to the qualia criterion.

The reason these three problems are not fatal
to functionalism is that they are equally damaging
to logical behaviorism and the mental state-brain
state identity thesis. Also, functionalism does do
a credible job with respect to the other component
of the third condition (Fodor, 1981): intentional
content.

INTENTIONAL CONTENT COMPONENT A mental
event has intentional content if it possesses semantic properties. A mental event has semantic properties if it expresses some kind of knowledge. For
instance, a belief has semantic properties and expresses some kind of knowledge. A symbol also possesses intentional content: it achieves meaning by
referring to or representing something outside of
itself. Human language is the prototypical example
of a symbol system. It is natural to conjoin the
notions of mental event and symbol, such that mental
symbols exist. Another way of expressing the same
thing is that mental representation exists. Mind
operates on and processes symbols. There is no mental computation without mental representation (Fodor, 1981). It should not be surprising that contemporary cognitive behaviorism is attempting to
provide a unified treatment of language and mentation: much mental computation (representation) involves language symbols.

The classic approach to mental representation
is the Humean resemblance view, as a component of
British associationism: a mental idea is an image
that resembles the thing represented (Hume, 1748).
Functionalism replaces the classic view with a causal role/relations approach: the proposition expressed by a given mental representation depends on the
causal properties of the mental states in which the
mental representation figures (Fodor, 1981). This
merely amounts to the fundamental proposition of
functionalism expressed at a higher level of abstraction.

Incidentally, it would be possible to handle
qualia by an extension of this same fundamental
proposition. Specifically, qualia can be conceptualized as a qualitative state of another mental
state. The qualitative state of the mental state
can then be defined in terms of its causal, relational role. Also note that self-consciousness, being aware of one's consciousness, can be handled analogously: self-awareness is a qualitative state of
the mental state of being conscious and can be functionally defined in terms of its causal role. It
could be argued that either of these applications of
the fundamental proposition violates one's intui-
tions about the nature of qualia or self-consciousness, but this is a topic for Chapter 9.

Functionalism's conception of mental representation explains cognitive behaviorism's virtual rev-
erence for the mind-computer analogy. Computers operate on symbols, usually those subsumed by some
programming language. There is no computer computation without some form of functional representation.

Both the computer and the mind, as computational devices, are representational systems operating on
symbols with intentional content. A computer can
only consist of functionally defined states with intentional content specified in terms of causal role
(not resemblance). Qualia are irrelevant for a computer. It is as if the introduction of computers
has opened up a whole new level of reality for the
philosopher, one that externalizes all the problems
involved in the task of modeling and accounting for
human mentation.

RELATIONAL COMPARISON: EVOLUTION OF MENTATION

Cartesian interactionist dualism formalizes the
everyday view that mental events determine behavior.
His doctrine ran into trouble because it violates
one of the basic tenets of physical science: the
conservation of energy (see Bunge, 1980). Whenever
mind affects the body, energy is created. Conversely, when body affects the mind, energy is dissipa-
ted. To the best of my knowledge, no one has ever
argued that the respective energy creations and dis-
sipations offset each other, such that there is no
net change in energy and it is functionally conser-
ved.

Given the pre-eminence of the nontranscendental
view of the human being (see Chapter 6), the intuition that mentation exists and is causative must be
given a physicalistic interpretation. This makes
the many variants of materialism and functionalism
the only philosophically viable approaches to mentation.

If a psychologist merely is interested in predicting and/or controlling overt behavior, then des-

criptive behaviorism or eliminative materialism is
an acceptable characterization of mentation. In
this approach, mentation, or what passes for mentation, simply is a property of the behavioral output
itself. The organism is a black box, such that response output is a direct, linear function of stimulus input.

The simplest way to separate mentation from output is to conceive of mental events as behavioral
dispositions, as done in logical behaviorism or reductive materialism. Behavioral dispositions are
relationally defined in terms of stimulus input and
response output, but they perform no causal role.
They merely serve as structural descriptions specifying what behaviors are probable in given situations.

Central state identity theses give mental states physical realization as some kind of causative
physiological entity: brain state, neuronal process,
biochemical event, and the like. Since mental
events are physical events, they can perform all the
functions of the Cartesian mind without violating
naturalistic or mechanistic doctrine. There is
nothing inconceivable about one physiological event
(mentation as a brain state) determining another
physiological event (behavior as the activation of
some effector system). The type theory version of
mind state-brain state identity suffers the compositional problem: since a mental state is not defined
relationally, but rather in terms of its existential
components, specification of the exact physiological
property by which a brain state is a mental state
eludes final resolution.

Emergentist materialism is a refinement over the psychophysical identity thesis in that it makes human mentation a unique physical process; however, its basic conceptual advance derives from the fact that its fundamental compositional elements, plastic neuronal systems, are defined in a relational manner.

The functional approach to mentation combines the relational specification characteristic of logical behaviorism and the causative features of central state identity theory. Conversely, it eliminates the noncausative features of logical behaviorism and the compositional criteria of central state identity theory. Functionalism does this, informally, by specifying a mental state in terms of its causal role between input and output and its association with other mental states and, formally, by the additional requirement of a Turing machine table state correspondence thesis. This approach eliminates mentation as an exclusive property of the human being, or other biological organism, and makes it a characteristic of any functionally organized conceptual system, such as a computer, irrespective of its compositional realization. Like all philosophical conceptions of the mind, functionalism has problems with qualia; but it is eminently successful with respect to intentional content and the problem of mental representation. Since human mentation subsumes a functionally organized conceptual system, other such systems as the computer, more readily accessible to analysis and manipulation, can serve as models for the mind.

CHAPTER 8

PSYCHOLOGICAL EXPLANATION

One of the functions of a psychologist is to explain
phenomena that are regarded as psychological in nature. Since such phenomena are contingent on the model of psychological reality that is used (as demonstrated in Chapters 3, 4, and 5), what constitutes
acceptable psychological explanation also depends on
the particular model that is employed. The various
models of psychological reality have different criteria and standards for explanation associated with
them. The ultimate value of a given approach to psychological explanation cannot be judged independently
of the goals of the system with which it is associated, and this fact contributes to the continued pluralistic state of contemporary psychology.

        We are going to analyze the approaches to psy-
chological explanation that are characteristic of
five of the six contemporary systems discussed in
Chapter 5: radical behaviorism, cognitive behaviorism, psychoanalysis, humanism, and dialectical psychology. Five different conceptions of psychological explanation will be presented: (1) low level,
descriptive scientific explanation or explanation by
control, (2) high level, theoretical scientific explanation or explanation by deduction, (3) function-
analytical explanation, (4) interpretive consistency,

and (5) intuitive understanding. The many variants
of behaviorism and dialectical psychology must employ some form of scientific explanation; cognitive
behaviorism subsumes function-analytical explanation
in addition to scientific explanation; Freudian
depth psychology uses interpretive consistency; and
humanism involves intuitive understanding.

     The nature of explanation is just as much a
philosophical issue as the mind-body problem and the
nature of the human being (Cummins, 1983). In this
context, the criteria, standards, and even implications of acceptable explanation are more developed
in those systems that assume an explicit nontranscendental and physical monistic orientation than in
others. Therefore, the overall scientific approach
to psychological explanation that is advocated by
the various forms of behaviorism must serve as the
essential focal point of the chapter. This does not
mean that we are abandoning our neutral approach to
analyzing the task of constructing a model of psychological reality; it simply means that we have
reached a point in our analysis where it is relevant
to emphasize certain systems over others.

     It will become apparent later in the chapter
that a fundamental difference exists between the two
types of scientific explanation and the internal
consistency and intuitive understanding approaches.
Scientific explanation prescribes both the form that
an acceptable explanation can take and the manner in
which it is evaluated. The other two approaches are
mute with respect to form and really constitute
evaluational criteria for explanations that violate
one or more of the characteristics of a scientific

explanation.

One of the correlates of scientific explanation
is determinism. Scientific explanation and determinism mutually imply each other (see Underwood, 1957).
The various interpretations of determinism associated with the dominant forms of behaviorism must be
discussed. Four unscientific types of explanation
also must be considered: (1) circular, (2) teleological, (3) ethical, and (4) rational. A behaviorist
can be guilty of using any one of these types of explanation, but they primarily are associated with
the interpretive consistency and intuitive understanding approaches.

SCIENTIFIC EXPLANATION

Two interrelated hierarchical levels of scientific explanation exist: (1) descriptive and (2)
theoretical. Watson (1913) and Skinner (1938, 1953)
advocate descriptive behaviorism. They only allow
descriptive explanation. Contemporary cognitive behaviorism and the many variants of logical behaviorism (see Chapter 3) use theoretical explanation, _in_
addition _to_ descriptive explanation. Descriptive
explanation will be analyzed first, for two basic
reasons: (1) A descriptive explanation is the specific entity to which a given theoretical explanation
usually is applied, and (2) a descriptive explanation is more directly related to both the correlate
of determinism and the four types of unscientific
explanation.

DESCRIPTIVE EXPLANATION A given psychological
phenomenon, such as behavior, is descriptively explained by relating it to the real-time and real-
space environmental events that control its occur-

rence.   A descriptive explanation entails the specific causal law or functional relationship that underlies the occurrence of a given behavioral phenomenon (see Hillner, 1978).   The notion of a descriptive explanation was implicit in Chapter 3.   It amounts to the input-output relationship that constitutes the content of observation for the Watsonian
and Skinnerian behavioristic systems.   Recall that
the primary descriptive variables for Watson and
Skinner involve conditioning and/or reinforcement
contingencies.

      Descriptive explanation imposes two restric-
tions on the environmental events that can serve as
input variables: (1) they can only precede or be concurrent with the output variable in time, and (2)
the total number of preceding and concurrent environmental events associated with a given output variable must be finite.   Sometimes the second restric-
tion is referred to as the assumption of finite causation (Underwood, 1957).

      The primary advantage of descriptive explana-
tion is that it affords prediction and control.
Once a particular behavioral phenomenon has become
part of a given input-output relationship and has
been descriptively explained, in principle its future occurrence can be predicted or controlled.
Knowledge of the values of the input variables allows predictive statements to be made about the occurrence of the output phenomena; active manipulation of the values of the input variables allows the
occurrence of the output phenomena to be controlled.

      The distinction between prediction and control
merely is semantic in nature.   Which of the two is

occurring in any given case is a function of the
psychologist's intentions. The conceptual relationship existing between prediction and control has
changed over the years as descriptive behaviorism
has evolved. In Watsonian behaviorism, which assumed a hard-core interpretation of determinism,
prediction is logically prior to control; and the
ability to predict behavior underlies the ability to
control behavior. In Skinnerian behaviorism, which
takes a softer view of determinism, control is logically prior to prediction; and the ability to control behavior underlies the ability to predict behavior.

It is in the context of the softer view of determinism that Skinner (1953) is said to explain by
control. For Skinner, once a specific piece of behavior is controllable, all possible relevant empirical knowledge about the behavior has been exhaust-
ed. One need not dig deeper and seek other levels
of explanation.

THEORETICAL EXPLANATION Logical behaviorism
and cognitive behaviorism go beyond the descriptive
level of analysis. Determining the set of empirical
variables of which a particular piece of behavior is
a function does not constitute a complete explanation of the behavior. These forms of behaviorism
ask the question "Why is behavior Y a function of
variables X_1, X_2, X_3, . . . , X_N?" Resolving this
question requires reference to a higher order level
of explanation, commonly called the theoretical level. The explanatory device existing at this level
is called a theory.

A theory (see Hillner, 1978, 1979) is a set of

verbal statements (blueprints, rules, or axiomatic
system) which, if explicitly actualized, would generate an aspect of the descriptive level of analysis, either the input situation, the output situation, or both (an input-output relationship). Behavioristic theories come in all shapes and sizes,
ranging from a simple, informal theory composed of
a few sentences in the vernacular to a complex,
highly abstract, formal theory stated in axiomatic
and mathematical form.

A theory constitutes a higher order explanation
of some aspect of the descriptive level of analysis
in the sense that the descriptive aspect is derivable from it. In the ideal case, derivation occurs
through explicit logical deduction; in less than the
ideal case, derivation is done implicitly: the descriptive statement is an informal implication of the
theory.

A theory must fulfill a crucial requirement if
it is to be taken seriously: empirical testability.
A theory must be amenable to empirical validation in
order to serve as a source of higher order explanation in the context of science. Functionally this
means that the theory must generate one or more predictions, commonly called hypotheses, other than the
input-output relationship it putatively explains,
that are capable of empirical assessment in a specific laboratory or research situation. So a scientific theory not only explains; it also must predict.

The substantive content of a theory involves
reference to one or more so-called theoretical constructs. Theoretical constructs, as is the case
with theories themselves, come in all shapes and

sizes.   A theoretical construct usually can be given
a specification on each of two independent dimensions (Hillner, 1978): (1) level of reality and (2)
existence status.

1. Two general levels of reality exist: constructive and reductive.   A constructive theoretical
concept is stated at the same level of reality as
the descriptive fact to be explained: behavioral or
psychological.   A reductive theoretical construct is
stated at some level of reality lower than the fact
to be explained, usually the physiological level.
Explaining a behavioral fact in terms of the underlying physiology involved technically is referred to
as reductionism (Turner, 1967).

2. Existence status refers to whether or not
the denotation of the theoretical construct actually
exists.   Theoretical constructs that possess the existence property usually are called hypothetical
constructs; theoretical constructs that do not possess the existence property usually are called intervening variables (MacCorquodale and Meehl, 1948;
Marx, 1951).

The history of logical behaviorism, as a learning psychology, can be characterized in terms of
four theoretical cycles (Hillner, 1979):

1. The macrotheoretical era (1930-1950) in
which attempts were made by Hull (1943, 1951, 1952),
Guthrie (1935), and Tolman (1932) to explain the
overall process of learning.

2. The microtheoretical era (1930-now) in which
attempts were and are made by Osgood (1949), Postman (1962), Underwood (with Schulz, 1960), Neal Miller (1944, 1959), and Amsel (1958, 1962) to explain

the learning that occurs in a specific situation.

3. The macromodel era (1950-1960) in which attempts were made by Estes (1950, 1960), Bush (with
Mosteller, 1951, 1955), Mosteller, and Restle (1962,
1975) to mathematically formalize the learning process.

4. The micromodel era (1960-now) in which attempts are made by Bower (1959, 1962), Suppes (with
Atkinson, 1960), and Atkinson (1957) to mathematically formalize the learning that occurs in a specific situation. Many of the current micromodels of
learning are cognitive in nature and involve computer programs and simulation (see Chapter 5). There
is no hard and fast dividing line between current
information processing psychology and the micromodel
investigation of learning.

The general shift in orientation from logical
behaviorism to cognitive behaviorism that occurred
during the 1960s was accompanied by the replacement
of mechanistic, peripherally locused theoretical
constructs with constructional, centrally locused
theoretical mechanisms. Such concepts as habit
strength, drive, response threshold, and behavioral
oscillation (see Hull, 1943) were replaced by such
constructs as strategy selection, attention, stimulus salience, short term memory, coding, and cuing
(see Restle, 1975).

DESCRIPTIVE VERSUS THEORETICAL EXPLANATION Explanation by control and explanation by deduction
are continuous and complementary entities. The former inputs into the latter, and the latter completes
the former. Either type of explanation is perfectly
acceptable in the context of an objective, external-

ly based resolution of overt behavior. Skinner limits himself to the descriptive level because his goal is control. Logical and cognitive behaviorists
use an additional theoretical level because they
seek a more comprehensive understanding. Neither
type of explanation will ever supplant the other.
Descriptive will never replace theoretical because
of the sheer fun of theory construction and evaluation; theoretical will never replace descriptive because of the exigencies of practical application.

The mechanics of progress are completely different in the context of descriptive and theoretical
explanation. The success of explanation by control
is a function of such factors as hardware technology;
ethical standards or judicial decisions; and selection, training, and ability of behavioral modification specialists. The success of explanation by deduction is a more subjective and elusive notion that
is contingent on standards of precision and predictability, strictness of empirical evaluation criteria, available modes of acceptable theory construction, and faddish cycles in theoretical construct
preference. Explanation by control is constrained
mostly by externally imposed procedural factors,
while explanation by deduction is constrained by
considerations that are an inherent part of the theory construction and evaluation process, specifically dicta associated with the philosophy of science.
DETERMINISM
The principle of determinism is a metaphysical
assumption, associated with the natural view of the
human being, that the behaviorist applies to overt
behavior (see Chapter 6). Because of its metaphysi-

cal status, no amount of empirical research can ever
validate the principle. The experimental psychologist does not perform research to demonstrate the
validity of the assumption of determinism; the assumption justifies laboratory investigation of behavior in the first place. Likewise, attempts to
control behavior in the natural environment outside
the laboratory constitute applications, not vindica-
tions, of the principle of determinism. Psychologists that do not accept the principle of determinism profess a vastly different psychology (cf. humanism in Chapters 3 and 5).

        As is true of any metaphysical concept, the
principle of determinism admits of numerous interpretations. We shall simplify our analysis somewhat
by assuming that there are only two broad interpretations of the notion of determinism: (1) a traditional strict one and (2) a more contemporary flexible one. Each of these versions of determinism not
only has differential consequences for the relationship between prediction and control (as indicated
previously in the chapter), but also has differential consequences for the acceptability of the use
of various behavioral control techniques for the
general public.

        TRADITIONAL INTERPRETATION In the strict view
of determinism, the input conditions are true causes;
and the output phenomenon, usually behavior, is a
true effect. The notion of an empirical relationship encompasses a bona fide causal law. Causation
is physical in nature (see Nagel, 1961, especially
Chapter 10). Mechanical systems serve as the model
of causation. The activity or movement of one phys-

ical body, as cause, imparts the necessary energy or force for the activity or movement of another physical body, as effect. Cause and effect is an explicit, automatic sequence. Determinism is absolutistic in nature. Effects are deterministic, as opposed to probabilistic, occurrences. Knowledge of the causal law governing the occurrence of a specific natural event is sufficient to control the occurrence of that behavioral event. Prediction is logically prior to control. This interpretation of determinism tends to give the notion of behavioral control a bad name in our surrounding culture: viz., George Orwell's 1984.

CLASSICAL WATSONIAN BEHAVIORISM Watsonian descriptive behaviorism can be construed as advocating a strict interpretation of determinism and serves as the best example of this interpretation in the behavioristic context. Watson (1913, 1925) made extreme environmentalism the cornerstone of his system, in part, to justify his objective approach to human behavior. Of course, stimuli did not cause responses in a direct, mechanical, transformation of energy sense; however, Watson's emphasis on the reflex made the organism a prisoner of its environment. Although Watson did not appeal to underlying physiology to explain overt behavior, he assumed the classic, push-pull conception of a reflex in which response output is an automatic function of a telephone type neuronal hookup system. The primary source of behavioral change was classical conditioning. All learning was assumed to be an instance of classical conditioning. Classical conditioning was an automatic process over which the organism had no

real control. Both the unconditioned response and
the conditioned response were regarded as involuntary in nature.

     CONTEMPORARY INTERPRETATION In the current,
more flexible view of determinism, input variables
and output variables merely are natural events that
are related to each other and covary. An empirical
relationship subsumes a functional relationship in
which the dependent variable is some function of the
independent variables. The notion of "is some function of" is not all that explicit; however, it can
entail more than mere correlation. Perhaps a good
analogy is that of a mathematical equation in which
a rule specifies how many units of one variable is
equivalent to so many units of another variable.
Determinism is symbolic and relativistic in nature
(see Nagel, 1961, especially Chapter 14). Response
output basically is a probabilistic, as opposed to
deterministic, event. Since behavioral events are
probabilistic, the ability to control underlies the
ability to predict. Control is logically prior to
prediction.

     It can be argued that logical behaviorism,
Skinnerian radical behaviorism, and contemporary
cognitive behaviorism either do assume or only can
assume this more diluted form of determinism. The
implications of this interpretation of determinism
for the public at large will become apparent very
shortly in the context of Skinner's system.

          LOGICAL BEHAVIORISM Recall that the many
variants of logical behaviorism encompass both descriptive and theoretical explanation. Overt behavior is related to both external environmental events

and postulated theoretical constructs intervening between the stimulus input and response output. The
many possible hypothetical relationships existing
among the intervening theoretical constructs admit
an element of randomness into any experimental situation. Hull (1951) even built a formal oscillation
factor into his system. The kinds of experiments
that such learning macrotheorists as Hull (1951),
Guthrie (1935), and Tolman (1932) performed did not
afford a high degree of control over the organism's
behavior; and they had to absorb the consequent lack
of predictability into the theoretical level of analysis. As extensions of classical learning macrotheory, both the macromodel and micromodel approaches
construct probabilistic models of learning and explicitly make response probability the primary dependent variable for representing behavioral occurrence
(for instance, Estes, 1950; Bower, 1962).

SKINNERIAN RADICAL BEHAVIORISM Recall that
Skinnerian radical behaviorism strictly is a descriptive system in which behavior is related only to external environmental events. Psychological reality
in Skinner's (1953, 1974) system is structured in
terms of correlations between classes of stimulus
events and classes of response events. In this context, Skinner focuses on only one response variable,
rate, and manipulates only two kinds of operational
contingencies: reinforcement and stimulus discrimination. This particular combination of input and output events (generating the Skinnerian contingencies)
allows a pre-emptory degree of behavioral control
and, consequently, predictability.

It would be misleading to presume that Skinner

is a strict, or unidirectional, determinist. Skinner does assume that organismic behavior is controlled by environmental contingencies. But the response term is a component of such contingencies, and
Skinner also assumes that the organism can change
the environment. The environment and organismic behavior mutually influence each other, much as in the
case of dialectical psychology. Determinism is reciprocal or bidirectional, as opposed to unidirectional. In prototypical laboratory operant conditioning, the experimenter is conditioning the subject; but the subject is also conditioning the experimenter. The subject's response rate increases
as a function of reinforcement delivery, and the experimenter's rate of reinforcement delivery increases as a function of the subject's responding. The
basic theme of Skinner's <u>Walden</u> <u>Two</u> and <u>Beyond</u> <u>Free-</u>
<u>dom</u> <u>and</u> <u>Dignity</u> is the design and construction of
environments that encompass benign contingencies for
the control of human behavior.

   The application of Skinnerian operant conditioning principles to certain applied settings, known as
behavior modification, can be interpreted to involve
a contractual determinism, whereby the organism
yields certain power to the psychologist through a
kind of contractual social agreement (Erwin, 1978):
the behavioral psychologist assumes control over the
means of access to reinforcement and its delivery
for the betterment of the organism. The arbitrariness of control in this setup is demonstrated by the
fact that the terms of the social contract can be
resisted and changed, for any number of reasons.
Behavior modification specialists engaged in private

practice are encouraged to use actual physical contracts specifying the terms, goals, and techniques
of the treatment program.

The ultimate in behavioral control is self or
personal control, as opposed to external or social
control (Lazarus, 1971). For example, the best way
to prevent crime is not by having policemen station-
ed every fifty feet in the environment, but rather
by conditioning people to refrain from criminal behavior regardless of the state of the external stimulus situation. In other words, people carry the
environment with them: the relevant controlling
stimuli have become internalized. Skinner's (1974)
admission of internal stimuli that can be discrimin-
ated through proper training, and of self-planned
and self-generated reinforcement, makes the individual organism more than a mere prisoner of its immediate physical surroundings. The object of many behavior modification programs is self-improvement
through self-control: improved study skills, weight
reduction and control, efficient use of work or recreational time, and extinction of smoking behavior.

COGNITIVE BEHAVIORISM The information processing approach to human cognition relates overt
behavior to hypothetical internal cognitive processes. Responding is not a direct function of external, physical stimulus events, but rather of how
they are processed by the cognitive mechanisms in
the organism's brain (Anderson, 1980). The locus of
behavioral control is internal in cognitive behaviorism, as it is in the context of logical behaviorism. A strict interpretation of determinism is impossible in this context. Prediction and control

constitute much more elusive goals in cognitive behaviorism (Neisser, 1976). The ultimate source of
behavior makes it very difficult to control and, consequently, very difficult to predict.

FUNCTION-ANALYTICAL EXPLANATION

Just as explanation by control and explanation
by deduction are continuous and complementary entities, scientific explanation as a whole and function-
analytical explanation are continuous and complementary strategies of explanation. Scientific explanation involves a subsumption strategy: an empirical
phenomenon is treated as an instance or application
of some descriptive causal law that in turn is resolvable in the context of some general covering
theory or higher order explanation. Function-analytical explanation involves a systems analysis strategy: the function of an empirical phenomenon is determined, and then the manner in which the function
is performed is specified (Cummins, 1975).

A scientist in general and an experimental psychologist in particular must take a function as giv-
en: the function of the entity to be explained usually is assumed to be its customary use, which is
equivalent operationally to the task that the entity
performs. Otherwise, the notion of function gets
confounded with the notion of purpose; and problems
associated with Aristotelian final cause or teleology might ensue.

The creative aspect of function-analytical explanation resides at the level of specifying exactly
how the task performed by the entity is accomplished.
This is typically done by analyzing the overall task
into a series of subtasks or suboperations and then

relating them via some organizational program or
combinatorial sequence. Everyday examples of this
include (1) a flow chart for the components of a production line, (2) a diagram of the circuitry of some
electronic device, (3) an organizational chart for
the departments of a hospital, and (4) an outline of
the subroutines of a computer program. Note that in
these simple physical examples even the subcompon-
ents or suboperations are given or obvious.

The systems analysis strategy can be applied to
any psychological phenomenon requiring explanation.
Wundt (1896) and Titchener (1898) implicitly used it
in their analysis by synthesis approach to the content of conscious experience. Watson (1916) analyzed a piece of behavior into a concatenation of conditioned response units. The complex mental abilities studied by contemporary cognitive behaviorism
are particularly amenable to functional analysis.
Genuine theoretical creativity is involved in the
cognitive context because neither the suboperations
nor the combinatorial rule are given or obvious:
they must be postulated and evaluated (see Chapter
5).

A successful function-analytical explanation in
psychology, especially cognitive psychology, possesses three characteristics (Cummins, 1975):

1. The suboperations are simple, unsophistica-
ted, or merely mechanical in nature. It is possible
to break down a specific suboperation into a series
of subsuboperations, with their own combinatorial
rule; however, to prevent an infinite regression
with respect to the postulation of sub . . . suboperations, somewhere along the line of reduction a

subsumption type of explanation must be used or the
current level of suboperations must be accepted at
face value.

2. The suboperations are different from the
phenomenon to be explained with respect to typology.
Use of suboperations that only differ from the entity to be explained with respect to complexity and
not typology makes the function-analytical form of
explanation degenerate.

3. The organizing program or combinatorial rule
is sophisticated. This is necessary to reduce the
gap between the differential complexities and typol-
ogies of the entity to be explained and the suboperations.

Ideal function-analytical explanation is approached in the context of automata theory (Boden,
1981), where a complex cognitive process is analyzed
into a concatenation of simple computational steps.
The contemporary functionalist approach to mind (see
Chapter 7) is a subset of the systems analysis strategy. A mental event is defined in terms of its
causal role, or function, in the overall mentation
system and related to the input and output of the
system. A mental event isolated in this manner can
either be analyzed into subproperties or serve as
a subproperty of a higher level event.

INTERPRETIVE CONSISTENCY

Interpretive consistency is the mode of understanding ultimately used by depth psychology, in
general, and Freudian psychoanalysis, in particular.
Any depth psychology encompasses an extensive, even
complex, set of theoretical propositions. At a superficial level, the theoretical propositions of

depth psychology have the same structure and form as
those of many behavioristic approaches using the theoretical level of analysis.   But there is at least
one critical difference between Freudian theory and
behavioristic theory.   Freud's theoretical propositions are not subject to empirical test.   Freudian
theory is not scientific theory.   Freudian propositions amount to a belief system that must be accepted on faith (Robinson, 1979).   Using a religious
analogy, Freudian psychology amounts to dogma.   As
everyone knows, dogmatic disputes only can be resolved by emotional or irrational means.

There are many reasons why Freudian propositions are impervious to empirical test, only two of
which need be mentioned here:

1. Recall that Freudian psychoanalysis is a
description of an organism's inner psychic world.
Most, if not all, of Freud's theoretical constructs,
such as libido, id, or dream censor, are not operationally definable.   They cannot be reduced to a set
of empirical operations that can be physicalized in
the laboratory (Grünbaum, 1980).

2. Even if operational specification were possible in the context of Freudian psychology, its
psychodynamics would still overdetermine and multi-
predict the psychological phenomena of interest (Von
Eckardt, 1983).   Overdetermination means that a
given psychological phenomenon can be the result of
numerous alternative mechanisms.   Multiprediction
means that a given mechanism can be the source of
numerous alternative psychological phenomena.   Overdetermination prevents experimental isolation of the
"true" cause of a given psychological phenomenon.

Multiprediction prevents specification of what particular psychological phenomenon will occur ahead of
time.   Both Freud and behaviorists assume determinism, but Freud's determinism is psychic in nature
and does not allow one-to-one linkages between specific input and output events.   Freud's determinism
has too much indeterminism built into it.   Overdetermination and multiprediction collectively result
in multilinkages between specific input and output
events, preventing meaningful empirical assessment
of Freud's psychodynamic system.

POST HOC EXPLANATION AND INTERNAL CONSISTENCY
Freudian theory only allows after-the-fact or post
hoc explanation (Cummins, 1983).   Freudian dynamics
can readily account for a given psychological phenomenon once it has already occurred.   It is possible
to trace the exact path through the multilinkage
system that led up to the psychological phenomenon
in post hoc fashion.   After-the-fact explanation
supplies a kind of understanding that only can be
judged in terms of interpretive consistency.   The
notion of interpretive consistency possesses at
least two possible meanings (Kendler, 1981):

1. Freudian theory is consistent to the extent
that it provides a coherent interpretation of psychological phenomena.   Coherent is a subjective notion.   What is coherent for one person is not necessarily coherent for another.   The notion of coheren-
cy frequently reduces to the notion of reasonableness.   The reasonableness of Freudian theory is
self-obvious to the general public.

2. A set of propositions is technically consistent if no contradictory statement is logically de-

ducible from it. Since Freudian theory is so loosely formulated and open-ended, no psychologist claims
that psychoanalysis is consistent in this second,
technical sense.

The notion of interpretive consistency can be
further explicated if it is described in terms of
the internal consistency that can exist in a diagnostic clinical situation, such as a psychoanalytic
therapy session. Freud made diagnoses of his patients' problems, as revealed during psychoanalysis.
Since his diagnoses lacked any significant empirical
content, they could not be evaluated in terms of any
external validity assessment: the degree to which
Freud's diagnoses corresponded to objective reality
was indeterminable. Freud could only evaluate the
internal consistency of his conclusions. He continually cross-checked different aspects and levels of
his overall interpretive conclusions with each other.
A given diagnosis was correct to the extent that its
components "hung together" by whatever subjective
criterion of consistency that Freud used.

INTUITIVE UNDERSTANDING

Intuitive understanding is characteristic of
humanistic, phenomenological, existential psychology.
Considering the purpose of the humanistic approach,
this conception of psychological explanation is the
most subjective of all. The aim of humanistic psychology is to interpret an organism's conscious
feeling state and overall psychological status in
terms of its conception of psychological reality
(see Chapter 5). The components of the prior sen-
tence specify the content of observation in humanistic psychology. But how do humanistic psychologists

know that their reactions to the subject's phenomenological report have validity? No objective criterion exists to determine this.

One of the fundamental concepts in humanistic
psychology is meaning (Keen, 1975). An authentic
psychological phenomenon is one that possesses meaning for the individual. Meaning in this context
does not necessarily connote denotational reference;
meaning should be interpreted as significance or
relevance. The humanist must induce the meaning a
phenomenalizer attaches to something from self-report. For want of a better term, it is assumed that
the psychologist "intuits" the person's meaning or
"intuitively understands" the person's meaning.

The psychological nature of intuition is open-
ended: it can be a rationalistic process, an emotional process involving identification, or a combination of both. Psychologists simply know when some
intuitive understanding of the person has been
achieved; psychologists simply know when they can
resolve the individual's psychological status in
terms of its view of psychological reality (Abel,
1948).

Intuitive understanding is similar to the "ah-
hah" experience one often enjoys in the context of
problem solving. Solution of the problem eventually
seems to appear out of nowhere and is immediately ap-
prehended as being correct without knowing why
(Duncker, 1945). My own preference is to assume
that the "ah-hah" experience is perfectly predictable and a function of factors of which the problem
solver is not immediately aware. One of the factors
that inputs into a successful "ah-hah" occurrence is

degree of prior exposure to similar problems.

Intuitive understanding is not limited to judgments about a phenomenalizer's conscious state and beliefs. It occurs in mathematics, science, aesthetic judgments (beauty, symmetry, simplicity, harmony), philosophy, ethics, morality, and the like.

Intuitive understanding amounts to a kind of personal knowledge (Kendler, 1981). It could even be argued that it constitutes some type of prescientific or preobjective knowledge. The humanist simply opts for personal knowledge as an end goal. A depth psychologist attempts to transform personal knowledge into consistent knowledge, such that the substance of the knowledge is not self-contradictory. The behaviorist, as scientist, goes all the way and evaluates whether the content of intuitive understanding possesses empirical content and passes all the tests of objective knowledge.

Personal knowledge is most easily communicated via literary or artistic creations. Although the communication of any kind of knowledge involves symbols and descriptive constraints, the literary/artistic format is less restrictive than the scientific format. One of the humanistic criticisms of behaviorism is that it oversymbolizes, overabstracts, and overcategorizes (Correnti, 1965). Denying personal knowledge dehumanizes the individual and destroys the individual's uniqueness. The typical behaviorist rejoinder is that if the concept of personal knowledge is taken to the extreme, such knowledge becomes ineffable.

Personal knowledge, by definition, is subjective and idiosyncratic. It is much more intimately

associated with a psychologist's value system and
metaphysical beliefs than objective scientific knowledge that is subject to consensual agreement, even
if only tacit in nature. One humanist's view of humankind need not correspond to another humanist's
view of humankind: contrast Maslow's (1970) and Rogers' (1961) conceptions of self-realization.

FOUR TYPES OF UNSCIENTIFIC EXPLANATION

This section analyzes four classes of explanation of behavioral phenomena that violate one or
more of the presuppositions or characteristics of
descriptive scientific explanation: (1) circular explanation, nominal explanation, or explanation by
labeling; (2) teleological explanation or explanation by immanent purpose; (3) ethical explanation or
the concept of rule governed behavior; and (4) reasonable or rational explanation. These types of explanation seem intuitively plausible to the average
person, pose no conceptual problems for psychologists operating in an interpretive consistency or
intuitive understanding context, and constitute a
"no-no" for the behaviorally oriented experimental
psychologist. Circular explanation is the most pervasive of the four and appears in virtually every
system of psychology. Teleological explanation is
primarily associated with cognitive psychology and
the humanistic approach. Ethical explanation is
characteristic of many cognitive theories. Reasonable explanation primarily occurs in an applied context, such that its discussion serves as a convenient transition to Chapter 10.

CIRCULAR EXPLANATION Circular explanation arises when some name is given to a particular behavior,

treated as a separate event, and then used to account
for the behavior. This procedure is called circular
explanation because the only evidence for the cause
of the behavior is the behavioral effect itself
(Hillner, 1978).

The classic example of a circular explanation
in the psychological literature is the concept of instinct (McDougall, 1923). Countless behaviors have
been categorized as instinctive in nature and, therefore, putatively explained. For instance: nest building behavior, which seems to be particularly characteristic of birds. The bird presumably possesses
a nest building instinct. But how do we know that
the bird possesses a nest building instinct? Because we see it building a nest. This is the very
behavior that required explanation in the first
place.

Stated more formally, a circular explanation
involves the conjunction of the following two conditions:

1. The evidence for conceptual entity X is the
behavior of engaging in Y.

2. The explanation of behavior Y is the conceptual entity X.

The evidence for the conceptual entity X and
the phenomenon the conceptual entity X is supposed
to explain are the same event: the occurrence of behavior Y. The existence of conceptual entity X is
not postulated independently of the evidential behavior Y it is supposed to explain.

Circular explanations are after-the-fact explanations (Cummins, 1983). The existence of the
explanatory conceptual entity X is not postulated

until instances of behavior Y are observed to occur.
This characteristic of a circular explanation is illustrated best in a demonology context. A demonologist explains behavior, especially socially undesirable behavior, by an appeal to the notion of an evil
spirit. For instance: John Jones murders his wife.
Why? Because he is possessed by an evil spirit.
But the only reason the demonologist knows John
Jones is possessed by an evil spirit is the fact
that he killed his wife.

     Other examples of circular explanation, in ad-
dition to instinct and demonic possession, include
(1) the classic nineteenth century phrenological
traits, such as adhesiveness, submissiveness, and
amatoriness (see Temkin, 1947); (2) Freudian psychoanalytic concepts, such as id, ego, superego, and
libido (see Chapter 5); and (3) the concept of human
nature--explaining a person's behavior by saying
that it is characteristically human: it is human to
kill, cheat, lie, or be hostile (see the Bible).
(Note that it is also human to love, be honest, or
be friendly.)

     With circular explanations such as instinct and
phrenological trait you run the risk of postulating
an infinite number of conceptual entities, one for
each new class of behavior that is observed. The
classic instinct doctrine, as promulgated by William
McDougall (1923), fell into disrepute because he
never could resolve the total number of instincts or
how they were interrelated. A nineteenth century
phrenologist, such as Gall or Spurzheim (Gall and
Spurzheim, 1810-1819), fared somewhat better. The
human skull can only accommodate a limited number of

bumps!

Introductory psychology students find it very difficult to reject the acceptability of circular explanation. It is too soon for them to understand why a notion such as instinct or phrenological trait can never serve as an input variable in a descriptive level functional relationship. An input variable must be a physical event in the naturally occurring universe, possessing real-space and real-time properties. Such an event usually exists in degrees and can be manipulated. It also must exist or be observable independently of the output variable to which it is relatable. The factors of which a given behavioral output is a function must precede or be simultaneous with it in time. The input and output variables of a functional relationship constitute two separate events and observational entities. This permits the prediction and control of the behavioral output through knowledge of and manipulation of the input factors. Circular explanatory entities typically do not possess real-space and real-time properties, do not exist in degrees, are not manipulable, are not observable independently of the phenomenon to be explained, and do not permit prediction and control of behavor.

The existence of the possibility of circular explanation does have an effect on the day-to-day research activities of experimental psychologists. They must make sure that the situation in which a particular descriptive explanation of a piece of behavior is used is different from the specific situation in which the evidence for that explanation of the behavior was originally obtained. Recall the

circularity discussion in Chapter 5 relative to the
distinction between (1) the specific situation in
which the possible reinforcing properties of a stimulus are assessed and (2) the situations in which its
assessed reinforcing properties can be used as an explanation.

TELEOLOGICAL EXPLANATION   A teleological explanation arises when ongoing behavior is resolved in
terms of some future event.   The behavior is putatively being performed to achieve some end result;
the immanent purpose of the behavior is the attainment of some goal (Hillner, 1978).   Although teleological explanation presumes a relationship between
a behavioral term and a causal input term, it violates the fundamental dictum of a causal law: the
causes of a piece of behavior must precede or be simultaneous with the behavior in time.   Resolving a
piece of behavior in terms of an appeal to a future
happening prevents the prediction and control of that
behavior.   Teleological explanation in a behavioral
context seems so plausible that it is best to start
with examples of teleology from physics, biology,
and theology before proceeding to a couple of examples of teleology in psychology.

PHYSICS   One of the fundamental characteristics of water is that it runs downhill, rather
than uphill.   A teleologist could explain this by
saying that it is the goal of water to return to the
sea.   Water runs downhill in order to get to the sea,
as its immanent purpose.   While such a statement
seems poetic, no one would take it seriously.   The
commonly accepted descriptive explanation of the behavior of water is simply that it obeys the laws of

gravity.

       BIOLOGY   Practically every kind of organism
has some distinguishing, or extreme, anatomical feature: special or unusual coloring, some very well
developed sensory system, some unusual prehensile,
or the like. For instance, the distinguishing feature of a giraffe is its long neck; the distinguishing feature of an elephant is its long trunk. A teleological explanation for the giraffe's long neck
and the elephant's long trunk is that these anatomical features allow the giraffe and elephant to reach
the young, tender leaves at the top of trees. Teleology says nothing about why the giraffe has a long
neck, instead of a long trunk, or why the elephant
has a long trunk, instead of a long neck. Biological science resolves extreme anatomical features in
an evolutionary context (Darwin, 1859, 1871): variation, natural selection, and survival of the fittest.
Anatomical features evolve, and the only reason a
specific feature appears to be ultradeveloped in a
certain organism is that intermediate links in the
evolutionary chain have disappeared.

       THEOLOGY   One of the fundamental mysteries
of life is why humankind exists on earth. This question often is resolved at a theological level. For
instance, the Western Christian tradition responds
to this query by postulating that we were placed on
earth by God in order to serve Him, do good deeds,
and earn our way into Heaven. Our immanent purpose,
as creatures of God, is earthly service and eternal
reward. This theological explanation of our existence is blatantly teleological. Sometimes this general theological, teleological approach is extended

to cover why the universe itself exists. The universe exists in order for us to develop and serve God.
There is no one monolithic scientific explanation
for either the origin of human life or the origin of
the universe, but these problems are dealt with in an
overall evolutionary framework (Mayr, 1982; Schrödinger, 1945).

PSYCHOLOGY Two examples of teleological
explanation will be presented in the context of psychology. The first relates to the bar press behavior
of a rat in a Skinner box; the second relates to college attendance behavior. The second example is a
logical extension of the first and, in many respects,
is an application of the principles derived in the
first example.

BAR PRESS BEHAVIOR Let us assume
that a rat is banging away at a depressible bar in a
Skinner box and is receiving a pellet of food subsequent to each bar press response. This is the prototypical operant conditioning situation, as described
in Chapter 5. It is obvious to the average person
or the college freshman why the rat is pressing the
bar. The rat is pressing the bar in order to get
food; the purpose of the bar press response is to obtain food. This explanation is teleological because
the current bar press response is resolved in terms
of the delivery of the next food pellet.

We already know how a Skinnerian operant psychologist prefers to interpret the rat's bar press
responding. It is a function of the reinforcement
history of the rat; namely, its exposure to past
food pellet deliveries (Skinner, 1938). Resolution
of the rat's bar press response in terms of rein-

forcement history is an acceptable descriptive explanation for the Skinnerian.

Why should the Skinnerian descriptive explanation of bar pressing behavior be preferred over the everyday teleological explanation of bar pressing behavior? Beyond appeal to the general fact that descriptive explanation allows the bar press response to be predicted and controlled, we can refer to at least six specific arguments in favor of the scientific approach.

1. The teleological explanation cannot explain why the rat presses the bar for the very first time. Since the rat has never pressed the bar before and received food for its efforts, it does not know that the food delivery will follow. The reinforcement history explanation does not sufficiently resolve the first bar press response occurrence either. There is no reinforcement history prior to the occurrence of the first bar press response. But the operant psychologist is aware of this deficiency and can postulate any one of a number of other scientifically acceptable mechanisms for resolving the first bar press response occurrence: for instance, transfer of training response, drive stimulus elicited response, or exploratory activity (Kimble, 1961).

2. The teleological explanation does not take cognizance of the fact that the rat will press the bar independently of food delivery. There are times when the rat presses the bar ostensibly to obtain nothing; that is, nothing under the control of the experimenter. The rat's food independent rate of bar pressing is called the operant rate by the operant psychologist (Skinner, 1938). It is the rate at

which the rat presses the bar before food delivery
is ever instituted. The experimenter takes advan-
tage of the operant rate and eventually begins to
reinforce bar press responding. Operant conditioning merely increases the rat's rate of responding
above the initial operant rate. If a particular
rat's operant rate is zero, food delivery cannot be
instituted unless the experimenter uses specific
means by which to shape the occurrence of the very
first bar press response.

   3. The teleological explanation assigns special
goal properties to the food. The food is a nutri-
tive substance, having caloric value, necessary for
the rat's survival. At a teleological level, the
rat is pressing the bar in order to procure a valuable goal object. What the teleological explanation
does not take cognizance of is the fact that practically any detectable stimulus change, many of which
are not valuable, can come to control the rat's bar
press responding. For instance, the onset of a dim
light and the presentation of a substance with no
caloric value, such as saccharine, serve as reinforcing stimuli (Kimble, 1961).

   4. The teleological explanation, just as it
cannot explain the beginning of bar press responding, cannot account for the final cessation of bar
press responding. The rat does not respond in order
to get food indefinitely. Eventually the rat slows
down, stops responding, and perhaps goes to sleep in
the corner of the Skinner box. The operant psychologist explains bar press response cessation in terms
of satiation. Eventually the food pellet is no longer reinforcing to the rat because the effects of

the initial food deprivation operation have worn off
(Skinner, 1938).

   5. The teleological explanation cannot account
for the fact that the rat continues to press the bar
after delivery of food is discontinued. The rat's
responding no longer serves the purpose of securing
a future food delivery, but responding continues to
occur anyway. The failure to deliver reinforcement,
after a period of exposure to reinforcement, technically is called the extinction procedure (Skinner,
1938; Kimble, 1961). The typical rat demonstrates
an appreciable degree of resistance to extinction by
continuing to respond in the face of no reinforcement. The operant psychologist explains the resistance to extinction of the rat in terms of the rat's
specific reinforcement history. For instance, the
rat's resistance to extinction actually is greater
following exposure to some partial reinforcement
schedule than following exposure to continuous reinforcement (Ferster and Skinner, 1957).

   6. The teleological explanation has no way of
explaining the many parametric effects that food
delivery has on the rat's rate of responding. Simply stating that the rat is pressing the bar in order to obtain food does not provide for the subtle
effects that variations in the amount, hedonic quality, immediacy, or schedule of food delivery have on
the rat's rate of bar press responding (see Chapter
5). The operant psychologist easily explains these
parametric effects in terms of the rat's specific
reinforcement history. For example, a reinforcement
history of a large pellet delivery per response is
different from a reinforcement history of a small

pellet delivery per response: differential amount of
reinforcement per response can come to control the
rat's exact rate of bar press responding (Kimble,
1961).

COLLEGE ATTENDANCE BEHAVIOR If you
ask college students why they are attending college,
the invariable answer is "in order to obtain a degree." It is implicit in the students' response
that the earning of the degree leads to later financial gain or economic security, social or professional recognition, some self-satisfaction, and the
life style of an educated person. This explanation
of college attendance behavior is teleological. It
is impossible to argue back to the students that
they are not attending college to obtain a degree.

The appropriate approach is to conceptualize
current, ongoing college attendance behavior as an
operant response, or a combination of operant responses, under discriminative stimulus and reinforcement control (see Chapter 5). Although every student
ostensibly is attending college in order to attain a
degree, students vary widely with respect to the nature of their college behavior. Some study hard and
achieve good grades; some engage in many athletic,
recreational, or social activities. The point is
that the day-to-day behavior of a college student,
as with the case of the behavior of the rat in the
Skinner box, cannot be sufficiently explained by an
appeal to some common monolithic goal. Rather it is
a function of the individual student's stimulus environment and reinforcement situation. Many students
leave college before graduating, not because the ultimate goal of a degree has changed, but rather be-

cause the college environment no longer serves as the source of discriminative stimuli and reinforcements sufficient to maintain ongoing college attendance behavior.

ETHICAL EXPLANATION   An ethical explanation arises when behavior is said to be in accord with a specific moral precept or law.   Behavior is assumed to be determined by a certain ethically relevant rule (Robert Brown, 1970).   Ethical explanation admits of the validity of the notion of rule governed behavior in general, just as cognitive psychology does (Berlyne, 1965; Skinner, 1977).   For instance, verbal behavior follows grammatical, phonetic, and morphemic rules (Chomsky, 1968).   Advocates of ethical explanation treat it as a sufficient form of explanation and even meld it with descriptive explanation.   The rule serves as an input variable in a functional relationship.

The notion of rule governed behavior is subject to two very severe criticisms: (1) Moral and legal rules are not coextensive and often conflict, and (2) a specific rule is not followed just as often as it is obeyed.   The first criticism suggests that ethical precepts in general cannot provide a consistent guide for overt action or cannot serve as the source of consistent, stable stimulus situations. The second criticism implies that an ethical precept is not a sufficient explanation for overt behavior. Statement of the rule alone is not sufficient for predicting whether the organism is going to follow or break it.   Each of these criticisms should be analyzed in more detail.

CRITICISM ONE   There are certain behaviors

that are prohibited at both a legal and moral level:
murder, stealing, bigamy. But to demonstrate the
lack of an absolute consistency between moral and
legal rules, consider the following examples:

1. Stopping the car at a stop sign or red light
is a legal rule, not a moral precept. It is illegal
not to stop, but not immoral not to stop.

2. Adhering to the so-called Golden Rule (do unto others as you would have them do unto you) is a
moral precept, not a legal rule. It might be immoral to break the Golden Rule, but not illegal to do
so.

Examples of conflict between legal rules and
moral dicta are endless:

1. Refusing to sign up for the draft or refusing to be inducted for reasons of conscience.

2. Civil disobedience or passive resistance to
demonstrate some valid moral point.

3. Refusing to inform on a friend as a witness
in a court of law for reasons of personal conscience
and loyalty.

4. Participating in or abetting a so-called
mercy killing.

CRITICISM TWO It can be argued that the
critical missing element in an ethical explanation
is the possible consequences incurred by either following or breaking the rule. Specifying the rule
plus consequences would make this type of explanation more like a Skinnerian contingency (see Chapter
5). Taking the consequences into consideration
could account for many of the behavioral violations
of the rule. Whenever the consequences of following
or breaking the rule are the same and positive, more

than likely the rule will be broken. Whenever the consequences of following the rule are positive and the consequences of breaking the rule are negative, more than likely the rule will be followed. Consider the rule of stopping at a stop sign or red light. Either stopping or not stopping in response to a stop sign located at an isolated country intersection at three o'clock in the morning has the same consequence: no accident and an uninterrupted trip. Either stopping or not stopping in response to a red light at a high density city intersection at five o'clock in the afternoon can have vastly different consequences: no accident versus almost certain accident. The notion of rule plus consequences also applies to individuals who habitually break the rules: the psychopath or sociopath. These are people for whom no consequences are meaningful or negative (White and Watt, 1973).

REASONABLE EXPLANATION A reasonable explanation of behavior is one that is stated in input-output functional relationship form, but never is actually subjected to empirical test. It usually is a hypothesis that is derived from naturalistic observation or a review of the technical literature. The lack of empirical validation of the postulated input-output relationship prevents it from achieving the status of a causal law. The sole criterion of the truth value of the postulated relationship is its reasonableness. Does it make sense, or is it logically consistent with other bona fide causal laws? Reasonableness is a notoriously deficient criterion for evaluating the sufficiency of an explanation, even if it is in functional relationship form. The

criterion is personalistic, idiosyncratic, and subjective (Kendler, 1981).

Reasonable explanation is prevalent in an applied context, such as clinical psychology, where a
therapist makes hypotheses about the source of a client's psychological problems that are not subject to
independent, empirical assessment. Applied psychologists in general (industrial, educational, community psychologists) operate in a framework where they
are required to make reasonable explanations, or
even predictions, of behavior. In a sense, the applied psychologist is in an advocate position, much
as a lawyer is. Given knowledge of a certain body
of theoretical propositions, programmatic assumptions, and operating principles and given knowledge
of a set of facts about a specific problem situation,
the applied psychologist must devise a reasonable
explanation, a reasonable prediction, or a reasonable course of action.

CHAPTER 9

BEHAVIOR VERSUS EXPERIENCE

The content of this chapter derives from a consideration of two conceptual points made earlier in the
analysis:

1. It is reasonable to treat behavior and conscious experience as a psychologist's basic objects
of direct observation. These are the aspects of human experience that traditionally have been interpreted as being inherently psychological in nature.
They constitute the fundamental metaphysical categories of psychology, and psychological reality must
be constructed in terms of either or both of them
(cf. Chapter 3).

2. It is impossible to give a technical specification to psychological phenomena that would be
acceptable to every professional psychologist. The
unique or indigenously characteristic property of a
psychological event is a philosophical question, not
admissable to final resolution (cf. Chapter 2).

These two propositions might seem to contradict
each other. But such is not the case, for two basic
reasons:

1. No universally accepted conception of either
behavior or conscious experience exists. There is
no standard approach as to why or in what sense

these two kinds of events are psychological in nature.

2. The objects of direct observation merely are
of ancillary concern to many psychologists who make
inferences from them to various loci of determination that constitute the real foci of interest.

Cartesian philosophy set up the basic dichotomy
between conscious experience and behavior. By postulating two separate, but interacting, entities--
mind and body--Descartes (1650, 1662) created two
potential objects of psychological interest. His rational approach to mind led to British empiricism
and its implicit cognitive psychology that eventually
became physicalized in the structuralist approach to
conscious experience. His basically materialistic
account of the body separated animate motion from inanimate motion. Inanimate motion became a matter of
physics; animate motion became a problem of physiology and ultimately psychology via functionalism and
Watsonian behaviorism.

There is nothing inherently psychological about
either conscious experience or behavior. Wundt
(1873-1874) studied conscious experience because he
combined expertise in both epistemological philosophy and experimental sensory physiology. Watson
(1913) focused on behavior for methodological reasons, after functionalism related mental activity to
organismic adaptation. As argued in Chapter 4, a
one-step jump from structuralism with its focus on
conscious experience to descriptive behaviorism with
its focus on behavior would have been impossible: it
certainly did not happen in Europe where no analogue
to functionalism existed. European psychology re-

tained its initial focus on conscious experience via
the Gestalt approach.

Although the basic objects of direct observation constituted a crucial metaphysical battleground
during the classical school era, contemporary psychologists realize that the distinction between conscious experience and behavior is strictly semantic
(see Chapter 2). Neither category of description is
conceptually or methodologically distinct from the
other. The skin cannot even be used as an arbitrary
dividing line separating conscious experience from
behavior: virtually every internal physiological activity is currently conceptualized as behavior. Conscious experience can only be externalized through
behavior (self-report or third person inferences),
and behavior only can be given meaning by reference
to some external framework that usually includes
knowledge of an organism's mental states (intentions,
desires, and the like).

Whether contemporary psychologists refer to
their focus of interest as conscious experience or
behavior primarily is a function of goals. Epistemological psychology and understanding psychology primarily focus on conscious experience. An action system is constructed in terms of behavior. Dialectical psychology treats both conscious experience and
behavior. Only depth psychology focuses on a metaphysical category not resolvable in terms of conscious experience or behavior: the unconscious.

Contemporary psychology perpetuates the pluralism of classical psychology because both conscious
experience and behavior can occupy either slot of
the content of observation. Even more critically,

whenever conscious experience or behavior occupies
the object of direct observation slot, it is never
measured or quantified independently of its presumed
locus of causation. What is meant by conscious experience or behavior in a given case is, in part, determined by its associated locus of causation.

   We are going to assess the metaphysical properties of both conscious experience and behavior by
comparing them on some relevant dimensions: (1) access, (2) objectivity versus subjectivity, (3) composition, (4) use or value, (5) modeling techniques,
and (6) relationship to substrata (physiology) and
superstrata (social processes).

ACCESS

   CONSCIOUS EXPERIENCE Two modes of access to
the content of conscious experience exist: (1) first
person and (2) third person.

   In first person access, the organism, as observer, merely divulges the content of consciousness
via verbal or written report. Methods of self-report vary from constrained structuralist introspection and the freewheeling phenomenology of Gestalt
psychology, both of which are designed to tap sensory
or perceptual consciousness, to Freudian free association techniques and Rogerian client centered therapy that externalize the content of emotional consciousness.

   First person access often is criticized on two
bases (for instance, Comte, 1830-1842; Maudsley,
1867; Watson, 1913): (1) Many philosophers and psychologists argue that the mind cannot observe itself;
and (2) the act of self-report can interfere with,
if not destroy, the content of consciousness. The

act of externalizing the content of current emotional consciousness is particularly susceptible to the
second criticism.   Reporting on past emotional consciousness, as in therapy, is immune from the second
criticism, but is subject to errors of memory and
distortion.

Third person access is required for nonverbals
and preverbals: for instance, animals, retardates,
chronic schizophrenics, children, and the like.
(Freud (1939, 1949) never psychoanalyzed children,
not because they could not talk, but because they
did not have sufficient past experience.)   In third
person access, the experimenter, as observer, attempts to infer the content of an organism's consciousness from its overt behavior.   People engage
in third person access in the context of their everyday life, as when they attempt to infer a friend's
or relative's mood, disposition, or mental state in
general via observation of overt behavior.   Structuralists engaged in introspection by analogy with
subjects that could not engage in self-report.   Functionalists introspected about animal consciousness.

The basic weakness of third person access derives from the fact that it is strictly constructional in nature (Mackenzie, 1977).   Third person inferences require some surrogate psychological theory
that is usually implicit, idiosyncratic, and analog-
ically based.   (Notice how a person will introspect
about the mental states of a pet dog or cat, but
will not do so about a fly or cockroach that happens
to be in the room.   The validity of introspective
analogies decreases the farther down one goes on the
phylogenetic ladder.)   The historical standards as-

sociated with this type of access have changed, such
that virtually no contemporary psychologist attempts
third person judgments of conscious experience or
constructs a model of psychological reality from
them.

BEHAVIOR   An organism's <u>overt</u> behavior is only
susceptible to third person access under standard observational conditions. First person access to behavior is limited, unless a mirror is used or the behavior is filmed or videotaped.   There are contexts
in psychology where an organism is allowed to see
its current behavior, usually not for quantification
purposes, but rather because it serves as a kind of
feedback (see Shapiro et al., 1973).

Third person access to overt behavior can be
direct or indirect. In direct access, the experimenter observes the behavior in the raw as it is being
produced. Quite often, automated recording equipment serves as a surrogate experimenter to prevent
errors of perception or judgment on the part of a
human observer. In indirect access, some residual
of the prior behavior of an organism is observed:
for instance, some kind of art work, intellectual
construction, manufactured object, and the like.
This kind of access is more prevalent in anthropology and nonlaboratory psychological contexts, such
as a therapeutic relationship or a psychoanalytic
session. Group mental or psychological testing typically only affords indirect access. Individual,
one-on-one testing allows both direct and indirect
access, with the residual test performance serving
as the major component.

The digital aspects of responding (all-or-none

occurrence) usually can be observed by the naked
eye, but analogical attributes of a behavioral event
usually are only measurable with the use of sophisticated recording equipment: for instance, the latency
of a salivary response, the intensity of a bar press,
or the loudness of a nonsense syllable. When behavior is conceived as occurring within the skin (for
instance, brain waves, heart rate, stomach secretion,
individual neuron or receptor firing) such activity
only permits indirect access in the sense that only
some residual physiological recording of the event
can be observed and measured.

     An organism's verbal behavior is perfectly sus-
ceptible to third person access, under the assumption that it is simply a surrogate motor response.
For instance, an individual saying "yes" is equivalent to hand raising or button pushing. It is possible for the semantic meaning and symbolic content
of verbal responding to be analyzed, but not for purposes of inferring about the nature of consciousness.
A behaviorist does not treat verbal behavior as an
external indicant of inner consciousness. Verbal
responses elicited by Rorschach (1942) ink blot
cards in a projection situation typically do not constitute part of a behaviorist's content of observation.

OBJECTIVITY VERSUS SUBJECTIVITY

     Third person access to overt behavior ostensib-
ly is possible because it is an external, public,
objective event; access to conscious experience is
limited to the first person presumably because it is
an internal, private, subjective event. Behavior is
external and public, but it is not objective in any

absolute or simplistic sense; likewise, conscious experience is internal and private, but it is not subjective in any absolute or simplistic sense. Behavior
is much less objective than its public image belies;
conscious experience is much less subjective than its
public image belies. In many respects, behavior is
just as subjective as conscious experience; and conscious experience is just as objective as behavior.

BEHAVIOR Since behavior is a metaphysical concept, what qualifies as an instance of behavior is
contingent on the conceptual sunglasses that a psychologist wears. A reflexive response is behavior
for Watson or Skinner; it is not such for a Gestalt
or humanistic psychologist. Blind, trial and error
activity in a Thorndike puzzle box or a Skinner box
is behavior for an S-R associational learning theorist, such as Hull; it is not for a Gestalt psychologist or an S-S expectancy learning theorist, such as
Tolman. Button pushing is significant behavior for
Skinner; it is meaningless activity for a humanist.
Seeing is behavior for a Skinnerian; seeing is a perceptual process for a cognitive psychologist; seeing
is experiencing for a humanist.

What constitutes behavior in a specific model
of psychological reality depends on the assumptions
of the model, especially those pertaining to the locus of causation and permissible methodology. Each
system sets its own criteria for identifying and interpreting certain natural events as behavior. At a
more basic level, a system determines the kind of relationships or laws in which behavior is supposed to
participate. For Watson, behavior is a concatenation
of reflexive responses, amenable to classical condi-

tioning. For Skinner, behavior is an operant under
stimulus or reinforcement control. For a Gestalt
psychologist, behavior is molar activity, representing the structure and dynamics of the organism's
psychological environment. For Riegel, behavior is
a dialectically determined event.

Given this variety of metaphysical conceptions
of behavior, it should not be surprising that the operational specification of behavior in any research
context is a complex matter. Consider operant psychology (Skinner, 1938). A legitimate operant response must be

1. easily performable by the organism,
2. part of its natural behavioral repertoire,
3. easily isolatable and discretely countable,
4. autonomous or self-reifying,
5. subject to reinforcement and stimulus control, and
6. physicalized as activation of some environmental manipulandum that is independent of
   the organism's effector system.

Even this listing does not specify how an operant is
technically measured and recorded.

Granted that an instance of behavior is external, public, and identifiable in the context of a
given conceptual approach to psychology, the notion
of behavior itself is subjective. Some systems--
structuralism, depth psychology, conceivably even
humanism--do not even consider behavior to be a component of the psychological universe. Even in the
various action systems, there is no basic continuity
between one psychologist's conception of behavior
and that of another. Different psychologists liter-

ally see different things in the same circumstances
or the same thing in different circumstances. Humanistic psychologists talk about each organism living
in its own private experiential world. A specific
psychologist's conception of behavior is part of a
private world view. One of the functions of graduate
training in psychology is to indoctrinate future psychologists in one or more world view, so that they
can automatically or implicitly "see" behavior.

        The experimental psychologist is forced to cre-
ate the illusion that behavior is objective, in addition to being bona fidely external and public.
Elaborate techniques are employed to guarantee that
observations of behavior result in reliable and valid
measurements: use of sophisticated or precalibrated
recording apparati, elaborate experimental designs,
standardized or uniform instructions, restricted response categories, highly trained or practiced observers, multiple observers when the behavioral phenomenon is particularly esoteric or elusive, and the
like. Although behavior is external and public, the
objectification of behavior is the result of a psychologist's construction and imposition of a certain
psychological reality.

        CONSCIOUS EXPERIENCE Although the notion of
conscious experience is as metaphysical in nature as
that of behavior, it presents a vastly different problem for the psychologist. Because conscious experience is internal and private, admitting of only first
person access, many psychologists are not willing to
assume the existence of other minds--the so-called
other mind problem in philosophy (see Churchland,
1984). What is certain is that the qualia or charac-

teristic nature of an organism's consciousness--the
actual phenomenal experience of some essence, say
red, brightness, pleasure, or pain--is ineffable and
noncommunicable. It might be that my red is your
green or that my feeling of pleasure is your feeling
of pain. But this is irrelevant, except on the
strictest construal of a phenomenology of psychological or mental states. The fact that people can label aspects of their conscious experience consistently or the fact that mental states in general have a
consistent relationship to behavior demonstrates that
some degree of objectivity can be attained in the
study of conscious experience. The psychology of
sensation and perception, the transcendence of various emotional states in a therapeutic setting, or
the human being's self-awareness in general would be
impossible if consciousness were subjective in an
absolute sense.

Psychologists have to create and objectify conscious experience, just as they do behavior. What
is primitive or given in consciousness and what is
derivative in consciousness are unknown. What constitutes the fundamental elements of consciousness
and what constitutes the phenomenal output of these
elements are arbitrary. The qualitative aspect of
conscious experience might be automatic or implicit,
but externalization and interpretation of the content of consciousness are not. The content of consciousness is only expressible in words--the language function of Chapter 1. It is uninterpretable
independently of a model of consciousness. Structuralists, Gestaltists, Freudian depth psychologists,
humanistic, existential psychologists, even Skinner-

ian descriptive behaviorists have different conceptions of the concept of consciousness and impose differing strictures and categories of verbal self-report.

In the context of a given technique of externalization and a given model of conscious experience,
first person reports of conscious content must be
taken at face value. What the observer expresses
must be accepted as true for that observer. Since
no external reliability or validity check is possible, the content of one person's phenomenalizing
cannot be generalized to other organisms. First
person reports of consciousness only allow construction of the psychological world of the observer;
they cannot be used to construct a universal psychological reality applying to all organisms. The notion of interpersonal or interorganism objectivity
simply does not apply when conscious experience is
the psychologist's focus of interest. But in the
limited confines of individualistic consciousness,
the experimental datum is just as objective (or subjective) as that associated with the overt behavior
of a group of organisms.

COMPOSITION

BEHAVIOR Composition in the context of behavior can be interpreted to mean existential reality
level. What is the substantive content of behavior
as a psychological entity? Assuming behavior occurs
outside the skin, an instance of behavior consists
of two things: (1) activation of some effector system and (2) physical movement of some limb or the
body through space. The first component gives behavior a physiological reality: behavior is physio-

logical activity of some sort. The second component
gives behavior a physical reality: behavior can be
measured in terms of concepts indigenous to physics.

Note that my compositional specification of behavior does not define behavior or identify instances of behavioral occurrence: it merely delineates
its compositional content. Behavior possesses more
than a physiological and physical reality: it also
has a psychological reality, but the substance of
its psychological reality is model-contingent. Definition and identification of behavior require reference to its characteristic psychological reality,
and these cannot be done independently of a specific
model of the psychological universe. Once the psychological features of behavior are specified by a
model, the absence of effector activation and overt
movement can constitute a meaningful piece of behavior in some contexts.

Much has been made historically of the distinction between involuntary and voluntary behavior (for
instance, see Flanagan, 1984). Although the notions
of involuntary and voluntary are impossible to operationally define (Rescorla and Solomon, 1967), we
are going to assume that the Skinnerian respondent-
operant dichotomy (see Chapter 5) approximates the
involuntary-voluntary behavior distinction.

A respondent is behavior that is given no psychological representation above and beyond its physiological and physical composition. It is pure physiological activity resulting in some kind of physical movement in space. A respondent is elicited by
a specific stimulus and in psychological jargon usually is referred to as a reflexive response. A res-

pondent can be defined and identified strictly in
terms of its stimulus elicitor and compositional effector activation. Respondents served as the model
for all behavior in Cartesian philosophy because at
the time the notion of movement was equivalent to
that of behavior (Henle, Jaynes, and Sullivan,
1966). Watson (1916) also reduced behavior exclusively to individual respondents or a concatenation
of respondents, at least at the conceptual level.

An operant is behavior that is given functional
specification in terms of its causal role (see Chapter 7). The classic example of an operant is the
bar press response of a rat in a Skinner box. An operant possesses physiological and physical composition, but they are irrelevant for its definition and
identification. The psychological reality of an operant derives from its role in an environmental contingency. In Skinner's (1938) system, it is the reinforcement contingency that provides the necessary
functional context. An operant is a response that
activates the response manipulandum and duly gets
reinforced. Using non-Skinnerian terminology, an operant is an act that manipulates the environment and
has consequences for its performer.

In nonbehavioristic systems that focus on behavior, such as Gestalt psychology and humanism, the
psychological composition of a meaningful piece of
behavior is highly abstract and much more elusive.
True behavior in Gestalt psychology is embedded in a
behavioral environment; meaningful behavior in a humanistic context must represent the fact that its
performer is self-aware.

CONSCIOUS EXPERIENCE Although conscious exper-

ience, interpreted as specific mental or psychological states, can be assumed to possess physiological/
physical reality, its composition cannot be reduced
to specific physiological/physical states (see Chapter 7): the compositional problem. The psychological reality of conscious experience is given or axiomatic, in the sense that no other academic discipline attempts to empirically study the content of
consciousness. This was why Wundt (1873-1874) constructed psychological reality in terms of conscious
experience in the first place.

     Although the psychology of conscious experience
is both heterogeneous and fragmented, a basic theme
does run through psychology's perennial attempts to
deal with consciousness; namely, the assumption that
consciousness has two components (see Mueller-Freienfels, 1935). One component is the fact that consciousness possesses content that can be experienced
and verbalized. The other component refers to the
fact that an organism is aware of this content or
realizes that certain processes are occurring that
allow the content to be experienced. The second component often is expressed by the notion that human
beings are aware of their consciousness. (The existence of consciousness in the content sense in an
animal is a matter of the now discredited third person access mode; the existence of consciousness in
the self-aware sense in an animal is strictly a metaphysical issue, with no empirical concomitants.)

     The structuralist and Gestalt approaches merely
focused on the first component of consciousness,
particularly the content of sensory and perceptual
consciousness. These approaches assumed that an ob-

server could objectively focus on its static mental
states. Contemporary humanistic and phenomenological psychology stresses the second component of consciousness, particularly as it relates to the content of emotional consciousness. This kind of psychology focuses on an organism's quality and degree
of self-awareness and feelings. It should be noted
that epistemological psychological approaches exist
that treat the two components as indissoluble aspects
of a whole: for instance, Brentano's (1874) act psychology that fuses experiential content and the process of knowing into the notion of a mental act.

Recall from Chapter 5 that Skinner (1957, 1974)
accounts for introspecting about the content of consciousness in terms of tacting responses under the
control of reinforcement contingencies subsumed by
the surrounding verbal community. All Skinner has
to do to account for self-awareness is assume that
tacting responses about tacting responses exist.

The first component of consciousness subsumes
the problem of qualia, as introduced in Chapter 7.
Qualia are an irresolvable philosophical (metaphysical) and psychological (empirical) problem (for instance, see Fodor, 1981). All philosophical and psychological attempts to analyze consciousness bypass
the qualia problem. Every analysis or reduction of
conscious contents involve verbal, or semantic,
transformations; but qualia themselves cannot be
represented by words. They can be abstracted, classified, and the like. But their inner essence cannot be described by the language function. From another perspective, qualia cannot be modeled in terms
of external, physical analogies or systems.

Attempting to explain qualia is analogous to accounting for why you are _you_. Why are you _you_? Why were you born of certain parents, in a certain locale, at a certain point in time? Such questions are unanswerable, even in a theological context.

The compositional status of conscious experience is a degenerate issue. No amount of functional specification of qualia in terms of causal role can alter the fundamental ineffability of qualia. The same is true for the experience of self-awareness. You either know what it is to be self-aware or you do not know.

USE OR VALUE

What are the respective uses or value of conscious experience and behavior as possible foci of psychology? The classical schools, specifically structuralism and Gestalt psychology, were interested in sensory and perceptual conscious experience solely as an intellectual endeavor. Contemporary interest in consciousness, as exemplified by humanistic psychology, revolves around the attempt to better understand the individual organism and its coming to terms with the environment. The classical schools, specifically functionalism and Watsonian behaviorism, focused on behavior because it is subsumed by the notion of organismic adaptation to the environment, with Watson's interest being supplemented by his methodological prescriptions. Contemporary psychology can construe virtually any event as being an instance of behavior, and the notion has achieved an aura of metaphysical neutrality and indifference; however, current psychology's basic interest in behavior is related to the fact that every

major contemporary system, exclusive of Skinnerian
radical behaviorism, allows and focuses on internal
determinants of behavior: mental processes for cognitive behaviorism and Piagetian structural psychology, unconscious forces for Freudian depth psychology, goals and striving for humanism, and dialectical processes for Riegelian psychology. Virtually
every contemporary psychologist focuses on behavior,
but not because it is the only acceptable one, as
dictated by classical and contemporary versions of
descriptive behaviorism.

BEHAVIOR   The material composition of behavior
allows psychology to be conducted as a scientific
endeavor. Instances of behavior can be related to
and studied as a function of discrete environmental
events. Experimental psychology seeks the uniform-
ities in behavioral expression subsumed by nomothetic
laws. It is the most efficient and practical approach to psychological intervention when a group of
organisms is involved in a common environmental situation.

Sometimes action psychology, especially its behavioristic versions, is criticized for being interested in behavior as an end in itself (for instance,
Maslow, 1971). But the criticism is misdirected because action psychology merely is implementing the
consequences of treating a living organism as a real-
space and real-time entity. The fact that behavior
is predictable and controllable should not detract
from the status of the human being when it is used
for benign goals and the betterment of the human condition.

CONSCIOUS EXPERIENCE   The privacy and inacces-

sibility of conscious experience, especially when
viewed from the level of qualia, highlight the fact
that each person is unique and exists in a private
psychological world. Certainly each one of us has
and lives in a psychological environment that cannot
be penetrated by another living organism. Humanistic
psychology continually reminds us that this fact
should not be forgotten. To a lesser degree, Freudian depth psychology does the same, although it does
presume the existence of a universal psychodynamics
or psychic determinism that must be taken into consideration.

     Sensory and perceptual consciousness no longer
is regarded as exhausting psychological reality, but
has devolved to merely one aspect of the psychological universe, as emphasized by cognitive behaviorism.
It is now realized that our mentation constructs
many different conscious realities: memorial, emotional, epistemological, even motor. The human being
is the only creature on the earth that we can be
reasonably sure possesses self-awareness. This is
the ultimate source of our ethical, moral, and perhaps even religious consciousness, all of which contribute to the necessity of investigating and understanding our psychological nature. Our intelligence
far exceeds that of any other living organism, and
it must be tempered by the reflection and rationality that self-consciousness allows.

MODELING TECHNIQUES

     People, in general, and other academic discip-
lines, in particular, look to psychology for guidance because of its task of comprehending our psychological nature. Ironically, the psychologist has

to look to other academic disciplines and intellectual pursuits for guidance in this task. The nature
of psychological reality is arbitrary. Psychology
must liberally borrow concepts and stratagems from
other fields of endeavor, and this practice is encouraged by the fact that psychology was one of the
last physical or social sciences to evolve (Hillner,
1984). First-rate contemporary psychologists, those
who have made significant scholarly contributions
to the discipline, invariably are experts in subject
matter other than psychology and have achieved their
fame by applying nonpsychological concepts and mechanisms to psychological material. The psychologist
must model both behavior and conscious experience,
and most of these models come from outside the confines of psychology itself.

BEHAVIOR Since behavior is an externally resolvable event and possesses material composition, it is
relatively easy to model. Strictly speaking, a model
of behavior only need provide an analytical framework for describing and classifying instances of behavioral occurrences. In actuality, a model of behavior typically is put forth as a component of a
larger, more comprehensive framework that also takes
the presumed locus of causation into account. Chapters 4 and 5 described how the major classical
schools and contemporary systems of psychology model
behavior in the context of the basic reference activity of "doing something."

CONSCIOUS EXPERIENCE Since the content of conscious experience is not an externally resolvable
event and possesses no monolithic material composition, it is very difficult to model. No contemporar

psychologist attempts to model the content of conscious experience in the structuralist sense or to
realistically account for qualia. Today the focus
is on consciousness as a locus of causation, i.e.,
mental activity in the philosophical functionalist
sense, and the computer and computer based analogies
serve as the source of various information processing
models (see Chapters 5 and 7). The life-like mentation of computers, robots, and other preprogrammed
devices serves as such an excellent source of models
for human mentation that philosophers currently de-
bate whether they possess consciousness, are self-
aware, can "think," and the like (for instance, see
Turner, 1971). (Remember hardware is irrelevant in
the functionalist approach to mind: if a machine and
a human fundamentally possess the same defined states, machine mentation is indistinct from human mentation.)

RELATIONSHIP TO SUBSTRATA AND SUPERSTRATA

     The human being is a biological creature: this
provides the substratum for our existence. Human
beings also are social creatures: this provides the
superstratum for our existence. Note that an organism can be a biological creature without being a
social creature, but an organism cannot be a social
creature without being a biological creature. Somewhat artificially, we can say that the human essentially is a biological creature within the skin and
a social creature outside the skin. How do behavior
and conscious experience interface with these two
aspects of an organism?

     BEHAVIOR   Behavior is always a biological enti-
ty and often a social entity. Its biological nature

is indigenous to its material composition. Any overt
behavioral occurrence involves effector system activation and entails some form of physiological activity. The social basis of behavior is more obscure:
It does not derive from its material composition.
When behavior is treated strictly as a reflexive response, or respondent, it is not social in nature.
The social aspect of behavior arises when behavior
is given some psychological representation beyond its
material composition. Specification of this psychological representation usually cannot be done without reference to an organism's social environment.
The very fact that an instance of behavior occurs in
some social framework that gives it meaning disting-
uishes behavior from the activity exhibited by matter
or material systems in general.

     The dual nature of behavior accounts for the
fact that it is very difficult to distinguish between a physiological psychologist and an experimental physiologist, or a social psychologist and a sociologist, at a conceptual level. In the context of
an action system, any distinction among biology, psychology, and sociology must be made at the level of
locus of causation.

     CONSCIOUS EXPERIENCE Conscious experience can
be either a biological entity, social entity, or
both, contingent on one's metaphysics. The materialist account of mind (see Chapter 7) would have no
trouble treating consciousness as some kind of physiological event; certain forms of functionalism (see
Chapter 7) deny any physiological status to mentation. The fact that mentation/consciousness is affected by all sorts of physiological manipulations

(drugs, lesions, food or water deprivation, and the like) demonstrates that conscious experience is at least indirectly tied in with an organism's substrata (Bunge, 1980).

Consciousness is not a social entity in structuralism or Gestalt psychology. It is implicitly social in the functionalist school, cognitive behaviorism, Piagetian structural psychology, humanism, and depth psychology. The surrogate for consciousness in descriptive behaviorism is explicitly social in nature. Consciousness is an explicit social entity in dialectical psychology, as an offshoot of dialectical materialism (Marx, 1867), and strictly social in origin.

The ambiguous nature of conscious experience makes those psychological systems that focus on the individual organism as the unit of analysis, such as depth psychology and humanism, share overlapping boundaries with philosophy, theology, literature, and other humanities.

CHAPTER 10

APPLIED, PROFESSIONAL PSYCHOLOGY

Psychology exists in two forms: (1) pure, academic,
or experimental and (2) applied or professional.
Experimental psychologists conduct basic research in
such traditional substantive areas as sensation,
perception, learning and conditioning, motivation,
physiological, and comparative, typically without
regard for the possible practical applicability of
their research findings. Applied psychology consists of such substantive subareas as clinical, abnormal, psychoanalytic psychology, behavioral medicine, forensic psychology, counseling, industrial,
community psychology, vocational, child, educational, and military psychology. Such areas as developmental and social are more equivocal, possessing
both pure and applied aspects.

Not every psychologist would agree with this
rather strict dichotomization between pure and applied psychology. Many experimental psychologists
consider the results of basic laboratory research to
be inherently applicable to the behavior occurring
in the natural environment; and certainly many psychologists who classify themselves as applied in orientation conduct high level, meaningful research
possessing theoretical significance. Granted there

is much overlap between pure and applied psychology,
the distinction is relevant for at least four reasons.

1. The historical roots of the two forms of psychology differ (Hillner, 1984). The emergence of experimental psychology as an independent intellectual
discipline customarily is identified with certain
events that occurred in the Germanic university system under the influence of Wilhelm Wundt (1873-1874)
in the late 1870s, the founding of structuralism.
Structuralism, as the first recognized school of ac-
ademic/experimental psychology, eschewed any practical application value of a pure science of consciousness. The emergence of applied psychology, as a
whole, cannot be traced back to a specific historical event. Each type of applied psychology has its
own specific historical roots. If we use clinical
psychology as an illustrative reference point here,
the emergence of clinical psychology is associated
with the nineteenth century French--Charcot (1872-
1887), Janet (1892)--and Freudian (1939, 1949) conceptions of psychopathology and abnormal behavior.

2. The systems subsumed by academic/experimen-
tal psychology traditionally have served as models
for and the conceptual basis of applied psychology.
When the substance of psychology is analyzed at a
philosophical level, usually it is academic psychology that constitutes the basic reference point: for
instance, behaviorism, Gestalt psychology, conditioning as a world view, the organism as an information processor.

3. The educational, professional, and accredi-
tation requirements, as well as legal status and recognition, for an applied psychologist are appreciably

different from those of an academic psychologist (see
Woods, 1979; Lowman, 1980). The research psychologist working in academia need not have completed an
APA approved internship, need not fulfill state licensing or certification requirements, and in general cannot ethically engage in private practice.

   4. It is possible to refer to applied psychology, in general, and clinical psychology, in particular, as professional psychology. The state of development of academic and professional psychology, as
well as their degree of geographic spread, is not on
a par with each other (Sexton and Misiak, 1976).
Clinical psychology and psychometrics, or psychological testing, are nonexistent in the Soviet Union.
Clinical psychology is only germinal in Western
Europe and Japan. It is only fully developed as a
viable profession in such countries as the United
States, Canada, Great Britain, and Australia, and to
a lesser degree in other British Commonwealth nations. Academic psychology is still only germinal
in many regions of the world: South America, Africa,
the Middle East, and the lower Orient. There are
even countries where professional psychology is more
developed than experimental psychology, such as Mex-
ico. In areas where professional psychology is nonexistent or germinal, therapeutic intervention is
still a monopolistic function of the medical and/or
psychiatric establishment.

   Applied psychology in America today enjoys more
governmental, economic, and social support than experimental psychology does. The heyday of indiscrim-
inate governmental financial support for pure social
science research is over; academic psychology barely

is holding its own in the currently depressed state
of education; job openings for psychologists are pre-
dominantly in the applied areas; the APA basically is
oriented to the needs and concerns of the psychological practitioner; the significant ethical and pragmatic issues of our time relate directly to applied,
not experimental, psychology.

One of the basic reasons why the profession of
psychology is still evolving is that the relationship between the discipline and the means of production (see Chapter 1) has not as yet been finalized
(Clark, 1957). This is particularly true for applied psychology. Unlike medicine or law, the psychological establishment is unable to control en-
trance into the profession. It is unable to control
the use of the label of psychologist as a source of
livelihood. Although the APA exists, full membership in which is contingent on possession of the
doctorate, the profession has no real control over
who teaches psychology at any level of the educational spectrum, especially the high school level, or
who practices psychology in an applied setting.
This situation is exacerbated by a number of factors (McNamara and Barclay, 1982):

1. The current attack on state licensing or
certification requirements for the private or applied practice of psychology as constituting an il-
legitimate and unfair closed shop situation.

2. The continual spawning of new psychological
subspecialties, such as community psychology, forensic psychology, geriatric psychology, environmental
design psychology, and space psychology.

3. The continuing failure to resolve the pro-

fessional status of the M.A. or M.S. psychologist.

4. The recent appearance of the Psy.D. degree.

5. The voluminous increase in employment of so-
called behavioral technicians (B.A., B.S., M.A., or
M.S. people with special training in behavior modification techniques) who do the work of a psychologist,
but are not classified and paid as such.

6. The high degree of overlap between clinical
psychology and psychiatry, counseling, social work,
even the ministry. For instance, it is possible for
a person with an M.S.W., a master's degree in social
work, to engage in therapy. When was the last time
an academic psychologist processed the papers of
someone applying for welfare?

By way of contrast, we can point to the profession of physicist, whose relationship to the means
of production has been finalized. A professional
physicist must be theoretical in orientation, either
in a teaching or research context. Applied physics
does not constitute a profession. Engineers, elec-
tricians, mechanics, technicians in general are related to the means of production outside the confines of the physics establishment.

Applied psychology is heterogeneous and diverse.
Each of the distinct subareas of psychological application bears a differential relationship to academic
psychology. Because of this, our characterization
of the state of applied, professional psychology
must be selective and is based on the following two
orienting assumptions.

1. The specific variant of applied psychology
that is least historically and conceptually related
to experimental psychology, and its basic physical

realization as behaviorism, is abnormal and/or therapeutic psychology. Abnormal psychology and psychotherapy constitute the prototypical forms of nonacademic psychology. Concern for and treatment of various forms of abnormality have their historical and
conceptual origins in the medical and/or psychiatric
establishment (Zilboorg, 1967; Coleman, Butcher, and
Carson, 1980).

    2. The value system of an applied psychologist
working in a nonacademic setting is vastly different
from that of an experimental psychologist teaching
at a college or university. The applied psychologist's basic aim is to implement the change imperative (see Chapter 1) in a context that usually only
allows reasonable prediction in an advocate type of
setup (see Chapter 8). The academic psychologist's
basic aim is the generation and dissemination of new
research data and theoretical concepts. The typical
applied psychologist likes to be appreciated and
evaluated as a component of the helping profession,
while an experimental psychologist solely wants to
be judged as some kind of knowledge specialist: re-
searcher, instructor, intellectual synthesizer, or
theoretician.

    This chapter focuses on (1) the concept of ab-
normality and (2) the notion of therapy in order to
illustrate the pluralistic state of contemporary applied psychology. A brief discussion of the topic
of psychological testing is also included because of
its historical and conceptual relationship to both
abnormality and therapy.

ABNORMALITY

    The notion of abnormality is metaphysical in

nature.   The term can be applied to either overt behavior or the presumed internal framework underlying
overt behavior: mental events, thought processes,
physiological functioning, or neural activity.   Academic psychologists typically are not concerned with
abnormality at either level because they usually focus on general psychological laws characteristic of
some average or statistical subject in a framework
that reduces extreme individual variation to random
error.   Conversely, the physician/psychiatrist operates in a context in which the basic object of interest does not arise until normal functioning at either
level breaks down.   We shall focus on abnormal behavior and only refer to abnormal underlying processes
where necessary.

An analysis of abnormality is reducible to three
separate, but interrelated, questions: (1) What is
the existential reality level of abnormal behavior;
(2) what is the primary, or exclusive, source of abnormal behavior; and (3) how are instances of abnormal behavior operationally identified?

REALITY LEVEL   Two broad conceptual approaches
to the reality level of abnormal behavior exist: (1)
a traditional view, characteristic of the medical or
psychiatric establishment (Zilboorg, 1967), and (2)
a more contemporary view, characteristic of American
behavioristic psychology, especially Skinnerian radical behaviorism (Craighead, Kazdin, and Mahoney,
1981).

TRADITIONAL VIEW   Abnormal behaviors really exist, constituting real-space and real-time
events in the naturally occurring universe.   Abnormality is regarded as an absolute property of behav-

ior. A piece of behavior judged to be abnormal is
fundamentally different from a piece of behavior
judged to be normal. By extension, a person exhibiting abnormal behavior is fundamentally different
from a person exhibiting normal behavior; and abnormality can also be regarded as an absolute property
of the individual. It is perfectly meaningful to
categorize a person as insane, deranged, or mentally
ill, as if these were absolute features structurally
possessed by the individual (Page, 1971).

A good analogy for the traditional conception of
abnormality is that of physical disease or biological
defect. Either one of these is an absolute structural property of an organism. For instance, a person
diagnosed as having cancer is fundamentally different
from a person who does not have cancer; or a person
who is deaf is fundamentally different from a person
with no hearing loss.

It is presumed in the traditional approach that
a piece of behavior, or the organism exhibiting the
behavior, can be unambiguously classified as normal
or abnormal. Given a set of behaviors exhibited by
an individual, it is easy to assign the individual
to the normal or abnormal category. The psychiatric
establishment over the last one hundred years has
evolved an elaborate catalogue of specific classes
and subclasses of abnormality, one which is analogous to the voluminous catalogue of physical dis-
eases/biological defects developed by the medical
profession. The latest version of such a catalogue
is the DSM-III (Williams, 1980).

CONTEMPORARY VIEW Abnormality merely is a
descriptive label attached to a piece of behavior or

to the organism exhibiting the behavior by culture
and society (Szasz, 1961, 1970). The notions of normal and abnormal are like the descriptive social labels of (1) Democrat and Republican, (2) Catholic
and Protestant, or (3) liberal and conservative.
These are characteristics that can be used to differ-
entiate people, but they are not regarded as absolute properties of the organism.

Abnormality is a subjective, relative notion.
Abnormality and normality merely constitute opposite
ends of the same continuum, and the boundary line
separating these two categories of behavior is arbitrary. An organism and/or its behavior cannot be unambiguously classified as normal or abnormal. Contemporary behaviorism, as exemplified by the behavior
modification approach (Craighead, Kazdin, and Mahoney,
1981), does not place much value on a systematic typology of abnormality. Behavior modification rejects
any elaborate attempt to assign specific behaviors
and individuals to the traditional psychiatric diagnostic classificatory slots. It deals directly with
the content of the specific behavior in question, independently of any descriptive labeling it could re-
ceive. As a consequence of this, behavior modification can and does focus on certain maladaptive behaviors that are not regarded as abnormal in the traditional, psychiatric sense of the term: test anxiety,
smoking, poor study habits, overeating, and such.

PRIMARY SOURCE There are two classic interpretations of the etiology of abnormal behavior (Zilboorg, 1967): (1) a somatogenic view, characteristic
of nineteenth century German psychiatry, and (2) a
psychogenic view, associated with the nineteenth cen-

tury French psychopathological movement.

SOMATOGENIC VIEW This interpretation relates abnormal behavior exclusively to disturbances
in bodily, physiological, or neuronal activity. The
somatogenic view of abnormality was emphasized by
nineteenth century German psychiatry. Wilhelm Griesinger (1845) believed that the brain and its pathology was the essential factor in all forms of mental
illness. He recognized no distinction between neurology and psychology, and any instance of abnormal
behavior had to be diagnosed as possessing a physiological cause. Emil Kraepelin (1883, 1892) postulated two major classes of psychoses: dementia praecox and manic-depressive. He related dementia praecox to sex gland activity and manic-depressive psychosis to metabolic dysfunction. Eugen Bleuler
(1911) later reconceptualized the monolithic notion
of dementia praecox as the more heterogeneous concept
of schizophrenia. The somatogenic view allowed orthodox clinical medicine to absorb psychiatry and
its focus on extreme forms of abnormality, such as
the psychoses. This interpretation of the source of
abnormality survives today, not monolithically, but
in the context of the organic psychoses--those psychoses with known physiological causes.

PSYCHOGENIC VIEW This interpretation relates abnormal behavior exclusively to psychological
causes. The psychogenic interpretation of abnormality primarily originated with nineteenth century
French psychopathology. The chief figures in this
movement were Charcot (1872-1887), Liébeault (1866),
Bernheim (1891), and Janet (1892). Charcot and Janet
were neurologists; Liébeault and Bernheim were prac-

ticing physicians.   They were concerned with (1) hyp-
nosis, (2) hysteria, and (3) their interrelationship.
Hysteria is a classic form of neurosis, involving
limb paralysis, body anesthesia, blindness, or deaf-
ness, all with no known neurological cause.   The
French psychopathologists demonstrated that hysterical symptoms were both treatable and reproducible
through the use of hypnotic suggestion, either alone
or in combination with other operations.   Janet form-
ulatcd the first formal psychogenic theory for hysteria in particular and neuroses in general, employing the concept of dissociation of consciousness.

     Freudian psychology can be regarded as a logi-
cal extension of the French psychopathological movement (Hillner, 1984).   Freud (1939, 1949) studied under both Charcot (1872-1887) and Bernheim (1891) and
also treated hysterical patients, along with Breuer
(with Freud, 1895), in Vienna.   Freud's interpretation and treatment of hysterical neuroses led to the
founding of psychoanalysis, the most inclusive psychogenic approach to abnormality ever devised (see
Chapter 5).   Freud's resolution of the neuroses, a
less extreme form of abnormal behavior than the psychoses, at a psychogenic level institutionalized the
psychotherapeutic approach to the treatment of abnormal behavior.   Every contemporary form of psychotherapy is an outgrowth of or reaction to psychoanalysis
(White and Watt, 1973).   Freudian and non-Freudian
psychotherapeutic techniques basically differ with
respect to the denotation of the critical psychological factors leading to abnormal behavior.   Psychoanalysis, as a depth psychology, stresses internal, organismic events.   Many contemporary non-Freudian psy-

chotherapeutic techniques, such as behavior modification, emphasize external, environmental events. The
psychogenic view of abnormal behavior survives in the
context of the neuroses, the functional psychoses,
and any form of maladaptive behavior that is assigned
only the descriptive label of abnormal.

OPERATIONAL IDENTIFICATION Regardless of how
the existential and etiological aspects of abnormal
behavior are resolved, we still have the problem of
identifying instances of abnormality when they occur.
While it could be argued that this usually is done
capriciously, there are three general classes of operational definitions for the specification of abnormality (Wright et al., 1970, Chapter 20): (1) the
statistical or frequency approach, (2) the cultural
or relative approach, and (3) the personal adjustment criterion. These three classes of operational
specification are not mutually exclusive. Quite often the same piece of behavior will be classified as
abnormal by all three operational criteria. Each of
these approaches to abnormality identification is in-
adequate in at least one respect, and this fact will
be emphasized in the ensuing discussion. To provide
some continuity in presentation, each of the operational criteria will be illustrated in terms of the
same example; namely, homosexuality as an instance
of abnormality.

STATISTICAL, FREQUENCY APPROACH The notions of normal and abnormal are resolved at a quan-
titative level. The most frequently occurring behaviors in a population of behaviors are classified
as normal, and the least frequently occurring behaviors in a population of behaviors are classified as

abnormal. Modal behavior is normal; rare behavior is
abnormal. What the vast majority of people do is
considered normal; what the small minority of people
do is considered abnormal (Coleman, Butcher, and Carson, 1980). Homosexuality is abnormal because only
a few individuals engage in homosexual behavior relative to the entire population.

This operational approach to abnormality involves no qualitative considerations whatsoever. It
just so happens that the population of people living
outside mental institutions exceeds the population of
people consigned to institutional incarceration. The
total number of people who commit behaviors that lead
to institutional commitment is less than the total
number of people who do not commit behaviors that
lead to institutional commitment. If the situation
were the reverse, the people who commit behaviors
that are regarded as normal according to the current
situation would have to be forcibly separated from
society. For instance, if most people hallucinated,
nonhallucinators would be abnormal and have to be removed from society. The statistical criterion of abnormality really is a variant of Thomas Hobbes'
(1650, 1651) ethical principle that "might makes
right."

There are two problems associated with the statistical, frequency approach to abnormality: (1) More
often than not, the exact distribution of a class of
behavior in the general population is unknown; and
(2) even if the distribution is known, the cutoff
line separating the normal and abnormal categories
is arbitrary. For instance, with respect to the
first problem, we do not really know the exact fre-

quency of occurrence of different variants of heterosexual and homosexual behavior in the general population (Masters and Johnson, 1979). We can illustrate
the second problem by an appeal to a psychological
characteristic whose exact distribution in the general population is known; namely, the intelligence quotient or IQ. An organism's IQ level is not a piece
of behavior, but certainly is an inference based on
overt behavior. IQ is distributed randomly, or nor-
mally, in the general, unselected population with a
mean of 100 and a standard deviation of approximately
15. This is the case because of the way in which IQ
tests are constructed (Kamin, 1974). The partition-
ing of the overall distribution into distinct sub-
normal and supernormal categories of intelligence is
strictly arbitrary. Designations of idiot, imbecile,
moron, gifted, genius, and the like are strictly capricious.

 CULTURAL, RELATIVE APPROACH This approach
to identification is indigenous to sociology, but is
readily extendable to psychology. Sociologists distinguish between so-called deviant behavior and nondeviant behavior, or between deviant individuals and
nondeviant individuals (Scheff, 1966). The notion of
deviant in sociology corresponds to that of abnormal
in psychology; the notion of nondeviant corresponds
to that of normal. Deviancy and nondeviancy are operationally defined by reference to the social norms
that are characteristic of a given culture or sub-
culture. A piece of behavior that is in accord with
the social norm is nondeviant; a piece of behavior
that violates the social norm is deviant.

 Society, in general, does not value deviancy,

probably because one of the purposes of a social norm
is to preserve the integrity and continuity of society. This is unfortunate because deviancy serves as a
primary source of social/cultural change. Heterosex-
uality is nondeviant because it is in accord with the
overall social norm specifying appropriate sexual expression. Homosexuality is deviant because it violates the overall social norm regarding proper sexual
expression. Heterosexual behavior helps maintain the
continued integrity of society because it leads to re-
cruitment, the acquisition of new members for society.
Homosexual activity does not lead to societal recruit-
ment.

The basic problem with the cultural approach to
abnormality derives from its relativity, both with
respect to (1) space and (2) time.

1. At a given point in time, two spatially separated cultures, or two subcultures existing in the
same essential space, can have different social norms.
For instance, in ancient Greece homosexuality was acceptable among members of the upper class, but not
among members of the lower class (Churchill, 1967).
Analogously, there are subcultures in America today
in which homosexuality is the norm: in San Francisco
and New York City. As an example of this kind of relativity not involving sexual behavior, consider a
man with long hair in a flowing white gown claiming
to be revealed to by God. If this happened on a
mountain top in rural North Carolina, the man probably would be revered by the local population; if this
happened on Times Square in New York City, the men
in the little white coats would eventually come and
take him to Bellevue.

2. At a given point in space, two temporally
separated cultures can have different social norms.
For instance, while homosexuality flourished in ancient Greece among the upper class, this is not true
of contemporary Greece (Churchill, 1967). As an example of this kind of relativity not involving sexual
behavior, we can refer to a woman in Salem, Massachu-
setts exhibiting certain bizarre behaviors. In Puri-
tan times, she would be labeled as a witch and perhaps burned at the stake; now she simply would be labeled as odd and perhaps encouraged to undergo some
form of therapy.

      PERSONAL ADJUSTMENT CRITERION Normality
and abnormality are defined in terms of the degree of
personal adjustment exhibited by the individual. An
organism is normal to the extent that its behaviors
do not interfere with its adjustment to life; that
is, do not interfere wih its everyday interaction
with the surrounding physical and social environment
(White and Watt, 1973). At the level of behavior, a
response activity is normal to the extent that it is
adaptive. Normality and abnormality are not all-or-
none, digital states; rather they coexist in certain
degrees.

The personal adjustment criterion suffers the
same deficiency that the cultural approach does: relativity. This is easily illustrated with homosexuality. A nighttime janitor who is an avowed homosexual would not necessarily be classified as abnormal.
His homosexuality does not interfere with his life:
who cares if a nighttime janitor is a homosexual?
On the other hand, the star player of a college bas-
ketball team who is an avowed homosexual is in grave

danger of being labeled abnormal. His homosexuality
does interfere with his life: the alumni and alumnae
will not tolerate a homosexual scoring points.

Other examples of the relativity of the personal
adjustment criterion might be helpful. Assume a person avoids people, refuses to talk on the telephone,
and walks close to the wall down corridors. If the
person is a nighttime janitor, these behaviors do
not interfere with personal adjustment; if the person is a lawyer, doctor, or business executive, these
behaviors do interfere with personal adjustment.
Finally, consider the case of professional rock mu-
sicians: they can engage in all sorts of bizarre behaviors and wear all sorts of offbeat clothes. The
same behavior and clothing exhibited by a member of
the clergy would lead to immediate social disappro-
val and perhaps even expulsion from the pulpit.

OPERATIONAL SPECIFICATION AND THE APPLIED
PSYCHOLOGIST The operational specification of abnormality in the applied medical/clinical context tends
to be subjective (Page, 1971). Anyone who is in the
profession of treating abnormality (doctor, psychiatrist, psychoanalyst, psychotherapist, counselor,
clergyman, or behavior modification specialist) implicitly uses the personal adjustment criterion. A
psychological practitioner usually knows that a given
piece of behavior is maladaptive and, therefore, abnormal through the self-judgment and self-report of
the client/patient according to a personalistic criterion of adjustment. Quite often, the individual
only knows that something is wrong or reports anxiety
or unhappiness.

Many times the original identification of abnor-

mality is implicitly done by an informal link in the
overall helping chain, such as a spouse, minister, or
family doctor. The therapist accepts the client's
predetermined abnormal status at face value. This
testifies to the fact that abnormality is a constellation of related entities. Behavior that tends to
make one unhappy or anxious also tends to interfere,
to be against the social norm, and to be exhibited
by a small percentage of the population.

THERAPY

        Two basic classes of therapy exist (Coleman,
Butcher, and Carson, 1980): (1) somatotherapy and (2)
psychotherapy. Somatotherapy involves direct biological intervention and treatment of the abnormal individual: for instance, electroshock therapy, chemotherapy or drug therapy, narcotherapy, psychosurgery.
This kind of therapy is indigenous to the somatogenic approach to etiology, under the control of the
psychiatric establishment, and especially relevant
for the more severe forms of abnormality, such as
the psychoses (Berger, 1978; Kalinowski and Hippius,
1969; Kalinowski and Hoch, 1952). We are not going
to be concerned with direct biological interventionist therapies in this section.

        Psychotherapy presumes the psychogenic interpre-
tation of the source of abnormality. The therapeutic situation ideally is viewed as a microcosm of
the vast macrocosm of the psychological universe.
Since there are many different models of the psychological universe, there are many forms of psychotherapy: Freudian psychoanalysis; Rogerian phenomenologically based nondirective, client-centered therapy;
Skinnerian behavioral therapy; humanistically orien-

ted T-group or sensitivity training; and the like
(Prochaska, 1979).

It is convenient to distinguish between two
broad classes of approaches to psychotherapy: (1)
the medical or disease model, the primary exemplar
of which is psychoanalysis (Peterfreund, 1982), and
(2) the social learning or behavioral therapy model,
derivative of descriptive behaviorism (Bandura, 1964,
1977). The phrase "medical or disease model" is descriptive behavioristic terminology for the traditional forms of psychotherapy that include Freudian psychoanalysis and its many offshoots, such as client-
centered therapy, Gestalt therapy, role playing or
psychodrama techniques, play therapy, and group therapy. The social learning approach, as a derivative
of academic psychology, represents the application
of behavioristic conditioning principles to the therapeutic situation and is more popularly known as behavior modification.

We shall briefly abstract the basic assumptions
and characteristics of these two conceptual approaches to psychotherapy, highlight the status of
psychotherapy in applied psychology, and put psychotherapy in some final perspective.

MEDICAL MODEL   The traditional disease model of
psychotherapy is characterized by four basic assumptions (Bandura, 1967).

1. The medical model presumes the traditional
real-space, real-time conception of abnormality, as
discussed previously in the chapter. Abnormality is
an absolute property of the organism, and abnormal
behavior is discontinuous with normal behavior. This
model, in general, accepts the validity of the basic

psychiatric classification scheme for the various categories and subcategories of abnormality.

2. A specific constellation of abnormal behaviors exhibited by an organism is considered to be analogous to the symptoms that occur in the context of
an actual physical disease.   The analogy lies at the
heart of the medical model.

3. Abnormal behaviors are assumed to be the result of explicit psychological factors, the specific
denotation of which is contingent on the specific
therapeutic approach involved.   The behavior modification approach likes to emphasize that most traditional therapeutic approaches locate the critical
psychological events internally: they are mentalistic
processes.   Overt behavioral symptoms are indicants
of psychological malfunctioning occurring at some
other level of reality.   For instance, behavior pathology in the context of Freudian psychoanalysis is
resolved in terms of an elaborate internal, mentalistic psychodynamic system (see Chapter 5).

4. Therapy can be viewed as the attempt to elim-
inate or mitigate the symptoms by rectifying the
specific psychological factors responsible for the
symptoms.   Therapy is not directly applied to the
symptoms.   They are only indirectly dealt with by
focusing on the specific etiological factors.   The
content of therapy is contingent on the specific
therapeutic technique used, which in turn depends on
the specific conceptual approach to therapy that is
taken.   Most traditional forms of therapy require
some ultimate insight on the part of the patient/cli-
ent (see Prochaska, 1979).

BEHAVIOR MODIFICATION   The social learning ap-

proach to psychotherapy can be characterized by an
analogous set of four basic assumptions (Bandura,
1967).

1. The social learning approach presumes the
more contemporary relativistic, linguistic interpretation of abnormality, as discussed previously in the
chapter. Abnormality merely amounts to a descriptive
social label, and abnormal behavior is continuous
with normal behavior. Behavior modification specialists deal with any kind of maladaptive behavior, regardless of its status in the traditional psychiatric
classification system.

2. Behavior modification rejects the abnormal
behavior-physical symptom analogy characteristic of
the medical model. Abnormal behavior merely amounts
to maladaptive behavior, and the focus is on the content of the behavior itself. The basic problem is
the overt behavior, not something of which it might
be symptomatic.

3. Maladaptive behaviors are dealt with directly
and are assumed to be the result of past learning/
conditioning experiences. Inappropriate behavior is
learned, just as appropriate behavior is learned.
The social learning approach uses Skinnerian operant
conditioning contingencies as the model for the psychological universe (see Chapter 5).

4. Therapy can be viewed as the attempt to elim-
inate or mitigate undesired behavior through exposure
to new or remedial learning experiences. Therapy
simply amounts to exposure to new or remedial reinforcement and/or conditioning contingencies. The
analogy for a traditional therapy session in the social learning approach is exposure to some controlled

and objectively evaluated retraining regimen. The
psychological dynamics subsumed by behavioral therapy
encompass the active conditioning of desirable behavior and the active extinction or punishment of undesirable behavior (see Leitenberg, 1976).

STATUS OF THERAPY IN APPLIED PSYCHOLOGY The
status of therapy in applied psychology is different
in the context of the traditional medical model approach and the behavior modification approach. Psychoanalysis, as the germinal form of psychotherapy,
and the more contemporary behavior modification techniques possess different values on some critical
evaluative dimensions. Three such dimensions will be
considered for illustrative purposes.

THE THERAPEUTIC SITUATION AS A SOURCE OF
NEW PSYCHOLOGICAL KNOWLEDGE Freud (1939, 1949) induced his view of human nature and the content of
his psychoanalytical system from the therapeutic situation. The psychotherapeutic and world view aspects
of psychoanalysis actually evolved simultaneously.
The germinal years of psychoanalysis, approximately
1885 to 1895, partially overlap the first full decade
of development of academic psychology, as represented
by Wundtian (1896) structuralism. Freud had some
knowledge of academic psychology, but was not influenced by it. He identified with the medical establishment and its basic function of alleviation of
human illness, such that the doctor-patient relationship and role system constituted the natural source
of psychological truth for him. Most of the later
forms of psychotherapy that evolved from psychoanalysis also developed without any direct influence from
hard-core, academic, experimental psychology (Pro-

chaska, 1979).

Although the behavior modification approach to
psychological intervention constitutes an applied
psychology, it is a direct extension of academically
based Watsonian and Skinnerian conditioning principles (Bandura, 1964). Behavior modification does not
serve as the source of new psychological knowledge
at the system level, although it does serve to illustrate and solidify some of the precepts of descriptive behaviorism.

AMENABILITY OF THERAPY TO MEANINGFUL EMPIR-
ICAL EVALUATION Most of the traditional forms of
psychotherapy, including psychoanalysis, are beyond
meaningful empirical evaluation, for a number of reasons (see Eysenck, 1952; Smith and Glass, 1977):

1. The therapist can predelimit the specific
range of applicability of a technique.

2. The therapist can preclaim that a complete
"cure" is not a reasonably expectable outcome of the
use of a specific technique.

3. The therapist-patient relationship is of
such a nature that any attempt to vary one or more
of its critical components would automatically preclude any possibility of a successful outcome.

4. The therapist is both the generator and inter-
preter of the relevant clinical data and, therefore,
is subject to numerous experimenter expectation effects.

Traditional psychotherapy, in general, was not
concerned with empirical evaluation (Eysenck, 1952).
As an extension of medical psychology, the practice
of psychotherapy was insulated from objective, external evaluation. Carl Rogers (1951) was the first

therapist to attempt meaningful empirical evaluation
in the context of his client-centered, nondirective
therapy. It also should be mentioned that it was
primarily due to the efforts of Rogers that the dis-
pensing of psychotherapy became a legitimate, recognized function of the psychologist, instead of being
the exclusive domain of the psychiatrist and psychoanalyst.

A properly implemented behavior modification
technique is just as much an evaluative experimental
device as it is a form of therapy (Leitenberg, 1976).
The basic therapeutic manipulation is physicalized
in the context of an explicit design that affords
objective evaluation of the behavioral effect of the
manipulation. In many situations, the response feedback is immediate and can occasion a change in the
manipulation before the first therapeutic session is
even over. With behavior modification becoming increasingly more cognitive in its orientation, the
objective evaluation aspect of behavior modification
is increasingly becoming its critical defining feature (Erwin, 1978).

The objective evaluation feature of behavior
modification techniques has generalized to the practice of psychotherapy as a whole. Contemporary psy-
chotherapists, regardless of whether they are behaviorally oriented or not, are becoming concerned with
the general accountability of their methods (see Garfield and Bergin, 1978). This is all to the good
due to the current consumer oriented climate in America and the prevailing issue of whether therapy, as
dispensed by psychologists, should be covered by private health insurance plans and ultimately by any

federally financed medical system.

GOAL OF THERAPY Although both the traditional forms of psychotherapy and the behavior modification approach deal with specific behaviors, psychological problems, or complaints expressed by the
patient/client, the basic goal of the two approaches
to therapy differ. Traditional psychotherapy focused
on the adjustment of the individual as a whole, even
though the institution of therapy was due to concern
over a specific malady. Psychoanalysts and even
Rogerian therapists view the attempt at adjustment
as a constant, ongoing process that never really
ends. Psychoanalysis, in particular, is biased
against a clear-cut, short term termination of therapy; and a successful analysis usually takes years
to complete.

A particular behavior modification regimen is
applied to a specific behavior, or set of behaviors;
and its acquisition or disappearance is the only
goal. The termination point of therapy usually is
built into the design of the program, and a successful completion of the therapy is specified explicitly
in the terms of the contract (see Chapter 8).

THERAPY IN PERSPECTIVE Recall that the practicing psychotherapist, especially a traditional non-
behaviorally oriented one, has a different value system and set of operating ground rules than the academic, experimental psychologist. This is one reason why the practice of psychotherapy tends to be one
dimensional in nature and subject to fads, or even
frauds, with respect to popularity. Divorced from
any significant academic conceptual base, the acceptability of many traditional forms of therapy waxes

and wanes as a function of external, cultural and
social factors. Psychoanalysis was the rage in American urban areas during the '30s and '40s, only to
be replaced by more specifically focused, esoteric
therapeutic approaches, such as transactional analysis, transcendental meditation, encounter sessions
or sensitivity training (T) groups, primal therapy,
nude marathon sessions, and e.s.t. (see Belkin,
1980). The acceptability of behavior modification
techniques is less subject to fads and primarily is
a function of the development of more sophisticated
technology: biofeedback devices, response monitoring
devices, or reinforcement delivery devices (Leitenberg, 1976).

    Kendler (1981) has a rather interesting view of
the role of therapy in society. His basic thesis
suggests that therapy should not be evaluated solely
as a psychological entity. For many people in our
society therapy is a surrogate religious experience,
esthetic experience, recreational experience, or an
experience of extreme intimacy. In this context,
empirical assessment of the possible beneficial effects of therapy becomes irrelevant. A weekly trip
to the therapist is equivalent to a weekly trip to
the hair stylist. As long as the consumer perceives
intrinsic value in the visitation or experiences personal satisfaction, no other justification is needed.
PSYCHOLOGICAL TESTING
    Psychological tests and testing in America con-
stitute both a commercial enterprise and a social
phenomenon of gigantic proportions (see Kaplan and
Saccuzzo, 1982; Sweetland and Keyser, 1983). Such
companies as the Psychological Corporation and the

Educational Testing Service produce and market tests
that can have a profound effect on the educational
and professional future of virtually every American.
Tests are used as selection and placement devices in
industry, education, and the armed forces. Tests are
used as diagnostic devices for the detection of possible abnormality in intelligence, reading ability,
personality traits, or sensory and motor abilities.

America's initial interest in tests and individual differences derives from the work of Galton
(1869, 1879, 1889) and Cattell (1890, 1898), a British Jack-of-all-trades and early American functionalist respectively. They quantified individual differences in reaction times, psychophysical judgments,
and memory span. In effect, they measured low level
sensory and motor abilities. Their datum was magni-
ficent and pure, but it lacked interpretive significance: it did not correlate with academic performance, problem solving capacity, or creativity, phenomena that are presumed to be indicative of an organism's intelligence.

The massive growth of the testing movement in
the United States had to await the appearance of the
intelligence test for general verbal or scholastic
ability. The intelligence concept was originated in
France in 1905 by Binet (1903; with Simon, 1913) and
Simon, who were commissioned by the French government to construct a test that would identify mental
defectives (traditional terminology here). Their
test was further elaborated by Terman (1916) at Stan-
ford University in 1916. The intelligence quotient
became institutionalized in America during World War
I in the context of Yerkes' (1921) and Otis' work on

the Army Alpha and Beta tests.

Although the IQ test is not the only kind of psychological test, it constitutes the prototypical type. The only other kind of test that comes close to it in the consciousness of the American populace is the personality test. Perhaps the most widely known type of personality test is the projective variety, as exemplified by the Rorschach (1942) Ink Blot Test and the Murray (1938) and Morgan TAT (Thematic Apperception Test) (see Bellak, 1975). These projective tests are directly based on Freudian psychology and its concept of projection, whereby respondents presumably project their personalities into an ambiguous stimulus situation.

TESTING AS A FORM OF APPLIED PSYCHOLOGY Tests and testing constitute an applied psychology in its purest form, due to four basic reasons (Kaplan and Saccuzzo, 1982).

1. The testing movement by and large developed outside the confines of academia and uncontaminated by the influence of any major system of experimental psychology.

2. Psychometrics, the process of test construction, basically is atheoretical in nature. It is atheoretical in the sense that no psychological theory is involved. Test theory does exist; but it is mathematical, statistical, correlational, factor analytic in nature. Psychometrics amounts to applied statistics, not an applied behaviorism or humanism.

3. Tests are measuring devices. Although most tests exist in paper and pencil form, they are perfectly analogous to a yardstick, weight scale, or

measuring cup. A test is an objective sample of behavior in one situation that allows prediction of behavior in another situation. This aspect of a test
defines the notion of validity: a test is valid if
performance on the items composing the test is correlated with performance in another situation, usually called the criterion. For instance, the prototypical criterion situation for an IQ test is academic performance; the criterion situation for a personality test is more amorphous, but usually involves
some indicant of the overall level of adjustment of
the individual. From another perspective, test performance only contributes to predictive, correlational R-R laws. Tests are independent of and sum over
various stimulus situations. Tests do not function
as control devices. The poststructuralist systems
of academic, experimental psychology basically subsume causal S-R laws that allow control besides prediction (see Chapter 8).

    4. The cultural significance of testing is inde-
pendent of any real concern for the nature of the human organism, either as a psychological being or as
an object of psychological analysis. Tests perform
a certain distributive, allocational, or classificatory function in society. A test is more of a sociological tool than a psychological tool in many respects. A test assesses various psychological skills,
but these tend to be the ones society deems necessary for its survival. It is no accident that the
two periods of greatest expansion in the use of tests
in America corresponded to World Wars I and II. This
sociological, allocational aspect of tests and testing must be elaborated.

TESTS AS SOCIAL CONTRACTS OR POLITICAL INSTRU-
MENTS The content and purpose of any kind of test,
as an assessment device, are arbitrary. For instance,
the concept of IQ is a noncontingent notion. It is
our invention, not a God-given construct. The notion of IQ, and IQ test, amounts to a social contract
between psychometricians and the general public that
certain items and terms will be used in certain ways.

The problem with a social contract is that certain elements of society can view it as a social conspiracy (Garcia, 1974). When the terms and consequences of the social contract are interpreted as
being unfair to a certain segment of the population,
the contract becomes a conspiracy. The concept of
IQ, and IQ test, is undergoing much current criticism
because it is viewed as only being a fair assessment
device for, and consequently a political instrument
of, the WASP: White, Anglo-Saxon, Protestant (Kamin,
1974). The current controversy relative to Jensen's
(1969, 1973, 1980) and the physicist Shockley's belief in the genetic inferiority of the American Ne-
gro with respect to overall IQ level really is a social or political one, not a biological or genetic one.

A projective personality test also is a political instrument, not so much because the concept of
personality is arbitrary, but rather because the process of taking a projective personality test can violate one of the fundamental rights guaranteed by the
Fifth Amendment of the United States Constitution:
the right not to incriminate oneself (Ruch, 1974).
An American has the right not to answer an objective
question if the answer will incriminate in any way.
An item on a projective personality test possesses

no face validity whatsoever.   The responder has no
idea what is being tested for or how the response information will be interpreted and used.

CHAPTER 11

MODERATING INFLUENCES

Up to now in the text we have focused on why psychology lacks paradigmatic coherence and hopefully have
demonstrated that this state of affairs is perfectly
expectable, if not inevitable. But psychology's perennial pluralistic state is a double-edged sword. We
also face the problem of accounting for the fact that
the discipline's conceptual fragmentation does not
contain the seeds of its eventual demise. What makes
it possible for psychology to be so diverse at a conceptual level and yet retain a high degree of disci-
plinary stability and professional coherence?

The basic reason is that the discipline's pluralism is subject to a number of moderating influences.
Four of these were mentioned in the Preface and have
been implicit in the analysis so far:

1. The pluralism is a product of various philosophical and historical factors that by and large
are immutable.

2. The pluralism is to a large extent superficial or semantically based.

3. The content of psychology is leavened by the
fact that each system must face the same basic set of
problems.

4. A system of psychology only can be evaluated

in terms of extra-disciplinary considerations and
value judgments.

The purpose of this chapter is to focus on some
indigenous aspects of psychology that function as
moderating influences. These include (1) uniqueness,
(2) complementary contributions of the different
types of psychology, (3) reciprocal relationship between pure and applied psychology, (4) metaphysical
neutrality of behavior and consciousness, (5) status
of methodology, (6) professional specification, (7)
national character of psychology, (8) ephemeral
truth, and (9) recipient status.

UNIQUENESS

Psychology is unlike any other academic discipline or intellectual endeavor in at least two critical respects: (1) irresolvability of its content of
observation and (2) arbitrariness of its orientation.

IRRESOLVABILITY OF CONTENT OF OBSERVATION Psychology possesses no fundamental agreed upon units
of analysis or loci of causation. The defining properties of an event deemed to be psychological in nature cannot be specified in a manner acceptable to
all psychologists (see Chapter 9). The indetermin-
acy of the domain of psychology primarily derives
from the fact that the human organism is an open-ended and infinitely descriptive creature. The substratum of the human organism (biology) makes it a
chemical, bioelectrical, biophysical, neurophysiological, and genetic reality. The superstratum of the
human organism (social world) makes it have a political, legal, ethical, and ecological reality. Psychology must interface with all these aspects, and
no one standard content of observation can do it.

The irresolvability of the content of observation serves as a moderating influence because practically any interpretation of the notion can be
found to possess some psychological relevance. Historically, specific systems of psychology have been
criticized for being too limited, not for being too
comprehensive (see Robinson, 1979). The discipline
is in no danger of disintegration when its dominant
models of psychological reality individually only
tap separate subportions of a potentially infinite
psychological universe.

ARBITRARINESS OF ORIENTATION Psychology can
focus on the self, as in humanism, or on a significant other, as in behaviorism. Focusing on the self
creates a psychology epistemologically and ontolog-
ically contingent on human consciousness; focusing
on a significant other creates a psychology devoid
of human consciousness (see Chapter 1). In the first
approach, psychological reality is divorced from and
not a component of physical reality; in the second
approach, psychological reality is continuous with
and a component of physical reality. Although the
first kind of psychological reality is more personal
than the second, it is strictly received, or given,
and cannot easily be manipulated. The second kind
of psychological reality is impersonal, but is derivative, or not given, and admits of relatively easy
manipulation.

The arbitrariness of orientation has a moderating effect because it results in vastly different,
incommensurate psychologies that appeal to individuals of disparate outlooks, goals, and the like. This
feature of psychology guarantees a place in the dis-

cipline for virtually any kind of psychological prac-
tice or practitioner.
COMPLEMENTARY CONTRIBUTIONS OF DIFFERENT TYPES OF
PSYCHOLOGY

     Five types of psychology were derived in Chap-
ter 3: (1) epistemological or cognitive, (2) understanding, (3) action, (4) depth, and (5) dialectical.
Each type makes a distinctive contribution to psychology, by fulfilling certain perceived needs and
being responsive to different elements of society
and the demands they put on the discipline. As such,
they complement each other and perform a moderating
function.

     EPISTEMOLOGICAL; COGNITIVE The first recognized
system of experimental psychology, structuralism,
was of the epistemological type (see Chapter 4). It
focused on the content of consciousness, through the
first person access of highly trained, verbally facile graduate students. Its content of observation
represented a technical, professional adjustment by
Wilhelm Wundt (1896), who combined the talents of a
philosopher and an experimental physiologist in the
empirical study of the structure of the mind. Structuralism constituted a pure psychology, with no practical application relevance, and succeeded in effec-
ting psychology's acceptance by the academic community as a legitimate intellectual discipline.

     Although the seeds of structuralism were plan-
ted in the United States by Titchener (1898), the
practical and pragmatic orientation of American culture fostered a concern for the utility of consciousness that was physically realized in the context of
a loosely formulated epistemological system called

functionalism (see Chapter 4). In this conceptual
approach, the activities of consciousness constitute
the loci of determination and overt behavior, for all
practical purposes, serves as the object of direct
observation. Functionalism provided the necessary
context for America's interest in mental testing,
child and adolescent psychology, educational psychology, effective teaching and learning techniques, and
the like.

Gestalt psychology (see Chapter 4) was a formal,
academically oriented cognitive system that revolutionized the psychology of perception, kept the epistemological orientation alive during the heyday of
descriptive behaviorism, and functioned as a germinal form of humanistic, understanding psychology. At
a conceptual level, it served as an antithesis to the
molecular, associationistic focus of both structuralism and behaviorism.

Cognitive behaviorism constitutes the dominant
contemporary American physical realization of an
epistemological psychology (see Chapter 5). It effects a third person access to mentation by employing a computer-brain analogy at both a conceptual
(modeling) and evaluational (methodological) level.
Cognitive behaviorism is an advanced, or more sophisticated, form of functionalism with overt behavior
related to highly formalized and codified mental
events.

Piagetian structural, genetic-epistemological
psychology (see Chapter 5) mapped the rational, intellectual side of our nature, just as Freud (1939,
1949) did for the irrational, instinctual components.
It constitutes the canonical cognitive-developmental

system to which other conceptual approaches to mentation invariably are compared. Piaget's system continues the traditional Continental emphasis on mind
and epistemology: structuralism, act psychology, Gestalt psychology, and the like. It also derived from
the general Kantian framework in which structure,
both in a logical and physical realization sense, is
regarded as a necessary component of anyone's world
view. Piagetian thought transcends psychology and
is unorthodox by strict behavioristic, experimental
standards; but this fact makes Piaget similar to
Freud in that his contributions to intellectual history belie his classification as a mere psychologist.

UNDERSTANDING This kind of psychology is best
exemplified in a contemporary context by humanistic,
phenomenological, existential psychology (see Chapter 5). First person access to the content of an organism's emotional consciousness, or general feeling
state, is used to infer the quality and degree of its
self-awareness, the nature of its overall adjustment
to life, and the like. Humanistic psychology literally constructs the psychological world in which each
individual exists. It is a conceptual extension of
Gestalt psychology and represents a rebirth of interest in consciousness after decades of neglect due to
the dominance of descriptive behaviorism. Although
empirical in nature, humanistic psychology is not an
experimental system and basically amounts to a form
of therapeutic intervention.

ACTION This type of psychology fills the need
for an objectively based, experimentally oriented
psychology by focusing on overt behavior as the object of direct observation. Functionalism constitu-

ted an implicit action system and served as a necessary transitional school between structuralism and
Watsonian behaviorism. Any kind of behaviorism is
an action psychology (see Chapter 3). Watsonian and
Skinnerian behaviorism are strictly descriptive in
nature, in the sense that external stimulus events
exhaust the locus of causation. Logical behaviorism,
or learning macrotheory, relates overt behavior to
postulated internal events, most of which are assumed peripheral in nature. Cognitive behaviorism,
in the tradition of Tolmanian learning theory, relates overt behavior to presumed internal, central
brain events.

Descriptive behaviorism, especially the Skinnerian variety (see Chapter 5), constitutes an applied
psychology par excellence: for instance, behavior
therapy, contingency management, token economies,
self-help programs, and programmed learning. Its interpretation of the content of observation as an input-output relation affords a pre-emptory degree of
control of behavior. Because its content of observation also de-emphasizes the specific type of organism exhibiting behavior, it permits a methodologically viable animal psychology: Commercial animal training, animal psychophysics, animal psychopharmacology,
and animal psychophysiology are made possible by
Skinnerian operant conditioning techniques.

DEPTH Many variants of depth psychology exist,
although Freudian psychoanalysis constitutes the canonical form (see Chapter 5). Depth psychology has
no formal concept of behavior and de-emphasizes rational, cognitive mentation occurring at the level
of immediate awareness. It regards the individual

organism as a psychic entity, subject to conflicting strivings, wishes, and forces, many of which are assumed to be unconscious. The psychological universe is strictly localized within the skin and subsumes a psychodynamic system incorporating psychic determinism. Psychoanalysis possesses a tremendous degree of face validity for the general public and exhausts psychology for the average person. It has had an immense influence on those disciplines that focus on the individual organism as the unit of analysis: for instance, art, literature, drama, history, and theology. Psychoanalysis heavily interfaces with the personality, developmental, and motivational areas of mainstream psychology. Freud (1939, 1949) put the psychogenic approach to abnormality and therapy on the psychological map. It was psychoanalysis, not one of the academic systems, that originally proffered the notion that the human organism is a psychological entity and that a characteristically unique psychological reality exists.

DIALECTICAL   This type of psychology is indigenous to Russia; however, beginning in the late 1960s, Klaus Riegel (1978, 1979) constructed an American version in an attempt to combine the objective orientation of behaviorism and the subjective orientation of humanism (see Chapters 3 and 5). What resulted was a hybrid cognitive-developmental psychology, quite similar to Skinner's (1974) descriptivism. Dialectical psychology, at this point in time, is strictly an academic system, although its potential practical application relevance is unlimited because it conceives of the individual organism as a point in a combined historical (developmental)-cultural (social environmental) space.

RECIPROCAL RELATIONSHIP BETWEEN PURE AND APPLIED
PSYCHOLOGY

The various conceptual approaches to psychology
possess differing proportions of pure and applied aspects.   The classical school of structuralism was
100% pure.   The mental testing movement is 100% applied.   The descriptive behavioristic and dialectical approaches are explicit academic systems with
indigenous applied relevance.   Depth psychology and
humanism are basically applied systems, but subsume
explicit world views.

The relationship between academic/experimental
psychology and applied/professional psychology is exceedingly complex (see Chapter 10).   The primary variable separating psychologists into different camps
today is not philosophical orientation, but professional identification as a pure or applied psychologist.   Conflicts are inevitable between psychologists
of such disparate goals and values; however, a reciprocal relationship also exists between pure and applied psychology that acts as a moderating influence
on the overall discipline.   No contemporary psychologist can construct a system, or a model in the context of a given system, devoid of any practical application relevance; likewise, no psychological practitioner can operate in a conceptual vacuum.   For instance, behavior modification has revolutionized the
care and treatment of the developmentally disabled
(erstwhile mental retardates) (see Whitney and Barnard, 1966); the applied area of industrial/organiza-
tional psychology serves as the source of new theories on job satisfaction, motivation, and optimal

group organization in the process of constructing a
vision of the industrial organism (see Muchinsky,
1983).

The basic distinction between a pure and an applied psychologist does not involve the system construction process.   Both kinds of psychologists must
operate in the context of some type of psychological
reality.   The traditional distinction between a normal organism and a so-called abnormal organism or
that between a fully functioning person and one with
some biological or psychological deficit is breaking
down.   Normal and abnormal situations and subjects
are serving as models for each other (Maser and Seligman, 1977).   Twentieth century life is so complex
and stressful that even the smallest psychological
aberration is considered conceptually important and
even the remotest psychological fact possesses practical relevance.

METAPHYSICAL NEUTRALITY OF BEHAVIOR AND CONSCIOUSNESS

It already has been noted that, with the transition from the classical school era to the contemporary system context, behavior and consciousness devolved from absolute metaphysical categories to mere
convenient, descriptive labels.   This change in status of psychology's traditional objects of study occurred for two reasons (Mueller-Freienfels, 1935):

1. The empirical study of behavior or consciousness ceased to be an end in itself.   Simply catalog-
uing the various behaviors that an organism could ex-
hibit à la functionalism became a meaningless exercise; simply externalizing the content of one's immediate consciousness à la structuralism became passe

2. Psychologists eventually realized that where

consciousness ends and behavior begins, or vice versa, strictly is arbitrary. Consciousness does not
exist in a vacuum; consciousness exists in a behaving
organism. Both the nature and quality of the content
of consciousness depend on one's overt behavior,
both in a short term, episodic sense and in a long
term, structural sense. Conversely, behavior does
not occur in a vacuum; behavior is the output of a
self-aware organism (or neuronal monitoring systems
in the brain). Meaningful behavior cannot occur
without some preliminary mentation, even if it is
conceptualized merely as some kind of physiological
or brain activity.

The basic semanticity of the behavior-conscious-
ness distinction is revealed by the isomorphism of
the Skinnerian and cognitive behaviorist approaches.
The way in which Skinner (1953) defines a piece of
behavior and the way in which a cognitive psychologist, such as Fodor (1981), defines a mental state
are exactly the same; namely, in terms of functional,
causal role. For Skinner, all experience is behavior: the contents of both introspective and perceptual awareness constitute reportable discriminable
responses. Experience merely is behavior occurring
within the skin, analyzable in terms of the same physical categories used to describe overt behavior.
For a cognitive psychologist, mentation is assumed
analogous to the behavior of some physical system,
such as a computer. Organismic mentation only differs from some form of mechanical information processing in terms of the hardware involved. For Skinner,
everything that occurs subsequent to the presentation
of some stimulus event is output; for a cognitive

psychologist, everything that happens prior to the
occurrence of a response event is <u>input</u>. The portion
of the <u>output</u> occurring within the skin for Skinner
and the portion of the <u>input</u> occurring within the
skin for a cognitive behaviorist consist of the
same functionally defined material events.

The metaphysical neutrality of behavior and consciousness is even more pronounced in the context of
a comparison between radical behaviorism and humanism. Both Skinner (1974) and a humanist, such as
Giorgi (1970), allow third person access to overt
behavior and first person access to mental events.
Skinner and a humanist only differ with respect to
the source of the reference point used to interpret
the output in each case: they differ merely with respect to the specification of the locus of causation.
Skinner interprets output strictly in terms of the
immediate environmental situation or the past history
of the organism. A humanist interprets output strictly in terms of the perceived psychological world of
the organism.

The metaphysical neutrality of behavior and consciousness in contemporary psychology serves as a
moderating influence because it reduces much of psychology's pluralism to a matter of linguistic usage.

STATUS OF METHODOLOGY

Correlative with the change of status of object
of study specification is a corresponding change in
attitude to methodology. When behavior and conscious
ness are regarded as absolute metaphysical categories, the question of appropriate methodology constitutes a critical metaphysical battleground. Choice
of focus on behavior or consciousness predetermines

the appropriate methodology. Once behavior and consciousness devolve to linguistic categories, the
question of appropriate methodology loses much of its
metaphysical significance.

Contemporary psychologists are concerned with
methodology, but for technical and logical reasons,
not for metaphysical reasons (Kendler, 1981). It is
virtually impossible today to deny credibility to research data solely on the basis of nonacceptance of
the specific experimental technique the psychologist
used. Methodology has devolved to a professional
and technical subspecialty that cross-cuts and super-
cedes the content and prescriptions of the various
systems, such that it is now viewed merely as a
means, rather than as an end in itself. For instance,
second and third generation operant psychologists no
longer generate and display data in exactly the same
manner that Skinner did (see Ferster, 1978); depth
psychologists accept data generated by developmental,
genetic methodology (Rapaport, 1959); states of consciousness are isolated and defined in terms of physiological measures, such as eye movements and brain
waves (for instance, Kleitman, 1963).

The new attitude to methodology serves as a moderating influence because it removes one possible
area of contention from affecting the construction
of a model of psychological reality.

PROFESSIONAL SPECIFICATION

A contemporary psychologist does not secure employment solely by professing adherence to a specific system of psychology. The profession, as a sociological and economic entity, simply is not structured in terms of systems. The primary professional

specification is done in terms of academic/research psychologist versus professional/applied psychologist. Within this basic dichotomy, job slots are defined in terms of specialties. For instance, an experimental psychologist can be a perceptual psychologist, comparative psychologist, learning psychologist, or the like; an applied psychologist can be a clinical psychologist, educational psychologist, industrial psychologist, or the like. Subspecialties within a given specialty also exist: for instance, a learning psychologist can be a conditioning, verbal learning, motor learning, animal learning, or human learning specialist.

System adherence can come into play at the level of subspecialty specification. For instance, a university might advertise an opening for a learning psychologist with expertise in operant conditioning (radical behaviorism), information processing (cognitive behavorism), or verbal learning (latter-day functionalism); a mental health center might advertise for a clinical psychologist with a Freudian, existential, Rogerian, behavioral, or Gestalt orientation. There are even "generalist" positions for psychologists who take an essentially eclectic orientation: it is very difficult for a hard-core Skinnerian or a committed Rogerian or Freudian to present a balanced introductory psychology course. An interest in system construction and evaluation (or theory construction and assessment) is <u>not</u> a viable subspecialty. A psychologist must combine this interest with some marketable subspecialty in order to secure employment.

System adherence can be a necessary condition,

but never a sufficient condition, for professional
job procurement and placement. This fact has a moderating effect on the discipline because it removes
the system construction and evaluation process from
the reward mechanisms that determine the currently
most desirable job slots.

NATIONAL CHARACTER

Unlike the physical sciences of chemistry and
physics, psychology possesses a distinctive national
character (Sexton and Misiak, 1976). American psychology, Russian psychology, French psychology, British psychology, Scandinavian psychology, and the
like have their own characteristic flavor and relative emphases, both at a system and institutional
level. The fact that psychology's pluralism has a
cultural aspect should not be surprising; however,
the degree to which these different national content
psychologies compete is surprising. Psychology is
part of the cultural competition among nations. Nations do not compete with respect to content chemistry or physics, although they might compete with respect to the products of their chemical or physical
technology.

The national character of psychology does not
necessarily demonstrate that psychological reality
is different from physical reality. It does indicate
that the construction of a psychological reality is
more susceptible to cultural and social variables
than the construction of a physical reality is. But
these very variables serve as a moderating influence
because they guarantee the continued maintenance of
many different simultaneous views of psychological
reality. Cultural relativism in psychology helps

sustain the vitality of the discipline.

EPHEMERAL TRUTH

A system of psychology entails only ephemeral truth: it rarely survives the death of its founder or principal adherents. Even when a system does survive, it is subject to evolutionary changes and adaptations. Only three systems of psychology have lasted more than half a century: (1) Freudian depth psychology, (2) Piagetian epistemological-genetic psychology, and (3) Skinnerian radical behaviorism.

Two factors determine the effective life span of a system: (1) the kind of psychology it subsumes and (2) the degree to which it has been institutionalized by its founder(s). Depth psychology and understanding psychology are not experimental systems: they are constructed as dogma accepted by faith. Epistemological, behavioristic, and dialectical psychology are experimental systems, continually subject to empirical validation and revision. The latter kind of system has virtually no chance of survival in original form.

Freud's psychology survived because he institutionalized his dogma and inspired future generations of neo-Freudians (Horney, 1950; Fromm, 1947; Sullivan, 1953). It is too early to tell whether Piaget's system will survive his recent death. Skinner is still alive and in a position to defend his system; however, second and third generation operant psychologists already have significantly altered his original system (for instance, Herrnstein, 1970; Staddon, 1967).

Structuralism, the many versions of learning macrotheory (logical behaviorism), and Gestalt psychology precipitously declined once their founders died. Watsonian behaviorism did not even survive its founder. Functionalism had no explicit founder(s) and ultimately was absorbed by behaviorism. Dialectical psychology more than likely was not sufficiently institutionalized prior to Riegel's death in 1977. Cognitive behaviorism probably is at mid life.

The extreme ephemerality of a system of psychology has a moderating effect on the discipline because it implicitly serves as a mechanism for redirection and change in system construction efforts. Some psychologists like to argue that systems (or theories) do not die, but merely are replaced (Lakatos, 1970); however, rarely is a system discarded as long as its original founder(s) and principal adherents are still alive to defend it. By way of comparison, we can appeal to physical science, especially physics, where Newton's and Einstein's theories were not affected by their deaths. In a science with paradigmatic coherence, the mechanism of change is impersonal (Kuhn, 1970).

RECIPIENT STATUS

Psychology is both a component of intellectual life and an aspect of intellectual history; however, with the exception of Freudian doctrine, it never has served as a catalyst for other intellectual disciplines. Psychology possesses recipient status: it is affected more by what happens in other fields, than by other disciplines being affected by it.

Structuralism, as the germinal form of experimental psychology, was the by-product of cognitive philosophy, experimental physiology, and physics. Functionalism represented a working out of the Dar-

winian biologically oriented evolutionary doctrine
in a psychological context. Gestalt psychology is
derivative of German rationalistic, idealistic philosophy and an explicit absorber of physical field
theory. Descriptive behaviorism is an expression of
the general philosophical doctrine of positivism,
and logical behaviorism is an explicit application
of logical positivism. Depth psychology physicalizes numerous philosophical doctrines: hedonism, the
unconscious, repression, and the like. Humanistic
psychology was inspired, in part, by existentialism.
Cognitive behaviorism is simply another instance of
the pervasive effect that the computer has had on
post World War II life. Piagetian structural psychology physicalizes and substantiates the basic
tenets of Kant's conception of the mind. Dialectical psychology merely is a semantic extension of
Marxist dialectical materialism.

      Contemporary psychology is rapidly expanding in
applied directions to meet needs that are defined by
and originate in other disciplines. For instance,
the interfacing of law and clinical psychology has
created the new subspecialty of forensic psychologist; space exploration requires a space psychology;
geriatric medicine has spawned a geriatric psychology.

      The recipient status of psychology functions as
a moderating influence because it sets limits to acceptable variation in psychological system construction. The pluralism of psychology must always reflect and can never exceed the diversity of the intellectual milieu of which it is a component.

CHAPTER 12

RELATIONAL ASPECTS

No relational question about the nature of contemporary psychology is resolvable independently of the
specific model of psychological reality that is used
as the evaluative reference point, as is the case
with any internal matter covered in Chapters 4 and 5.
It is the purpose of this chapter to evaluate a representative set of seven relational queries in order
to highlight the far-reaching consequences of psychology's pluralism:

1. In what sense is the human organism an object
of psychological analysis?

2. Is psychology a science? If so, what kind?

3. Is psychology reducible or autonomous?

4. Does psychology possess significant practical
application value?

5. How does psychology differ from other disciplines and endeavors concerned with the nature of the
human organism?

6. Is psychology relevant for ethics and morality?

7. Does psychology have to be taken into account in any rational consideration of the meaning
of life?

IN WHAT SENSE IS THE HUMAN ORGANISM AN OBJECT OF PSYCHOLOGICAL ANALYSIS?

The sense in which the human organism serves as an object of analysis for a system of psychology primarily is a function of its view of the organism. Chapter 6 abstracted three possible views: (1) explicitly nontranscendental, (2) explicitly transcendental, and (3) implicitly nontranscendental.

EXPLICITLY NONTRANSCENDENTAL   Any form of behaviorism is explicitly nontranscendental. There is nothing special about a human being. The human being is simply another kind of real-space and real-time entity. A person can be modeled as an animal or even a machine. In this approach, psychological reality corresponds to physical reality, and psychological analysis simply is another case of scientific analysis.

A behaviorist seeks scientific laws and generalizations that apply to a typical, or statistical, subject or to a group of organisms. Technically, this is called the nomothetic approach (Watson, 1967). The individual organism per se does not serve as a unit of psychological analysis. A subject in a behavioral experiment often is referred to as an ob-ject, because it is a repository of various psychological processes and mechanisms that constitute the behaviorist's actual focus of concern.

A behaviorist can focus on the behavior of an individual organism, either in an experimental context, à la Skinner (1938) or an operant psychologist, or in a therapeutic context, à la a behavior modifier. But the individual's behavior always is interpreted in terms of general, nomothetic laws; that is,

in terms of the all-encompassing "physical" psychological reality. For a behaviorist, the individual
organism does not constitute a psychological universe
unto itself.

EXPLICITLY TRANSCENDENTAL Humanistic psychology, in general, and phenomenological or existential
psychology, in particular, constitute the best examples of a contemporary system subsuming the explicitly transcendental view. The human being is a special
or unique form of life, characterized by self-consciousness. The term "human" is a technical one distinguishing us from every other form of life.

An individual organism serves as the unit of analysis and constitutes a psychological universe unto
itself. A person is a true subject, never an object,
a repository of accumulated experiences, personal
identities, and feelings that generate a true, efficacious self. Psychological analysis amounts to externalizing and resolving the content of a person's
psychological world. Psychological truth in this approach is idiographic (Watson, 1967). Humanists attempt to make people aware of things they already
know, but do not realize they know. In humanism, psychological analysis really amounts to an applied or
therapeutic endeavor.

IMPLICITLY NONTRANSCENDENTAL The remaining systems of psychology--structuralism, functionalism,
Gestalt, dialectical, genetic-epistemological, and
depth--would have to be classified as implicitly nontranscendental. These systems either assume some
form of determinism or consider the human being to be
amenable to scientific analysis; however, their nontranscendentalism is only implicit because they admit

of the efficacy or relevance of mentation.

     Each of these systems, except for depth psychol-
ogy, is an experimental one and views the human organism as an object of psychological analysis in the
same general sense that the behaviorist does. Unlike
the case of behavorism, consciousness can serve as a
focus of attention, either as input or as output.

     Depth psychology's approach to the organism as
an object of psychological analysis is a hybrid of
the behavioristic and humanistic views. The organism
is treated as a repository of psychological processes
and mechanisms, and a universally applicable psychodynamic system is assumed characteristic of each person; however, these are not externalized via physical
experimentation, but rather in terms of one-on-one
therapeutic intervention and analysis. Freud's
(1939, 1949) brand of depth psychology even gets its
name from the way it views the organism as an object
of psychological analysis: psycho-analysis (this hy-
phenated form is the characteristic English or Continental spelling of psychoanalysis).

     CONCEPTUAL SUMMARY There are really three sen-
ses in which the human organism can serve as an object of psychological analysis:

     1. The human is analyzed as a means to another
end. The output of the subject is used to create a
universal psychological reality, independent of human consciousness, that is continuous with physical
reality.

     2. The human is analyzed as an end in itself.
The output of the subject is used to create an individualistic psychological reality that has validity
solely for the reporting subject and takes cognizance

of consciousness.

3. The human is analyzed both as an end in itself and as a means to another end. The output of
the subject is used to create a personal psychodynamics that is assumed to be representative and derivative of a universal psychological reality existing
within the skin of every organism.

The first sense is characteristic of science
(Nagel, 1961); the second sense subsumes the general
understanding or Verstehen approach (Dilthey, 1924);
the third formalizes the psycho-analytical approach
(Munroe, 1955).

IS PSYCHOLOGY A SCIENCE? IF SO, WHAT KIND?

Whether psychology is a science or not depends
on one's conception of science, and the notion of
science is far from a monolithic entity (Turner,
1967). The basic defining properties of science constitute a philosophical question, specifically one
addressed by the philosophy of science. In recent
years, philosophers of science have focused on the
actual practices involved in the conduction of science in an attempt to formalize a coherent interpretation of the discipline (Fodor, 1981). Two things
mitigate against this strategy: (1) Most practicing
scientists do not let the philosophy of science get
in the way and conduct their activities according to
their own implicit criteria; and (2) physical science, especially physics, usually constitutes the
model for all science. Philosophy of science currently is in a state of turmoil because the traditional logical or empirical positivistic model has
spent its course and has not been replaced by a conception approaching anywhere near universal accep-

CHAPTER 12

tance (see Brodbeck, 1968). Consequently, we cannot
appeal to the philosophy of science for our defining
criteria of science.

Virtually all psychologists, regardless of system identification, even humanists and psychoanalysts, consider themselves to be engaged in science.
Such a view obviously means that different psychologists have differing conceptions of science or that
the criteria for science have changed over the years.

We need a criterion for science relevant for
psychology, and five possibilities are obvious:

1. Any system of psychology that is empirically
oriented, as opposed to rationalistic, is scientific.
Every system considered by our analysis is a science
according to this criterion.

2. Any system of psychology seeking to create a
psychological reality commensurate with physical reality is a science. This criterion only eliminates
humanism and psychoanalysis from being considered
scientific systems.

3. The conduction of science requires third person access. This criterion no longer allows structuralism, functionalism, or Gestalt psychology to be
scientific in an all-or-none sense.

4. Consciousness, either as locus of causation
or as object of direct observation, is beyond the
bounds of science. This criterion eliminates every
system, except for Watsonian behaviorism.

5. A system of psychology is not scientific unless it includes its own explicit philosophy of science. In other words, the system must be intentionally viewed as a philosophy of science for psychology. Only Skinnerian radical behaviorism survives

this criterion.

The first criterion is too liberal: it does not sufficiently discriminate between the vastly disparate conceptions and activities of a Skinnerian and a Freudian. The third criterion would operate as an after-the-fact measure because it would impose the stricter standards of a later historical era on the practices of a less methodologically sophisticated earlier historical era. The fourth criterion simply is too restrictive or radical. The fifth criterion is too chauvinistic or self-serving. The second criterion has the most to recommend it. It basically defines the conduction of science in terms of goals, independently of any other consideration: A system of psychology is a science if it attempts to construct a reality commensurate with that envisioned by physical science.

Adopting the second criterion, we shall assume that any epistemological, action, or dialectical system is a science. In the context of this criterion, I am not going to quibble with any humanist who claims to be engaged in "humanistic science" or any psychoanalyst who views depth psychology as a "psychiatric science."

It is possible to earn physical science, biological science, or social science credit for studying psychology, contingent on the specific college or university attended. These academic classifications are, in part, administrative and pragmatic and do not shed light on the question of just what kind of science psychology is. Begging the issue of criteria for these three types of science, the following summary conclusions seem reasonable:

1. Only descriptive behaviorism would be a realistic candidate for physical science status, specifically Skinnerian radical behaviorism because it is
the only currently viable descriptive behavioristic
approach. It does not possess analogues for abstract,
high level physical science theory; but no system of
psychology does. On the other hand, its capability
of generating reliable, valid, stable data is commensurate with that of physical science.

2. No system of psychology considered by our
analysis can be indigenously classified as a biological science. Wundt referred to his system as a physiological psychology, but for methodological reasons,
not content reasons. Functionalism does possess more
than a token degree of biological underpinning, but
it is not a biological psychology. Gestalt psychology certainly is physiologically oriented at a theoretical level, but has no realistic physiological representation at an empirical level. Both Watson and
Skinner decry physiology. The content of cognitive
behaviorism or Piagetian structural psychology currently only possesses the potential of being reduced
to neuronal and biochemical mechanisms. Dialectical
psychology emphasizes the mutual interaction of cultural and biological events, but only pays lip service to physiology at an experimental level. Both
general physiological theories, such as Hebb's (1949)
approach, and explicit physiological models for memory, color vision, conditioning, and schizophrenia
exist (see Koch, 1959, especially Volumes 1 and 4);
but it is problematical whether any of these construc-
tions constitutes a model of psychological reality in
the traditional sense of the term (for instance, see

Robinson, 1979).

3. Any system of psychology classifiable as a
science possesses social science status more-or-less
by default. This interpretation makes scientific
psychology commensurate with sociology, economics,
and political science. Psychology in general, including its humanistic and psychoanalytic versions, is
commensurate with anthropology and history.

IS PSYCHOLOGY REDUCIBLE OR AUTONOMOUS?

This query entails the classic problem of reductionism and is related to whether the various sciences are arranged in a hierarchy ordered from reducing
sciences to reducible sciences (Turner, 1971). When
psychological phenomena are assumed reducible, the
immediate reducing science is physiology; and the ultimate reducing science is physics, which occupies
the first rung of the hierarchy. When psychological
phenomena are not assumed reducible, no ordered hierarchy of the sciences need exist; and psychological
phenomena constitute an autonomous level of reality.

The problem of reductionism is a philosophical
one (Fodor, 1974). During the heyday of logical behaviorism, reduction constituted a desirable goal.
One of the basic tenets of logical positivism was
that any psychological concept, particularly a mentalistic one, could be translated into physical thing
language and thus ultimately reducible to physics
(see Chapter 7: logical behaviorism). This goal
strictly was programmatic in nature, requiring the
postulation of various models and logical interpretations of reduction. No actual reduction of psychological phenomena to physiological phenomena and physical phenomena was accomplished because the desir-

ability of reductionism merely was a matter of principle.

Contemporary philosophers and psychologists have
all but abandoned the principle of reductionism and
treat psychological phenomena as autonomous in nature, reflecting the demise of logical positivism
(for instance, Fodor, 1974). Psychologists have
found ways of legitimizing mentation other than by
reference to material composition; namely, the functional approach (see Chapter 7) in which mental
events are given constructive reality via causal role.
Contemporary philosophers of science, such as Jerry
Fodor (1974), assume that no hierarchy of sciences
exists: the various sciences merely cross-classify
the same phenomena. Isolated instances of reduction
might be possible; but each science, as a whole, requires its own constructive explanatory level and
theoretical constructs. The importance of the brain-
computer or the organism-computer analogy for psychology virtually guarantees the nonreducible status
of the discipline.

Abandoning the principle of reductionism also
means that psychology cannot be used as a reducing
entity for any science located above it on the hypothetical hierarchy of sciences: for instance, sociology or economics. Psychological interpretations are
currently given to certain sociological phenomena,
crowd behavior for example (viz. Latané and Darley,
1970, in a helping context), and to certain economic
phenomena, such as the buying habits of consumers
(Jacoby, 1976; Walters, 1978); but it is assumed that
sociology and economics constitute their own constructive levels of reality.

No system of psychology ever seriously accepted
reductionism as a programmatic goal, except for certain versions of logical behaviorism or learning macrotheory, such as Hull's (1943) hypothetico-deductive
approach.   Structuralism, functionalism, and Gestalt
psychology referred to physiology, but not to the
point of reductionism.   Watsonian and Skinnerian descriptive behaviorism actively argued against it.
Cognitive behaviorism treats mental events as emergent in nature, not reducible to more basic physical
processes.   Piagetian structural psychology is matur-
ationally based, but not biologically reducible.
Freud (1966) attempted to reduce his psychodynamics
to physiology, but eventually gave up.   Humanism conceives the organism as transcending biology: consciousness is not a material event.   Dialectical psychology gives equal weight to cultural and biological influences on the organism, and no reduction is
possible.

DOES PSYCHOLOGY POSSESS SIGNIFICANT PRACTICAL APPLI-CATION VALUE?

The purpose of this section is not to reiterate
that applied, professional psychology exists or that
certain types of psychology, such as action and understanding, possess inherent practical relevance.
Rather, accent should be put on the term "significant," such that we really are asking whether psychology has contributed to the progress of humankind
or fundamentally altered the cultural environment in
which the human being exists.   There follow three intellectual arguments in favor of the proposition that
psychology has not made a significant contribution
and one possible suggestion.

1. Psychology presumably is a codified profession, just as chemistry, physics, biology, or sociology is. People no longer act as their own chemists, physicists, biologists, or sociologists; but they still act as their own psychologists. The reason for this is obvious: the focus of psychology is people, and who knows people better than themselves? Who knows the self better than the self? A natural antagonism exists against taking advice from psychologists, because they are regarded as interlopers in the private psychological domain of the person.

Every human being carries around an implicit common-sense psychology in the head that is very difficult for the codified profession to penetrate (see Churchland, 1984, who refers to it as "folk psychology"). In fact, this implicit psychology is absolutely necessary for interpersonal interaction and organismic survival. Only two brands of psychology exist as cultural phenomena: Freudian psychology and to a lesser degree Skinnerian psychology. In both cases, the negative aspects of these systems usually are emphasized: sex, aggression, gratification, and the like for Freud; control, external inducement, unbridled determinism for Skinner.

2. A discrepancy between actuality (what is) and ideality (what should be) pervades life or human existence. The application of psychology to the real world is no exception to this truism. A discrepancy exists between what psychology actually accomplishes and what it should accomplish. There is no more ironic example of this than the behavior of psychologists, who consistently and predictably violate their own dicta with respect to proper or suggested courses

of action.   If it is argued that psychologists are
not immune from the action of psychological variables;
that is, they are prisoners of their own psychology,
it is just another piece of positive evidence that
psychology has failed.

In order that my argument is not misinterpreted
here (a discrepancy exists between what I intend and
what is interpreted), let me mention some analogous
cases.   This same discrepancy exists with respect to
government (democracy, dictatorship), religion (say
Christianity), economics (capitalism, socialism),
and education.   In each case there is a discrepancy
between what the entity is supposed to accomplish and
what it does accomplish.

An idealist finds it very difficult to adjust to
this pervasive discrepancy; a realist accepts it as
a fact of life.

3. Although every system of psychology sub-
scribes to the change imperative in its descriptive
or normative sense (see Chapter 1), no system of psy-
chology--with the possible exception of the dialectical approach (Riegel, 1978, 1979)--contains a realistic prescription for how psychological changes can
be implemented as part and parcel of its model of
psychological reality.   For instance, Skinnerian psychology is a virtual cookbook of descriptive change
mechanisms, but nowhere is it effectively specified
how they can be implemented; humanistic psychology
virtually institutionalizes the normative change imperative, but it is mute with respect to implementation of its goals.

In a realistic sense, psychology is just one institution among many competing institutions in soci-

ety with differential interests and goals; and an individual psychologist is just one professional among
other professionals with differential interests and
goals in a particular work setting. Psychology, as
an institution, especially in a democratic society,
must negotiate, compromise, and the like to accomplish its goals. An individual psychologist must
work within the "system"--pleasing the boss, acknow-
ledging the power structure and incentive situation,
adapting to various structural and legal restraints
on behavior, and the like--in order to successfully
carry out the job. The discipline of psychology, as
an intellectual, contentual entity, rarely takes cognizance of these factors.

     5. In an APA presidential address delivered by
George Miller (1969), the hope was expressed that
psychology would give itself away to the great unwashed. What Miller meant was that the discipline
should educate the general public in psychology so
that it could implement psychological principles and
knowledge for itself. This approach is not as laissez-faire as it appears. Minimally it would result
in a changed perception on the part of the public of
itself and in the execution of numerous self-help and
self-improvement programs.
HOW DOES PSYCHOLOGY DIFFER FROM OTHER DISCIPLINES
AND ENDEAVORS CONCERNED WITH THE NATURE AND CONDI-
TION OF THE HUMAN ORGANISM?

     Granted that not every system of psychology fo-
cuses on the human being exclusively, treats the individual person as the unit of analysis, or regards
humanity as associated with a characteristic condition, this is the basic perspective from which the

general public views the psychological enterprise.
Consequently, it is necessary to assess how psychology differs from other entities that also are concerned with the human organism.   These other entities
minimally include art, literature, theatre, religion,
philosophy, law, medicine, economics, sociology,
political science, and history. Psychology overlaps
with each of these or at least can be applied to each
of these. The nature of the interfacing is not our
concern here. Our focus is on how psychology supple-
ments or complements these entities.

ART, LITERATURE, THEATRE These are humanistic
pursuits and, as academic disciplines, usually are
referred to as humanities.   Artists, novelists, dram-
atists use their creations as vehicles for making
statements about life and reality, of which the human being can be one component.   Humanists are not
wedded to any specific view of human nature: they can
be either transcendentally or nontranscendentally oriented (see Scriven, 1964).

Psychology and a humanistic pursuit basically
differ in terms of form of expression, not content.
Humanists have much more freedom in defining and char-
acterizing the human organism.   They are not constrained by standard symbolization or logical criteria. A painting, novel, or play is supposed to be a
creation that uniquely and exhaustively captures the
"inner essence" of some facet of existence.   A humanistic creation not only informs and educates, but also is meant to be esthetically experienced or emo-
tionally felt.   A good painting, novel, or play is
the most efficient attitude and belief change device
ever devised.

The tenets of humanistic, existential psychology
and depth psychology are much more readily expressible
via a novel or play than by a dry, formal psychological tract because of their nonexperimental orientation. These systems are quite literally "literary"
psychologies that prefer to "paint" us and our condition in terms of our rich emotional complexity.

RELIGION Religion is one mode of assigning
meaning to life, the universe, or existence. The nature of humanity is resolved transcendentally: we are
a spiritual creature, with a relationship to a divine
being that has implications for virtually every facet
of our existence. For many people, religion either
functionally operates as a psychology or is allowed
to intrude on psychological truth. Conversely, for
a dedicated Skinnerian, psychology either functionally operates as a religion or is allowed to intrude
on theology. The relationship between psychology and
religion is exceedingly complex and multifaceted, and
either endeavor can serve as a model for the other
(Baillie, 1956).

Although Western psychology essentially is a non
theological enterprise and religion is not an exclusive or crucial component of the psychological universe, any system of psychology can incorporate religion in its dynamics. Cognitive, epistemological
psychology interfaces with religion at the level of
belief. An action system, such as Skinnerian behaviorism, can incorporate religion as a source of reinforcement or even punishment. Freudian depth psychology actually re-interprets religion in terms of
its psychodynamics. Humanistic psychology can focus
on religion as a type of goal or value. Dialectical

psychology can conceptualize religion as a factor in long term, structural, developmental change.

The basic difference between psychology and religion with respect to their relationship to the human organism is one of urgency. In the psychological approach, psychological reality is only one aspect of our existence; in the religious approach, religious reality exhausts reality or incorporates every other reality. In the context of co-model status, psychological malfunctioning is a mere inconvenience leading to some cognitive or emotional distress with no spiritual consequences, while a spiritual breakdown or a loss of faith can lead to dire psychological consequences, as well as eternal damnation.

PHILOSOPHY Philosophical psychology exists (for instance, Taylor, 1964); psychologically oriented philosophy exists (for instance, contemporary functionalism: see Fodor, 1981). Psychology, as most disciplines, can be construed as an applied philosophy in the sense that various philosophical beliefs determine whether psychology in general or a particular type of psychology is a viable intellectual endeavor. Since psychology must operate within the context of certain philosophical constraints, there is no fundamental difference between psychology and philosophy with regard to their respective views of human nature and the human condition.

The basic difference between psychology and philosophy resides at the evaluational level. Philosophical views of human nature stand on their own and are justified solely in terms of rational or logical arguments. Psychological views of human nature are indirectly testable via the evaluation techniques asso-

ciated with a given system. For instance, the behaviorist's view subsumes some experimentally testable
consequences; the humanist's view is a matter of intuitive understanding; the depth psychologist's view
achieves validity via internal consistency (see Chapter 8).

LAW The purpose of law, as a social institution,
is two-fold: (1) to affirm the ethical absolutes of
society and (2) to reduce the number of criminal acts
committed against society (see Sachar, 1963). The
first purpose entails moral condemnation and punishment of those who violate the ethical absolutes. The
second purpose involves the judicial penalty system
of deterrence and correction. Note that these two
purposes are not necessarily compatible: The application of retributive justice can interfere with meaningful rehabilitation efforts.

The function of law in society requires the legal establishment to take a transcendental view (see
Chapter 6). Specifically, it must be assumed that we
possess free will--our behavior is not determined--so
that we can be held responsible for our behavior.
Since we freely commit good or bad deeds, we freely
can be praised and rewarded or condemned and punished
The law only allows four classes of exceptions to the
doctrine of full criminal responsibility (Sachar,
1963): (1) self-defense, (2) duress, (3) juvenile
status, and (4) insanity. Note that in the last case
it still is assumed that the deed is freely committed
and not determined by some underlying pathology. Insane perpetrators are exempted from criminal responsibility only because they are incapable of moral
judgment and do not know the difference between right

and wrong.

The view held by the experimental psychology establishment, in general, and behaviorism, in particular, is diametrically opposed to the legal view.   In
nontranscendentalism, our behavior is assumed determined at some level of resolvability (see Chapter 6).
We cannot be held responsible for our actions.   It is
nonsensical to condemn an offender.   The offense per
se or the environmental context in which it occurs is
condemned, but only in the sense that they are
singled out as things that must change to prevent
repetition of the criminal deed.   In a behavioristic
context, responsibility is a social notion or a property of the overall environmental-behavioral system
(see Skinner, 1971).

The view of humanity associated with understanding psychology in general and humanism in particular
is similar to the legal view; however, the humanist's
stress on self-awareness, self-fulfillment, development of an authentic self, and the like is not germane to the legal context (Keen, 1975; Maslow, 1970).
The law's interest in a person strictly is instrumental in nature.   If a judge orders a convicted criminal to undergo some form of therapy or some enlightened rehabilitation program, it is only because the
law requires it.

A crime is a behavioral act.   The legal code really is a classification scheme for certain kinds of
behaviors.   The fact that the basic distinctions of
or in law evolved long before psychology became institutionalized means that an implicit common-sense
psychology has been reified by the legal establishment.   The law is not immutable.   As an instrument of

society, it does change to accommodate cultural, economic, and technological progress. But it will take
more than forensic psychology to effect a more equi-
table input of content psychology into the law. The
law possesses its own criterion of truth and acceptable evidence: the law determines and specifies who
is to be considered as an expert in matters of behavior. Currently, the legal establishment is much more
powerful and entrenched than the psychological establishment; and a psychologist or psychiatrist is allowed to operate in a legal context only at the dis-
cretion of the law.

MEDICINE Medicine is similar to law in the sense that it is a powerful social institution with distinct functions. Psychology is in the same position
with respect to the medical profession as it is with
respect to the legal establishment: The medical profession decides what and how many of the psychologist's activities are relevant to the practice of
medicine.

Medicine also is similar to psychology in the
sense that it constitutes a helping profession, and
the greatest degree of overlap between medicine and
psychology is in the area of psychiatry (Reisman,
1975). The medical profession is not committed to
any particular view of human nature over and above
its dealings with the organism as a biological creature whose various physiological systems are subject
to malfunctioning (Zilboorg, 1967). Some general
practitioners currently are becoming more aware of
their patients as psychological beings and are beginning to advocate the practice of holistic medicine
(see Engel, 1962; Szasz and Hollender, 1956). Psy-

chiatry historically emphasized biologically based
therapeutic intervention: for instance, electroshock
therapy and chemotherapy (see Chapter 10). It also
absorbed Freudian depth psychology, such that in the
United States at least most psychoanalysts also are
psychiatrists.

The basic differences between psychology and
psychiatry merely are a matter of degree, not kind,
and are institutional or professional in nature: they
involve "turf" identification and refinement. Therapy historically originated in the medical context;
only later did it also become a facet of the psychological universe and the primary component of clinical and counseling psychology. Psychology has a
richer tradition of basic psychological theorizing
from which to draw; psychiatry is committed to the
so-called medical model (see Chapter 10). A psychologist is better equipped to deal with abnormalities
of psychogenic origin; a psychiatrist is better equipped to deal with abnormalities of somatogenic origin.
A psychologist tends to place the human being in a
social or interactionist context; a psychiatrist primarily relates behavior to underlying biology. In
many current applied contexts, a team of psychiatrists and psychologists work on the same problem,
with a psychiatrist legally in charge.

ECONOMICS, SOCIOLOGY, POLITICAL SCIENCE, HISTORY
These disciplines constitute social sciences, among
which the discipline of psychology usually is grou-
ped. (Note: history is also classified as a humanity
in many academic institutions.) All these disciplines focus on the human organism and its condition,
typically from a third person perspective. Assuming

the validity of the notion of an ordered hierarchy of
sciences, psychology possesses a reducing relationship to each of these disciplines: they all make fre-
quent use of psychological interpretation and mechanisms.   The basic difference between psychology and
these other social sciences is subject matter, or
more technically, the content of observation.   These
disciplines primarily focus on behavior, but behavior
as resolved in a specialized context.   Economic, sociological, and political behavior are defined and
identified by reference to various systems that in
themselves are not usually regarded as reducible to
psychology: the economic system, culture and society,
and governmental and political structures.   History
involves a cross-cutting of all these disciplines,
specifically the change in economic, social, and political systems over time, although the discipline obviously subsumes more than this.

          ECONOMICS   There is no fundamental differ-
ence between an experimental system of psychology and
economics, except for the latter's focus on economic
behavior.   Classic economic theory presupposes the
existence of the "rational human being" (Katona,
1953; von Neumann and Morgenstern, 1947).   Microecon-
omic models currently are being used as analogues for
explaining performance in complex operant conditioning situations (for instance, see Staddon, 1980).

          SOCIOLOGY   The relationship between psychol-
ogy and sociology is very complex, with social psychology bridging the gap between the two disciplines.
It is very difficult to distinguish between a social
psychologist and a sociologist in any definitive way
(see Chapter 9).   Most of the distinctions between

psychology and sociology are arbitrary and idiosyncratic.

POLITICAL SCIENCE   There is no fundamental
difference between psychology and political science,
except for the latter's reputation of somehow being
less scientific. Political scientists are like as-
tronomers: it is impossible to bring the natural
phenomena of interest into the laboratory.

HISTORY   Although every social science
faces problems of orientation and perspective, these
seem to be particularly acute in historiography,
where a distinction must be made between the first
and third person view both in a current and past context (Berkhofer, 1969). History is not the mere
chronicling of physical events occurring in a temporal sequence. History cannot be written independently
of some interpretive scheme, as evidenced by the continual "reconstruction" of previously composed histories.

The practice of psychology basically is ahistor-
ical, except in certain applied contexts, such as
therapy. Psychology, with the possible exception of
depth and dialectical psychology, does not seek the
same kind of truth as history. The psychologist's
view of the human organism is only one aspect of a
historian's view.

The professional historian composes descriptive
narrative. One type of narrative focuses on the life
of an individual personage and is called biography.
In a biographical context, there is no basic distinction between historical description and the approach
taken by understanding or depth psychology. The last
two decades have seen an appreciable increase in the

construction of psychohistories, the analysis of famous historical figures from a latter-day depth psychology perspective (see Runyan, 1982).

The experimental systems can serve as objects of
historical analysis, but not vice versa.

IS PSYCHOLOGY RELEVANT FOR ETHICS AND MORALITY?

The answer to this question depends on whether
one takes a strict or liberal view of ethics (Dyck,
1977). In the strict view, the occurrence of virtually any instance of behavior is an ethical event or
has ethical connotations. In this context, any system of psychology dealing with behavior is implicitly
an ethical system.

The possible relevance of psychology for ethics
is a more meaningful query in the context of the liberal view, where behavioral activity per se does not
possess automatic ethical significance. In this context, a distinction must be made between means and
ends.

It is the function of ethics to postulate and
justify worthy goals. This process is almost universally regarded as metaphysical in nature, not subject
to scientific analysis and verification (for instance,
Kendler, 1981). Specification of what should or
ought to be, the ideal state of affairs, should not
be an empirical exercise. Otherwise certain goals
might be immediately dismissed as being unattainable,
and the notion of should or ought would become degenerate.

The specification and evaluation of means are
another matter entirely. Given a predetermined set
of worthy goals, it is considered appropriate to approach the issue of means empirically (Kendler, 1981).

What is the best, most effective, or most efficient
way of achieving a certain end? This is an empirical
question and can be assessed in the context of some
conceptual approach to behavior. A model of psychological reality serves as an ideal context for evaluating various alternative means of achieving a certain goal.

In an extended series of events, means can operate as subgoals or ends in themselves. No contradic-
tion is involved if it is realized that a subgoal
can be evaluated either as a means, or as an end, or
as both, contingent on the specific situation or problem.

Action systems, especially descriptive behaviorism, are explicitly designed to implement the means
of achieving certain goals. It is not generally realized that they are not designed to be the source of
worthy goals. Both Watson (1925) and Skinner (1971)
adhered to standardized American goals and values.
The contribution of dialectical psychology to ethics
is analogous to that of an action system, except it
is also possible for goals to be dialectically determined. Epistemological psychology, in general, is
not directly relevant for ethics; however, Gestalt
psychology, Piagetian structural psychology, and cognitive behaviorism can be used to evaluate means.

Humanistic psychology, as a nonexperimental approach, is wont to postulate worthy end goals. Recall from Chapter 5 that the value system inherent
in humanism is indistinguishable from that of Christianity. The other significant nonexperimental approach, depth psychology, often is used to delimit
goals: the psychic determinism inherent in Freudian

psychodynamics constrains human potentiality. Neither
humanism nor depth psychology can be meaningfully
used to implement the means of achieving certain
goals.

Both the psychological content of a system and
its view of human nature can be misinterpreted, mis-
applied, or exploited for the wrong ends: Skinnerian
radical behaviorism and Freudian psychoanalysis especially are subject to this.

DOES PSYCHOLOGY HAVE TO BE TAKEN INTO ACCOUNT IN ANY
RATIONAL CONSIDERATION OF THE MEANING OF LIFE?

There is no absolute yes or no answer to this
query. It certainly cannot be argued that psychology
is relevant in any normative sense. On the other
hand, at a descriptive level, psychological knowledge
does provide some input into a consideration of the
meaning of life:

1. Structuralism demonstrates that we possess an
active mental life.

2. Functionalism makes consciousness efficacious
and reminds us of our biological status.

3. Gestalt psychology originated the notion of
the subjective, psychological environment in which
each of us lives.

4. Watsonian behaviorism weds us to a specific
physicalistic system.

5. Skinnerian behaviorism presumes we can operate on and change our environment.

6. Cognitive behaviorism postulates that human
mentation is an emergent phenomenon.

7. Piagetian structural psychology resolves human mentation in terms of a fixed sequence of developmental, logical stages.

8. Depth psychology reveals that a seething psychological universe exists within each of us.

9. Humanistic psychology emphasizes our self-awareness and solidifies the Gestalt thesis of private, phenomenal worlds.

10. Dialectical psychology makes us a dialectically determined point in a combined historical-developmental space.

The realization that life must have a meaning more than likely originates in our self-consciousness. In this context, any rational account of the meaning of life must reconcile three fundamental psychological propositions:

1. We are both materially composed as some kind of biological organism and functionally characterizable as some kind of emergent being.

2. We possess a rich inner life, one of both cognitive and emotional experience.

3. We have an outer existence by which we constitute an active component of some kind of surrounding physical universe.

CHAPTER 13

FINAL PERSPECTIVE

The purpose of this chapter is to present some final
perspective on the system construction process by
(1) considering some historical statements relative
to the popularity and use of the four orientations
introduced in Chapter 3, (2) using the language function as a comparative reference point, (3) comment-
ing on "critical theory," as an example of spatial
pluralism, and (4) stating some personal opinions
with respect to the most promising directions for
future psychology to take.

FOUR ORIENTATIONS

The notion of orientation is central to the system construction process because it is associated
with the content of observation and permissible methodology employed by a system. The four orientations abstracted in Chapter 3--objective, subjective,
mixed or quasi-objective, and combined--divide into
two natural subclasses: (1) homogeneous and (2) heterogeneous.

The classic objective orientation underlying
descriptive behaviorism and the classic subjective
orientation, as represented by contemporary understanding psychology, constitute rather homogeneous,
mirror image approaches to the construction of psy-

chological reality.   Both orientations are strictly
monistic, but of opposite varieties; each orientation
is either explicitly transcendental or explicitly
nontranscendental.

The mixed and combined orientations, in which
objectivity and subjectivity are both involved, constitute less extreme, but more heterogeneous, approaches to the construction of psychological reality.
These orientations subsume the only contemporary systems that are both mentalistic and implicitly nontranscendental.

System construction efforts over the past century are characterized by two interrelated trends
(Rychlak, 1977): (1) a preference cycling over time
between the opposite poles (subjective, objective) of
the homogeneous subclass, and (2) a relatively constant, but high degree of interest in the heterogeneous subclass, primarily the mixed orientation.   In
this context, four conceptual summary statements are
relevant.

1. Every classical school of psychology, whether
experimental or not, used the subjective or mixed orientation until the advent of Watsonian descriptive
behaviorism.

2. The dominance of the strict objective orientation, associated with descriptive behaviorism, is
now over.   The newest attempts at constructing psychological reality involve either the mixed or combined orientation.

3. The subjective orientation survives only in
the context of the contemporary humanistic approach.

4. The mixed orientation has been the most popular and durable approach for constructing psycholog-

ical reality.

SUBJECTIVE, OBJECTIVE POLARITY   The creators of
the initial systems of academic psychology--structur-
alism, act psychology, Gestalt psychology (with respect to perceptual consciousness), and functionalism
(with respect to mental activities)--did not know
that their systems were subjective.   These systems
amounted to epistemological psychology, in which both
the content and function of consciousness served as
natural objects of interest.   The basic polarity between subjective and objective systems did not develop until the ascendance of descriptive behaviorism,
the epitome of an action psychology.   But a purely
objective system denies any uniqueness to the human
organism and removes any special status from psychological phenomena: every kind of matter behaves.   To
restore some uniqueness to psychological reality, the
subjective orientation was intentionally reintroduced
in the context of humanism.   The focus was on consciousness again: not every kind of matter presumably
possesses consciousness.   This time the focus was on
consciousness, as awareness or feelings.   Self-consciousness was irrelevant in the classical subjective
systems; self-awareness is the central feature of
contemporary understanding psychology.

MIXED ORIENTATION POPULARITY   The mixed orientation underlies depth psychology, functionalism (as a
whole), logical behaviorism, genetic-epistemological
psychology, and cognitive behaviorism.   The preval-
ence and longevity of this orientation primarily is
due to its balanced approach to psychological reality.
In this orientation the psychological universe consists of both observables and unobservables, with

many degrees of freedom with respect to the locus of
the latter. It provides a vehicle for constructing
a psychological reality with epiphenomena continuous
with the physical sciences and loci of causation
unique to living organisms. Its content of observation allows the quantification of objective behavioral events and the postulation of subjective psychological causative factors. The mixed orientation
serves as a convenient reference point for interpreting the significance of the more homogeneous objective and subjective orientations.

In an objective system, the elements of the content of observation, stimuli and responses, are both
physical events. The objective orientation necessarily reduces psychological reality to an aspect of
physical reality.

In the contemporary use of the subjective orientation, each element of the content of observation,
the content of awareness and the nature of the organism's psychological world, is a nonphysical and indigenously psychological entity. The contemporary
subjective orientation necessarily creates a psychological reality divorced from physical reality.

Historically only the mixed orientation generates a psychological reality composed of both physical and nonphysical elements. The recent use of the
combined orientation to construct dialectical psychology represents another attempt to unite the objective and subjective orientations, creating a psychological reality that is at least continuous with
those characteristic of the mixed orientation.
THE LANGUAGE FUNCTION

Recall from Chapter 1 that the only reason psy-

chology exists is the language function. It would be
instructive to compare how each of the four orientations interprets the language function in terms of
the dominant contemporary approach associated with
each orientation.

OBJECTIVE: SKINNERIAN RADICAL BEHAVIORISM Skinner (1957, 1974) focuses on verbal behavior, not
language in the linguistic sense of the term. He
submits verbal behavior to the same kind of functional analysis that is used for strictly physical, motor operants. A given utterance is assigned to a
specific class of verbal activity and is related to
its controlling stimulus condition or reinforcement
contingency. For instance, Skinner (1957) makes a
basic distinction between a mand and a tact. A mand
essentially is a request. A tact is some kind of
descriptive remark. The source of a mand is open-ended, but can only be reinforced by procurement of the
content of the mand: for instance, "Please give me a
glass of milk." The content of a tact is tied to
specific physical conditions, but is unrestricted
with respect to reinforcement: for instance, "It sure
is a nice day." The tact is Skinner's link to the
description of the content of one's perceptual or introspective consciousness, and the expression of
self-awareness involves tacting responses about tacting responses.

Skinner's analysis of verbal behavior has not
led to much research activity and has been bitterly
attacked by Noam Chomsky (1959), but it has never
been surpassed by any succeeding behavioristic analysis. It is a brillantly conceived and executed thesis that has never really been appreciated by Skin-

ner's more linguistic and literary oriented contem-
poraries (for instance, Fodor, Bever, and Garrett,
1974).

SUBJECTIVE: HUMANISM; PHENOMENOLOGY Phenomenologically based systems do not analyze verbal behavior or language in the sense of specifying relevant
mechanisms. (Humanistic psychology is mute with respect to mechanisms in general.) For the humanist,
such as Rogers (1961) or Keen (1975), language is the
primary mode of expression of the content of one's
consciousness. Recall that humanistic psychology
primarily deals with response or response-inferred
constructs, and the vast majority of these involve
language responses. The most elaborately constructed
psychology based almost exclusively on language responses was structuralism (Wundt, 1896; Titchener,
1898), which eventually was discarded because the
content of consciousness cannot be meaningfully resolved strictly in terms of itself.

MIXED: COGNITIVE BEHAVIORISM Most cognitive behaviorists, such as Anderson (1980), focus on language as a component of mentation. Language is treated
as a linguistic entity and consists of various subsystems, such as phonemics, morphemics, the lexicon,
syntax, and grammar. The ability to decode and en-
code language is assumed to represent some underlying
linguistic competence. Although not a behaviorist,
Chomsky (1968) is credited with making contemporary
cognitive research on language possible by distinguishing between linguistic performance and competence.
Chomsky explicitly assumes that the human being, and
only the human being, is biologically predisposed,
or prewired, to learn the different aspects of langu-

age by induction from samples of speech in the surrounding verbal community.   Although Chomsky's original stress on syntax and grammar has given way to a
current focus on semantics, his approach has inspired
a voluminous amount of research on language acquisition in the child (see Roger Brown, 1970, 1973).   The
psychology of language currently entails a technical
cognitive subspecialty called psycholinguistics.

COMBINED: DIALECTICAL PSYCHOLOGY   Language is a
crucial component of dialectical psychology: (1) It
is the usual medium of exchange involved in any short
term dialogue; and (2) it is the primary link between
the individual organism and its surrounding culture
with respect to long term, developmental changes.
Riegel (1978, 1979) postulates three different types
of language systems, proto-language, token language,
and transaction language, the last of which is assumed to be dialectically determined.   In dialectical psychology, language, like consciousness, is both
a social and socially sourced phenomenon.   Riegel
uses the monetary system as an analogue for language.
Speech is treated as a good/commodity produced by la-
bor.   These goods, i.e., sentences, can operate as
capital and serve as the basis of further production.

CONCEPTUAL SUMMARY   Each of the four orientations to the construction of psychological reality
taps a different aspect of the language function:

1. The objective orientation treats language as
a real-time, real-space output system controlled by
physical variables.

2. The subjective orientation formalizes the
general public's view of language as a method of expression.

3. The mixed orientation relates language to cognitive functioning in general and the notion of linguistic competence in particular.

4. The combined orientation views language as a
component of the overall dialectical process and
gives it an essentially social interpretation.

Given the diversity of psychology's treatment of
the language function itself, it is no wonder that
the overall discipline is pluralistic. Note that
these different interpretations do not contradict
each other, but perform a complementary function.

SPATIAL PLURALISM: CRITICAL THEORY

Although psychology possesses a distinctive national character and cultural relativism helps sustain the vitality of the discipline (see Chapter 11),
psychologists operating in different countries and
language spheres usually are unaware of those occa-
sions when their respective theoretical efforts con-
verge and really amount to the same thing. This results in an accidental or incidental spatial pluralism.

The best contemporary example of spatial pluralism involves so-called critical theory, characteristic of Habermas (1972, 1973), Horkheimer (1972), and
other members of the Frankfurt school of social philosophy. Critical theory amounts to a combined epistemological and sociological indictment of contemporary social science theory and practice that has implications for psychology. In critical theory, the
human being is not treated as a potential social object, or physical thing, amenable to scientific analysis; nor is it assumed that current cultural practices and institutional structures are designed for

our enlightened functioning. For Habermas, the construction of a social reality or the implementation
of a social practice is not a value-free process.
Social truth or knowledge really is a matter of ne-
gotiation among theorists with different constituent
interests and ideologies. The social practices and
institutions that derive from nonnegotiated truth
tend to reflect the ideology of the current political
establishment, maintain the status quo, and exploit
people.

CRITICAL PSYCHOLOGY Within the last fifteen
years, Sarason (1981) in the United States, Ingleby
(1972, 1974, 1980) in Great Britain, and Holzkamp
(1970, 1972, 1973, 1983) in Germany have severely
criticized the state of contemporary psychology from
a critical theory perspective; and their collective
efforts can be referred to as critical psychology.
The American, British, and German versions of critical psychology developed independently of each other,
with virtually no mutual influence. These critical
analyses have a distinct sociological bent and place
the organism in a dialectical arrangement with the
surrounding physical and social, or political, environment. Critical psychology possesses Marxist (1867)
elements, and many of its aspects are subsumable by
Riegel's dialectical psychology (see Chapter 5). Ingleby and Holzkamp, but not Sarason, consciously operate in the Marxist tradition. But Freud's (1939,
1949) view of the human psyche serves as the usual
reference point for critical psychological theorizing, primarily because it is constructed around the
organism's own interests and is not easily exploitable by the entrenched political establishment (in

Ingleby's (1980) view).

As with critical theory, the different versions
of critical psychology possess intertwined and insep-
arable epistemological and social action components.
Although the specific content psychology associated
with each version of critical psychology differs, the
approach as a whole regards the human organism as an
agent or enacter, generating behavior in a meaningful
contextual framework: the human being is not merely
a mechanical automaton, subject to inexorable physical, causal processes. One of Ingleby's favorite
terms is reification. This is used to describe what
happens when the meaningful activity of the human organism (as defined by some interpretive structure
such as psychoanalysis) is assumed to be the mere
outcome of an interplay of causal forces (as occurs
in behaviorism). The social action, or exploitation,
associated with the entrenched political establishment and its overweaning ideology is implemented and
maintained through this process of reification.

SARASON Sarason argues that contemporary
academic psychology is misdirected and ineffective
in the real world because it is nondialectical in its
approach to the human organism and its relationship
to society. He condemns the experimental psychologist for being the unwitting stooge of the governmental establishment by succumbing to the allure of fed-
eral research grants that maintain the status quo.
This explains why so many psychologists currently are
disillusioned with respect to the worth and viability
of their discipline.

INGLEBY Ingleby analyzes the ideological
basis of psychology and its effect on psychological

practice, specifically in the contexts of testing and
the IQ, personality and learning, mental health, and
child development. In each case he finds the discipline repressing the fact that an underlying ideology,
derivative of the political establishment, determines
both psychological theorizing and practice. In traditional behaviorism and humanism (linear or nondialectical approaches), political influences merely are
treated as sources of extraneous variance: if properly controlled in research, they presumably do not
yield biased, culture-bound truth. Ingleby's basic
thesis is that no ideological-free truth exists, such
that its denial automatically generates a politically
exploited organism. For Ingleby, truth is the joint
product of evidential input and the organism's information processing capacity. The latter inherently
encompasses the beliefs and assumptions of the dominant political order, i.e., its ideology.

HOLZKAMP Holzkamp is the leading figure of
the Berlin school of critical psychology, an explicit
attempt to create a latter-day Marxist-based psychological reality. At a structural level, the human
organism is conceptualized as the product of three
kinds of historical processes: phylogenesis, ontogen-
esis, and societal evolution. At a dynamic level,
the human organism is assumed to be in the continual
process of both creating and being created by an objective physical reality, the ultimate goal of which
is a more incisive control over the conditions of existence. Holzkamp's Marxism is explicitly shown by
his belief that this goal can only be realistically
attained by co-operation with others. Holzkamp and
his students have re-interpreted such traditional

psychological processes as perception, motivation, personality development, and therapy in this neo-Marxist critical framework.

SPATIAL PLURALISM IN PERSPECTIVE   Spatial plural-ism, as exemplified by the case of critical psychol-ogy, is more than a mere operational communication problem.   It demonstrates the shallowness of our dis-cipline's educational efforts and our laissez-faire attitude toward what constitutes a well-rounded psy-chologist.   If psychology, both as theory and prac-tice, is regarded as a distinctly social and ideo-logical endeavor, it is incumbent upon us to be aware of the different (but sometimes really the same) con-structions of psychological reality originating in different political and cultural contexts.

SOME PERSONAL PRESCRIPTIONS

For many years it was believed that an Einstein analogue would come along and rescue psychology from its pluralism (Koch, 1975).   This did not happen. The inability to attach an absolute defining property to an event deemed psychological in nature and the multiplicity of orientations from which psychological events can be studied preclude any final resolution of psychology's fragmented conceptual state.

Psychology is no longer characterizable strictly in terms of specific substantive content areas and processes.   Even a cursory review of any recent issue of the American Psychologist or the APA Monitor re-veals that psychology now basically is an adjudica-tive endeavor.   The discipline fundamentally deals with a person's psychological status and rights.   It basically concerns what psychologists should or should not be doing.   It is as if psychology is in

the process of fine tuning its relationship to society and the surrounding culture. Today's issues are
ethical, applied, or jurisdictional ones, not conceptual or content ones (McNamara and Barclay, 1982).
New psychological knowledge is being created by the
attempt to rectify past inequities with respect to
elitism, racism, sexism, and the like, not by new in-
sights with respect to human nature. It is as if the
conduction of psychology has become a sociological
endeavor. There is no such thing as a neutral psychological fact anymore. Today a psychological statement is some kind of social action statement. For
instance, thirty years ago such Hullian concepts as
habit strength, behavioral oscillation, and excita-
tory potential constituted the prototypical psychological concepts (Hull, 1952); today they are viewed
as valueless because they do not interface in any
significant way with an individual's psychological
status or rights.

        In this context, three prescriptions about sys-
tem construction seem particularly relevant for the
future of psychology.

        PRESCRIPTION ONE Psychology primarily should be
a descriptive, as opposed to explanatory, endeavor.
This prescription may seem to be a step backward.
But not really. Remember we are focusing here on
what psychology can do and do well. Psychologists
are specially trained to observe behavior, external-
izations of consciousness, and the milieu in which
these occur. Of course observation does not occur in
a conceptual vacuum or in the absence of some interpretive framework. But the purpose of observation
should not be the validation of some underlying the-

oretical scheme.

Emphasis on description puts a premium on the
objective and subjective orientations. Watsonian and
Skinnerian behaviorism are customarily recognized as
descriptive endeavors. But humanistic, phenomenological psychology also primarily is a descriptive enter-
prize. What is being described is the content of
one's emotional consciousness. Descriptive behaviorism exclusively deals with observables; humanism
deals with subject matter that is not immediately relatable to underlying theoretical entities.

High level theoretical explanation, in the traditional scientific sense, is primarily associated
with the mixed orientation: for instance, logical behaviorism, cognitive behaviorism, and Gestalt psychology. If the history of psychology over the past
one hundred years provides any lessons, it is that
general high level psychological explanation is an
elusive, if not unattainable, goal. The human being
can do and experience an infinite number of things
in infinitely many ways. Current theories are complex and sophisticated, but of such limited domain,
that they are irrelevant for policy or implementation
decisions. Sophisticated mathematical models and
computer simulation programs are fine for laboratory
research, but they have little or no relevance for
behavior in the natural environment. For instance,
when confronted by some learning problem in a classroom situation, psychologists do not appeal to a model or theory for guidance; rather they must deal with
the situation at a descriptive level. The problem
does not happen because the theoretical entities encompassed by some theory break down or malfunction--

after all, they do not even necessarily exist. The
problem happens because some internal or external
physical event has gone awry.

In a day when behavior and conscious experience
are mere semantic labels and when both mental and
physical events are functionally defined or materially composed entities, the descriptive approach to
system construction is a much more efficient and re-
sourceful strategy of representing psychological reality.

PRESCRIPTION TWO In order to give psychology
away to the great unwashed (see Chapter 12), pure
behavioral or phenomenological description is not
sufficient. Psychological phenomena, as output, do
require some form of interpretation or resolution.
But traditional psychological explanation is not germane. This is what makes Freudian depth psychology
so popular, although it is useless as a predictive or
control technique.

The general public sees behavior occurring in a
meaningful context; they view behavior as goal directed. The great unwashed demand common-sensical, mentalistic, dualistic explanatory entities. Psychology
should strive to formalize these kinds of entities.
There is nothing wrong with intention, purpose, expectation, goal, even the state of knowing as interpretive devices if they are properly defined and sim-
ulatable by some computer program. The subsystems of
an organism, such as perception, memory, inductive
reasoning, language generation, and the like, can be
resolved in isolation as mechanical or functional
systems; but the behavioral or experiential output of
the organism as a whole is best interpreted at a con-

structive, emergent level in terms of a general eclectic understanding approach. In a sense, the humanists and dialectical psychologists are correct:
the entities that are used to resolve human behavior
and experience must be self-validating or possess
face validity.

PRESCRIPTION THREE As a consequence of the
first two prescriptions, psychology's object of direct observation is not really a pure behavioral act
per se or a pure conscious content per se. It is
true that these entities must be observed, measured,
and classified; but in and of themselves they are
nothing. It is what they represent that is important.
Again we are back to the humanistic notion of meaning. The psychological meaning of an act or experiential event is not an objective part of the situation. It is imposed by the observer. This is what
makes psychology a participant in the overall cross-
classification process (see Chapter 2) and a relevant
discipline in the first place. Future psychology
must attempt to construct rational or logical representational schemes so that the properties of psychological phenomena can be formalized and evaluated.

The ultimate problem facing psychology today is
not whether it is scientific or nonscientific, nomothetic or idiographic, objective or subjective, behaviorally oriented or experientially oriented, or
emergent or reducible. The basic problem is whether
psychology's approach to cross-classification has
significant consequences for a conceptual understanding and interventionist reconstruction of the human
organism.

CONCEPTUAL SUMMARY The three prescriptions can

be summarized as follows:

    1. Psychology primarily should be a descriptive endeavor, focusing on behavioral occurrences and ex-periential episodes as manifested in a given contex-tual milieu.

    2. Acceptable explanation of these entities must involve a constructional level of reality that is congruent with the general public's conception of psychological determination.

    3. Entirely new rational or logical analyses of the process of assigning psychological meaning/reali-ty to behavior and experience must be performed.

    Ideally, the result of these prescriptions will be a psychology with real-space and real-time objects of interest resolvable in terms of an emergent frame-work that justifies the discipline's participation in the cross-classificational enterprize.

REFERENCES

Abel, T. The operation called Verstehen. American Journal of Sociology, 1948, 54, 211-218.

Adler, A. Practice and theory of individual psychology, 1909-1920. Paterson, N.J.: Littlefield, Adams, 1959.

Akhilananda, S. Hindu psychology. London: Routledge, 1953.

Allport, G.W. Becoming: Basic considerations for a psychology of personality. New Haven, Conn.: Yale University Press, 1955.

Allport, G.W. Traits revisited. American Psychologist, 1966, 21, 1-10.

Amsel, A. The role of frustrative nonreward in noncontinuous reward situations. Psychological Bulletin, 1958, 55, 102-119.

Amsel, A. Frustrative nonreward in partial reinforcement and discrimination learning: Some recent history and a theoretical extension. Psychological Review, 1962, 69, 306-328.

Anderson, J. Cognitive psychology and its implications. San Francisco: Freeman, 1980.

Angell, J.R. Psychology: An introductory study of the structure and function of human consciousness. New York: Holt, 1904.

Angell, J.R. The province of functional psychology. Psychological Review, 1907, 14, 61-91.

Angell, J.R. Imageless thought. Psychological Review, 1911, 18, 295-323.

Armstrong, D.M. The nature of mind. Brisbane: University of Queensland Press, 1980.

Atkinson, R.C. A stochastic model for rote serial learning. Psychometrika, 1957, 22, 87-96.

Attneave, F. Some informational aspects of visual perception. Psychological Review, 1954, 61, 183-193.

Baillie, J. The interpretation of religion. New York: Abingdon Press, 1956.

Bandura, A. Principles of behavior modification. New York: Holt, Rinehart, and Winston, 1964.

Bandura, A. Behavioral psychotherapy. Scientific American, 1967, 216, 78-87.

Bandura, A. Social learning theory. Englewood Cliffs, N.J.: Prentice-Hall, 1977.

Belkin, G.S. Contemporary psychotherapies. Chicago: Rand McNally 1980.

Bellak, L. The T.A.T., C.A.T., and S.A.T. in clinical use (3rd ed.). New York: Grune and Stratton, 1975.

Ben-David, J., and Collins, R. Social factors in the origin of a new science: The case of psychology. American Sociological Review, 1966, 31, 451-465.

Berger, P.A. Medical treatment of mental illness. Science, 1978, 200, 974-981.

Berkeley, G. A treatise concerning the principles of human knowledge. Dublin: Pepyat, 1710.

Berkhofer, Jr., R.F. A behavioral approach to historical analysis. New York: Free Press, 1969.

Berlyne, D.E. Structure and direction in thinking. New York: Wiley, 1965.

Bernheim, H. Hypnotisme, suggestion, psychothérapie. Paris: Doin, 1891.

Binet, A. L'étude expérimentale de l'intelligence. Paris: Schleicher, 1903.

Binet, A., and Simon, T. A method of measuring the development of the intelligence of young children (3rd ed.). Chicago: Medical Books, 1913.

Bleuler, E. Dementia praecox: Or the group of schizophrenias,
    1911. New York: International Universities Press, 1950.

Block, N. Troubles with functionalism. In C.W. Savage (Ed.),
    Perception and cognition: Issues in the foundations of
    psychology. Minnesota studies in the philosophy of science
    (Vol. 9). Minneapolis: University of Minnesota Press, 1978.

Block, N. What is functionalism? In N. Block (Ed.), Readings in
    philosophy of psychology (Vol. 1). Cambridge, Mass.: Har-
    vard University Press, 1980.

Block, N., and Fodor, J.A. What psychological states are not.
    Philosophical Review, 1972, 81, 159-182.

Blumenthal, A. A reappraisal of Wilhelm Wundt. American Psychol-
    ogist, 1975, 30, 1081-1088.

Boden, M. Artificial intelligence and natural man. New York:
    Harvester Press, 1977.

Boden, M. Minds and mechanisms: Philosophical psychology and
    computational models. Ithaca: Cornell University Press,
    1981.

Boring, E.G. The stimulus-error. American Journal of Psychology,
    1921, 32, 449-471.

Boring, E.G. A history of experimental psychology (2nd ed.).
    New York: Appleton-Century-Crofts, 1950.

Boring, E.G. A history of introspection. Psychological Bulletin,
    1953, 50, 169-189.

Boring, E.G. The trend toward mechanism. Proceedings of the
    American Philosophical Society, 1964, 108, 451-454.

Bower, G.H. Choice-point behavior. In R.R. Bush and W.K. Estes
    (Eds.), Studies in mathematical learning theory. Stanford:
    Stanford University Press, 1959.

Bower, G.H. An association model for response and training var-
    iables in paired-associate learning. Psychological Review,
    1962, 69, 34-53.

Brainerd, C.J. The stage question in cognitive-developmental
    theory. The Behavioral and Brain Sciences, 1978, 2, 173-
    213.

368   REFERENCES

Brentano, F. Psychologie vom empirischen Standpunkte. Leipzig:
Duncker, 1874.

Breuer, J., and Freud, S. Studien über Hysterie. Leipzig: Deuticke, 1895.

Brodbeck, M. (Ed.). Readings in the philosophy of the social
sciences. New York: Macmillan, 1968.

Bronowski, J., and Mazlish, B. The Western intellectual tradition. New York: Harper and Row, 1960.

Brown, R. (Robert). Explanation in social science. Chicago: Aldine, 1970.

Brown, R. (Roger). Psycholinguistics. New York: Free Press, 1970

Brown, R. (Roger). A first language: The early stages. Cambridge
Mass.: Harvard University Press, 1973.

Bunge, M. The mind-body problem: A psychobiological approach.
Oxford, England: Pergamon, 1980.

Burt, C. Mental and scholastic tests. London: King, 1921.

Burt, C. The inheritance of mental abilities. American Psychologist, 1958, 13, 1-15.

Bush, R.R., and Mosteller, F. A mathematical model for simple
learning. Psychological Review, 1951, 58, 313-322.

Bush, R.R., and Mosteller, F. Stochastic models of learning.
New York: Wiley, 1955.

Carnap, R. The unity of science. London: Kegan Paul, 1934.

Carnap, R. Psychology in physical language. In A.J. Ayer (Ed.),
Logical positivism. New York: Free Press, 1959.

Carnap, R. Logical structure of the world. Berkeley: University
of California Press, 1967.

Carr, H.A. Psychology: A study of mental activity. New York:
Longmans, Green, 1925.

Cattell, J.McK. Mental tests and measurements. Mind, 1890, 15,
373-381.

Cattell, J.McK. The advance of psychology. Science, 1898, 8,
533-541.

Charcot, J.M. Leçons sur les maladies du système nerveux. 3 vols.
    Paris: Delahaye, 1872-1887.

Chein, I. The science of behavior and the image of man. New York:
    Basic Books, 1972.

Chomsky, N. Review of Verbal Behavior, by B. F. Skinner.
    Language, 1959, 35, 26-58.

Chomsky, N. Language and mind. New York: Harcourt, 1968.

Churchill, W. Homosexual behavior among males: A cross-cultural
    and cross species investigation. New York: Hawthorn Books,
    1967.

Churchland, P.M. Matter and consciousness. Cambridge, Mass.:
    MIT Press, 1984.

Clark, K.E. America's psychologists: A survey of a growing pro-
    fession. Washington, D.C.: American Psychological Associa-
    tion, 1957.

Coleman, J.C., Butcher, J.N., and Carson, R.C. Abnormal psychol-
    ogy and modern life (6th ed.). Glenview, Ill.: Scott,
    Foresman, 1980.

Comte, A. Cours de philosophie positive. 6 vols. Paris: Bach-
    elier, 1830-1842.

Correnti, A. A comparison of behaviorism and psychoanalysis
    with existentialism. Journal of Existentialism, 1965, 5,
    379-388.

Craighead, W.E., Kazdin, A.E., and Mahoney, M.J. Behavior modi-
    fication: Principles, issues, and applications (2nd ed.).
    Boston: Houghton Mifflin, 1981.

Cummins, R. Functional analysis. Journal of Philosophy, 1975,
    72, 741-764.

Cummins, R. Psychological explanation. Cambridge, Mass.: MIT
    Press, 1983.

Darwin, C. Origin of species by means of natural selection or
    the preservation of favored races in the struggle for life.
    London: Murray, 1859.

Darwin, C. The descent of man and selection in relation to sex.
    2 vols. London: Murray, 1871.

Day, W.F. On certain similarities between the Philosophical In-
    vestigations of Ludwig Wittgenstein and the operationism
    of B. F. Skinner. Journal of the Experimental Analysis of
    Behavior, 1969, 12, 489-506.

Deese, J. Psychology as science and art. New York: Harcourt
    Brace Jovanovich, 1972.

Dennett, D. Artificial intelligence as philosophy and psycholo-
    gy. In D. Dennett, Brainstorms. Cambridge, Mass.: MIT
    Press, 1978a.

Dennett, D. Toward a cognitive theory of consciousness. In C.W.
    Savage (Ed.), Perception and cognition: Issues in the
    foundations of psychology. Minnesota studies in the phil-
    osophy of science (Vol. 9). Minneapolis: University of
    Minnesota Press, 1978b.

Descartes, R. Les passions de l'âme. Paris: Loyson, 1650.

Descartes, R. The treatise of man, 1662. Cambridge, Mass.:
    Harvard University Press, 1972.

Deutsch, J.A. The cholinergic synapse and the site of memory.
    Science, 1971, 174, 788-794.

Dewey, J. Psychology. New York: American Book, 1886.

Dewey, J. The reflex arc concept in psychology. Psychological
    Review, 1896, 3, 357-370.

Dilthey, W. Gesammelte Schriften. Leipzig: Teubner, 1924.

Donaldson, M. Children's minds. New York: Norton, 1978.

Dulany, D.C. The place of hypotheses and intention: An analysis
    of verbal control in verbal conditioning. In C.W. Eriksen
    (Ed.), Behavior and awareness. Durham, N.C.: Duke Univer-
    sity Press, 1962.

Duncker, K. On problem solving. Psychological Monographs, 1945,
    58 (5).

Dyck, A. On human care: An introduction to ethics. Nashville:
    Abingdon Press, 1977.

Engel, G.L. A unified concept of health and disease. In G.L.
    Engel, Psychological development in health and disease.
    Philadelphia: Saunders, 1962.

Erikson, E.H. Childhood and society (2nd ed.). New York: Norton,
     1963.

Erwin, E. Behavior therapy: Scientific, philosophical, and moral
     foundations. Cambridge, England: Cambridge University Press,
     1978.

Estes, W.K. Toward a statistical theory of learning. Psycholog-
     ical Review, 1950, 57, 94-107.

Estes, W.K. Learning theory and the new mental chemistry.
     Psychological Review, 1960, 67, 207-223.

Evans, R.B. E. B. Titchener and his lost system. Journal of the
     History of the Behavioral Sciences, 1972, 8, 168-180.

Eysenck, H.J. The effects of psychotherapy: An evaluation.
     Journal of Consulting Psychology, 1952, 16, 319-324.

Fancher, R.E. Psychoanalytic psychology: The development of
     Freud's thought. New York: Norton, 1973.

Fechner, G.T. Elemente der Psychophysik. Leipzig: Breitkopf and
     Härtel, 1860.

Ferster, C.B. Is operant conditioning getting bored with behav-
     ior? A review of Honig and Staddon's Handbook of Operant
     Behavior. Journal of the Experimental Analysis of Behavior,
     1978, 29, 347-349.

Ferster, C.B., and Skinner, B.F. Schedules of reinforcement.
     New York: Appleton-Century-Crofts, 1957.

Flanagan, Jr., O.J. The science of the mind. Cambridge, Mass.:
     MIT Press, 1984.

Flavell, J.H. The developmental psychology of Jean Piaget.
     Princeton, N.J.: Van Nostrand, 1963.

Fodor, J.A. Special sciences, or the disunity of science as a
     working hypothesis. Synthese, 1974, 28, 97-115.

Fodor, J.A. The language of thought. Cambridge, Mass.: Harvard
     University Press, 1979.

Fodor, J.A. The mind-body problem. Scientific American, 1981,
     244, 114-123.

Fodor, J.A., Bever, T.G., and Garrett, M.F. The psychology of
     language: An introduction to psycholinguistics and gener-
     ative grammar. New York: McGraw-Hill, 1974.

Freud, S. The interpretation of dreams. Leipzig and Vienna: Deuticke, 1900.

Freud, S. An outline of psychoanalysis. New York: Norton, 1939, 1949.

Freud, S. New introductory lectures on psychoanalysis. New York: Norton, 1965.

Freud, S. Project for a scientific psychology. In J. Strachey (Ed.), The standard edition of the complete psychological works of Sigmund Freud (Vol. 1). London: Hogarth, 1966.

Fromm, E. Man for himself. New York: Holt, Rinehart, and Winston, 1947.

Gall, F.J., and Spurzheim, J.K. Anatomie et physiologie du système nerveux en général. 4 vols. Paris: Schoell, 1810-1819.

Galton, F. Hereditary genius: An inquiry into its laws and consequences. London: Macmillan, 1869.

Galton, F. Psychometric experiments. Brain, 1879, 2, 149-162.

Galton, F. Natural inheritance. London: Macmillan, 1889.

Garcia, J. IQ: The conspiracy. In J.B. Maas (Ed.), Readings in Psychology Today (3rd ed.). Del Mar, Cal.: CRM, 1974.

Garfield, S.L., and Bergin, A.E. (Eds.). Handbook of psychotherapy and behavior change: An empirical analysis. New York: Wiley, 1978.

Gelman, R. Cognitive development. Annual Review of Psychology, 1978, 29, 297-332.

Giorgi, A. Psychology as a human science: A phenomenologically based approach. New York: Harper and Row, 1970.

Griesinger, W. The pathology and therapy of psychic disorders, 1845 (2nd ed.). London: The New Sydenham Society, 1867.

Grünbaum, A. Epistemological liabilities in the clinical appraisal of psychoanalytic theory. Nous, 1980, 14, 307-385.

Guthrie, E.R. The psychology of learning. New York: Harper and Row, 1935.

Habermas, J. Knowledge and human interests. Boston: Beacon Press, 1972.

Habermas, J. Theory and practice. Boston: Beacon Press, 1973.

Hall, G.S. Adolescence: Its psychology, and its relation to phy-
    siology, anthropology, sociology, sex, crime, religion, and
    education. 2 vols. New York: Appleton, 1904.

Hall, G.S. Senescence: The last half of life. New York: Appleton,
    1922.

Harlow, H.F. The formation of learning sets. Psychological Re-
    view, 1949, 56, 51-65.

Harré, R., and Lamb, R. (Eds.). The encyclopedic dictionary of
    psychology. Cambridge, Mass.: MIT Press, 1983.

Hebb, D.O. The organization of behavior. New York: Wiley, 1949.

Helmholtz, H. von. Handbuch der physiologischen Optik. 3 vols.
    Leipzig: Voss, 1856-1866.

Hempel, C.G. Logical positivism and the social sciences. In P.
    Achinstein and S.F. Barker (Eds.), The legacy of logical
    positivism. Baltimore: Johns Hopkins University Press,
    1969a.

Hempel, C.G. Reduction: Ontological and linguistic facets. In S.
    Morgenbesser, P. Suppes, and M. White (Eds.), Philosophy,
    science, and method. Essays in honor of Ernest Nagel. New
    York: St. Martin's Press, 1969b.

Hempel, C.G. The logical analysis of psychology. In A. Marras
    (Ed.), Intentionality, mind, and language. Urbana: Univer-
    sity of Illinois Press, 1972.

Henle, M., Jaynes, J., and Sullivan, J.J. (Eds.). A source book
    in the history of psychology. Cambridge, Mass.: Harvard
    University Press, 1966.

Herrnstein, R.J. On the law of effect. Journal of the Experimen-
    tal Analysis of Behavior, 1970, 13, 243-266.

Herrnstein, R.J. The evolution of behaviorism. American Psychol-
    ogist, 1977, 32, 593-603.

Hilgard, E.R., and Bower, G.H. Theories of learning (4th ed.).
    Englewood Cliffs, N.J.: Prentice-Hall, 1974.

Hillner, K.P. Psychology of learning: A conceptual analysis.
    Elmsford, N.Y.: Pergamon, 1978.

Hillner, K.P. Conditioning in contemporary perspective. New York:
    Springer, 1979.

Hillner, K.P. History and systems of modern psychology: A con-
    ceptual approach. New York: Gardner, 1984.

Hobbes, T. Human nature, or the fundamental elements of policy.
    London: Fra Bowman of Oxon, 1650.

Hobbes, T. Leviathan, or the matter, form and power of a common-
    wealth ecclesiastical and civil. London: Crooke, 1651.

Hochberg, J. Organization and the Gestalt tradition. In E. Car-
    terette and M. Friedman (Eds.), Handbook of perception:
    Historical and philosophical roots of perception (Vol. 1).
    New York: Academic Press, 1974.

Holzkamp, K. Wissenschaftstheoretische Voraussetzungen kritisch-
    emanzipatorischer Psychologie. Zeitschrift für Sozialpsy-
    chologie, 1970, 1, 5-21; 109-141.

Holzkamp, K. Kritische Psychologie: Vorbereitende Arbeiten.
    Frankfurt: Fischer Taschenbuch Verlag, 1972.

Holzkamp, K. Sinnliche Erkenntnis-Historischer Ursprung und
    gesellschaftliche Funktion der Wahrnemung. Frankfurt:
    Athenäum Fischer, 1973.

Holzkamp, K. Grundlegung der Psychologie. Frankfurt: Campus Ver-
    lag, 1983.

Horkheimer, M. Critical theory. New York: Seabury Press, 1972.

Horney, K. New ways in psychoanalysis. New York: Norton, 1939.

Horney, K. Neurosis and human growth. New York: Norton, 1950.

Hull, C.L. Principles of behavior. New York: Appleton-Century-
    Crofts, 1943.

Hull, C.L. Essentials of behavior. New Haven, Conn.: Yale Uni-
    versity Press, 1951.

Hull, C.L. A behavior system. New Haven, Conn.: Yale University
    Press, 1952.

Hume, D. An enquiry concerning human understanding, 1748.
    Oxford, England: Clarendon Press, 1902.

Ingleby, J.D. Ideology and the human sciences. In T. Pateman
    (Ed.), Counter course. London: Penguin, 1972.

Ingleby, J.D. The psychology of child psychology. In M.P.M. Rich-
    ards (Ed.), The integration of a child into a social world.
    London: Cambridge University Press, 1974.

Ingleby, J.D. (Ed.). Critical psychiatry. New York: Pantheon,
    1980.

Inhelder, B., and Piaget, J. The growth of logical thinking from
    childhood to adolescence. New York: Basic Books, 1958.

Jacoby, J. Consumer psychology: An octennium. Annual Review of
    Psychology, 1976, 27, 331-358.

James, W. The principles of psychology. 2 vols. New York: Holt,
    1890.

James, W. Pragmatism: A new name for some old ways of thinking.
    New York: Longmans, Green, 1907.

Janet, P. L'État mental des hysteriques. Paris: Rueff, 1892.

Jensen, A.R. How much can we boost IQ and scholastic achieve-
    ment? Harvard Educational Review, 1969, 39, 1-123.

Jensen, A.R. Educability and group differences. New York: Harper
    and Row, 1973.

Jensen, A.R. Bias in mental testing. New York: Free Press, 1980.

Jones, E. The life and work of Sigmund Freud, 1856-1900. 3 vols.
    New York: Basic Books, 1953, 1957, 1961.

Jones, M.C. A laboratory study of fear: The case of Peter.
    Pedagogical Seminary, 1924a, 31, 308-315.

Jones, M.C. Elimination of children's fears. Journal of Experi-
    mental Psychology, 1924b, 7, 383-390.

Jung, C.G. Analytical psychology. New York: Moffat-Yard, 1916.

Jung, C.G. Collected works. New York: Pantheon, 1953.

Jung, J. Verbal learning. New York: Holt, Rinehart, and Winston,
    1968.

Kaam, A. van. Existential and humanistic psychology. Review of
    Existential Psychology and Psychiatry, 1965, 5, 291-296.

Kaam, A. van. Existential foundations of psychology. Pittsburg,
   Pa.: Duquesne University Press, 1966.

Kalinowski, L.B., and Hippius, H. Pharmacological, convulsive,
   and other somatic treatments in psychiatry. New York: Grune
   and Stratton, 1969.

Kalinowski, L.B., and Hoch, P.H. Shock treatments, psychosurgery,
   and other somatic treatments in psychiatry. New York: Grune
   and Stratton, 1952.

Kamin, L.J. The science and politics of IQ. Potomoc, Md.: Erl-
   baum, 1974.

Kant, I. Kritik der reinen Vernunft. Riga: Hartknoch, 1781.

Kaplan, R.M., and Saccuzzo, D.P. Psychological testing: Principles, applications, and issues. Monterey, Cal.: Brooks/Cole
   1982.

Katona, G. Rational behavior and economic behavior. Psychological Review, 1953, 60, 307-318.

Kaufman, W. (Ed.). Existentialism from Dostoyevsky to Sartre.
   Cleveland: Minden Books, 1956.

Keen, E. A primer in phenomenological psychology. New York: Holt
   Rinehart, and Winston, 1975.

Keller, F.S. The definition of psychology. New York: Appleton-
   Century-Crofts, 1937.

Kendler, H. Psychology: A science in conflict. New York: Oxford
   University Press, 1981.

Kim, J. Phenomenal properties, psychophysical laws, and the
   identity theory. Monist, 1972, 56, 177-192.

Kimble, G.A. Hilgard and Marquis' Conditioning and learning
   (Rev. ed.). New York: Appleton-Century-Crofts, 1961.

Kleitman, N. Sleep and wakefulness. Chicago: University of Chicago Press, 1963.

Koch, S. (Ed.). Psychology: A study of a science. 7 vols. New
   York: McGraw-Hill, 1959.

Koch, S. Language communities, search cells, and the psycholog-
   ical studies. In J.K. Cole and W.J. Arnold (Eds.), Nebraska
   Symposium on Motivation, 1975, 23, 477-559. Lincoln, Neb.:
   University of Nebraska Press.

Koffka, K. Perception: An introduction to the Gestalttheorie.
    Psychological Bulletin, 1922, 19, 531-585.

Koffka, K. Principles of Gestalt psychology. New York: Harcourt
    Brace, 1935, 1963.

Kohlberg, L. Essays on moral development: The philosophy of
    moral development (Vol. 1). San Francisco: Harper and Row,
    1981.

Köhler, W. Intelligenz-prufungen an Menschenaffen. Berlin:
    Springer, 1917. (Trans. as The mentality of apes. London:
    Kegan Paul, 1924.)

Köhler, W. Die physischen Gestalten in Ruhe und im stationären
    Zustand. Erlangen: Weltkreisverlag, 1920.

Köhler, W. Gestalt psychology. New York: Liveright, 1929, 1947.

Kraepelin, E. Compendium der Psychiatrie, 1883. New York: Mac-
    millan, 1907.

Kraepelin, E. Über die Beeinflussung einfacher psychischer Vor-
    gänge durch Arzneimittel; experimentelle Untersuchungen.
    Jena: Fischer, 1892.

Krechevsky, I. (Krech, D.). "Hypotheses" in rats. Psychological
    Review, 1932, 39, 516-532.

Kuhn, T. The structure of scientific revolutions (2nd ed.).
    Chicago: University of Chicago Press, 1970.

Külpe, O. Grundriss der Psychologie (3rd ed.). Leipzig: Engle-
    mann, 1893.

Ladd, G.T. Elements of physiological psychology: A treatise of
    the activities and nature of the mind from the physical
    and experimental point of view. New York: Scribner, 1891.

Ladd, G.T. Psychology: Descriptive and explanatory. New York:
    Scribner, 1894.

Lakatos, I. History of science and its rational reconstruction.
    In R.C. Buck and R.S. Cohen (Eds.), Boston studies in the
    philosophy of science (Vol. 8). Dordrecht, Netherlands:
    Reidel, 1970.

LaMettrie, J.O. de. L'Homme machine. Leyden: Luzac, 1748.

Latané, B., and Darley, J.M. The unresponsive bystander: Why doesn't he help? New York: Appleton-Century-Crofts, 1970.

Lazarus, A.A. Behavior therapy and beyond. New York: McGraw-Hill, 1971.

Leary, D.E. The philosophical development of the conception of psychology in Germany, 1750-1850. Journal of the History of the Behavioral Sciences, 1978, 14, 113-121.

Leibnitz, G.W. New essays concerning human understanding, 1704. New York: Macmillan, 1896.

Leibnitz, G.W. Monadology, 1714. Oxford, England: Oxford University Press, 1898.

Leitenberg, H. (Ed.). Handbook of behavior modification and behavior therapy. New York: Prentice-Hall, 1976.

Lewis, D. Review of Art, Mind, and Religion. Journal of Philosophy, 1969, 66, 23-25.

Lewis, D. An argument for the identity theory. In D. Rosenthal (Ed.), Materialism and the mind-body problem. Englewood Cliffs, N.J.: Prentice-Hall, 1971.

Liébault, A.A. Du sommeil et des états analogues considérés surtout au point de vue de l'action du moral sur le physique. Paris: Musson, 1866.

Lindsay, P.H., and Norman, D.A. Human information processing (2nd ed.). New York: Academic Press, 1977.

Locke, J. An essay concerning human understanding. London: Basset, 1690.

Lowman, R.P. (Co-ordinator). Careers in psychology. Washington, D.C.: American Psychological Association, 1980.

Lundin, R.W. Theories and systems of psychology (2nd ed.). Lexington, Mass.: Heath, 1979.

MacCorquodale, K., and Meehl, P.E. On a distinction between hypothetical constructs and intervening variables. Psychological Review, 1948, 55, 95-107.

Mackenzie, B.D. Behaviorism and the limits of the scientific method. London: Routledge and Kegan Paul, 1977.

McDougall, W. Outline of psychology. New York: Scribner, 1923.

McNamara, J.R., and Barclay, A. (Eds.). Critical issues, trends, and developments in professional psychology. New York: Praeger, 1982.

Malebranche, N. De la recherche de la véritie. In Oeuvres de Malebranche, 1674 (Vol. 2). Paris: Charpentier, 1855.

Marx, K. Das Kapital. 3 vols. Hamburg: Meissner, 1867.

Marx, M.H. Intervening variable or hypothetical construct. Psychological Review, 1951, 58, 235-247.

Marx, M.H., and Hillix, W.A. Systems and theories in psychology (3rd ed.). New York: McGraw-Hill, 1979.

Maser, J.D., and Seligman, M.E.P. (Eds.). Psychotherapy: Experimental models. San Francisco: Freeman, 1977.

Maslow, A.H. Toward a psychology of being. Princeton, N.J.: Van Nostrand, 1962, 1968.

Maslow, A.H. Motivation and personality (2nd ed.). New York: Harper and Row, 1970.

Maslow, A.H. The farther reaches of human nature. New York: Viking, 1971.

Masters, W.H., and Johnson, V.E. Homosexuality in perspective. Boston: Little, Brown, 1979.

Maudsley, H. The physiology and pathology of the mind. London: Macmillan, 1867.

Mayr, E. The growth of biological thought: Diversity, evolution, and inheritance. Cambridge, Mass.: Harvard University Press, 1982.

Menninger, K.A., and Holzman, P.S. Theory of psychoanalytic technique (2nd ed.). New York: Basic Books, 1973.

Miller, G.A. Psychology as a means of promoting human welfare. American Psychologist, 1969, 24, 1063-1075.

Miller, G.A., Galanter, E.H., and Pribram, H.H. Plans and the structure of behavior. New York: Holt, 1960.

Miller, N.E. Experimental studies of conflict. In J.McV. Hunt (Ed.), Personality and the behavior disorders. New York: Ronald Press, 1944.

Miller, N.E. Liberalization of basic S-R concepts: Extensions to
    conflict behavior, motivation, and social learning. In S.
    Koch (Ed.), Psychology: A study of a science (Vol. 2).
    New York: McGraw-Hill, 1959.

Muchinsky, P.M. Psychology applied to work. Homewood, Ill.:
    Dorsey Press, 1983.

Mueller-Freienfels, R. The evolution of modern psychology. New
    Haven, Conn.: Yale University Press, 1935.

Munroe, R. Schools of psychoanalytic thought. New York: Holt,
    1955.

Murchison, C. (Ed.). A history of psychology in autobiography
    (Vol. 3). Worcester, Mass.: Clark University Press, 1936.

Murray, H.A. Explorations in personality. New York: Oxford Uni-
    versity Press, 1938.

Nagel, E. The structure of science. New York: Harcourt, Brace,
    and World, 1961.

Neisser, U. Cognition and reality. San Francisco: Freeman, 1976.

Nelson, S.D., and Stapp, J. Research activities in psychology:
    An update. American Psychologist, 1983, 38, 1321-1329.

Neumann, J. von, and Morgenstern, O. Theory of games and econ-
    omic behavior (2nd ed.). Princeton, N.J.: Princeton Univer-
    sity Press, 1947.

Newell, A., and Simon, H.A. Human problem solving. Englewood
    Cliffs, N.J.: Prentice-Hall, 1972.

Newell, A., and Simon, H.A. Computer science as empirical in-
    quiry: Symbols and search. In J. Haugeland (Ed.), Mind
    design. Cambridge, Mass.: MIT Press, 1981.

Nicholson, J. Men and women: How different are they? New York:
    Oxford University Press, 1984.

Ogden, R.M. Imageless thought. Psychological Bulletin, 1911, 8,
    183-197.

Orwell, G. 1984. London: Secker and Warburg, 1949.

Osgood, C.E. The similarity paradox in human learning: A reso-
    lution. Psychological Review, 1949, 56, 132-143.

Owens, J. A history of ancient Western philosophy. Englewood
    Cliffs, N.J.: Prentice-Hall, 1959.

Page, J.D. Psychotherapy. Chicago: Aldine-Atherton, 1971.

Pavlov, I.P. Conditioned reflexes. Trans. by G.V. Anrep. London:
    Oxford University Press, 1927.

Peterfreund, E. The process of psychoanalytic therapy: Models
    and strategies. Hillsdale, N.J.: Analytic Press, 1982.

Phares, E.J. Locus of control in personality. Morristown, N.J.:
    General Learning Press, 1976.

Piaget, J. Logic of epistemology. Manchester, England: Manches-
    ter University Press, 1953.

Piaget, J. The construction of reality in the child. New York:
    Basic Books, 1954.

Piaget, J. Genetic epistemology. New York: Columbia University
    Press, 1970.

Piaget, J. The development of thought: Equilibration of cogni-
    tive structure. New York: Viking, 1977.

Piaget, J., and Inhelder, B. The psychology of the child. New
    York: Basic Books, 1969.

Planck, M. The philosophy of physics. New York: Norton, 1936.

Polyani, M. Personal knowledge. Chicago: University of Chicago
    Press, 1958.

Postman, L. Rewards and punishments in human learning. In L.
    Postman (Ed.), Psychology in the making. New York: Knopf,
    1962.

Prochaska, J.O. Systems of psychotherapy: A transtheoretical
    analysis. Homewood, Ill.: Dorsey Press, 1979.

Putnam, H. The nature of mental states. In W.H. Capitan and
    D.D. Merrill (Eds.), Art, mind, and religion. Pittsburg,
    Pa.: University of Pittsburg Press, 1967.

Rapaport, D. The structure of psychoanalytic theory. In S. Koch
    (Ed.), Psychology: A study of a science (Vol. 3). New York:
    McGraw-Hill, 1959.

Reisman, J.M. History of clinical psychology. New York: Irving-
    ton, 1975.

Rescorla, R.A., and Solomon, R.L. Two-process learning theory:
    Relationships between Pavlovian conditioning and instrumen-
    tal learning. Psychological Review, 1967, 74, 151-182.

Restle, F. The selection of strategies in cue learning. Psycho-
    logical Review, 1962, 69, 329-343.

Restle, F. Learning: Animal behavior and human cognition. New
    York: McGraw-Hill, 1975.

Rieff, P. Freud: The mind of the moralist. New York: Viking,
    1959.

Riegel, K.F. (Ed.). The development of dialectical operations.
    Basel: Karger, 1975.

Riegel, K.F. Psychology mon amour: A countertext. Boston: Hough-
    ton Mifflin, 1978.

Riegel, K.F. Foundations of dialectical psychology. New York:
    Academic Press, 1979.

Roazen, P. Freud and his followers. New York: Knopf, 1975.

Robinson, D.N. Systems of modern psychology: A critical sketch.
    New York: Columbia University Press, 1979.

Rogers, C.R. Counseling and psychotherapy. Boston: Houghton
    Mifflin, 1942.

Rogers, C.R. Client-centered therapy. Boston: Houghton Mifflin,
    1951.

Rogers, C.R. Some issues concerning the control of behavior.
    Science, 1956, 124, 1057-1066.

Rogers, C.R. On becoming a person. Boston: Houghton Mifflin,
    1961.

Rorschach, H. Psychodiagnostics: A diagnostic test based on
    perception. New York: Grune and Stratton, 1942.

Royce, J.E. Man and his nature. New York: McGraw-Hill, 1961.

Rubinstein, S.L. Fundamentals of general psychology, 1940.
    (2nd ed.). Moscow: AN-SSSR, 1946.

Ruch, F.L. Personality: Public or private. In J.B. Maas (Ed.),
    Readings in Psychology Today (3rd ed.). Del Mar, Cal.:
    CRM, 1974.

Runyan, W.M. Life histories and psychobiography: Explorations in theory and method. New York: Oxford University Press, 1982.

Russell, B. An outline of philosophy. New York: Meridian, 1927.

Russell, B. A history of Western philosophy. New York: Simon and Schuster, 1945.

Rychlak, J.F. Dialectic: Humanistic rationale for behavior and development. Basel: Karger, 1976.

Rychlak, J.F. The psychology of rigorous humanism. New York: Wiley Interscience, 1977.

Ryle, G. The concept of mind. London: Hutchinson, 1949.

Sachar, E.L. Behavioral science and criminal law. Scientific American, 1963, 209, 39-45.

Sarason, S.B. Psychology misdirected. New York: Free Press, 1981.

Scheff, T.J. Being mentally ill: A sociological theory. Chicago: Aldine, 1966.

Schrödinger, E. What is life? Cambridge, England: Cambridge University Press, 1945.

Schur, M. Freud: Living and dying. New York: International Universities Press, 1972.

Schwartz, B. Psychology of learning and behavior. New York: Norton, 1978.

Scripture, E.W. The new psychology. New York: Scribner, 1897.

Scriven, M. Views of human nature. In T.W. Wann (Ed.), Behaviorism and phenomenology. Chicago: University of Chicago Press, 1964.

Sexton, V.S., and Misiak, H. (Eds.). Psychology around the world. Monterey, Cal.: Brooks/Cole, 1976.

Shapiro, D., Barber, T.X., DiCara, L.V., Kamiya, J., Miller, N.E., and Stoyva, J. (Eds.). Biofeedback and self-control 1972. Chicago: Aldine, 1973.

Shoemaker, S. Functionalism and qualia. Philosophical Studies, 1975, 27, 271-315.

Simon, H.A. The sciences of the artificial. Cambridge, Mass.:
    MIT Press, 1974.

Skinner, B.F. The behavior of organisms. New York: Appleton-
    Century-Crofts, 1938.

Skinner, B.F. Walden Two. New York: Macmillan, 1948, 1962.

Skinner, B.F. Science and human behavior. New York: Macmillan,
    1953.

Skinner, B.F. Critique of psychoanalytic concepts and theories.
    Scientific Monthly, 1954, 79, 302-307.

Skinner, B.F. A case study in scientific method. American Psy-
    chologist, 1956, 11, 221-233.

Skinner, B.F. Verbal behavior. New York: Appleton-Century-Crofts
    1957.

Skinner, B.F. Contingencies of reinforcement: A theoretical
    analysis. New York: Appleton-Century-Crofts, 1969.

Skinner, B.F. Beyond freedom and dignity. New York: Bantam/Vin-
    tage, 1971.

Skinner, B.F. About behaviorism. New York: Knopf, 1974.

Skinner, B.F. Particulars of my life. New York: Knopf, 1976.

Skinner, B.F. Why I am not a cognitive psychologist. Behavior-
    ism, 1977, 5, 1-10.

Small, W.S. An experimental study of the mental processes of
    the rat. American Journal of Psychology, 1901, 12, 206-239.

Smart, J.J.C. Sensations and brain processes. Philosophical
    Review, 1959, 68, 141-156.

Smith, M.L., and Glass, G.V. Meta-analysis of psychotherapy out-
    come studies. American Psychologist, 1977, 32, 752-760.

Solso, R.L. Cognitive psychology. New York: Harcourt Brace Jo-
    vanovich, 1979.

Spinoza, B. Ethics, 1677. New York: Dover, 1951.

Spranger, E. Psychologie des Jugendalters. Leipzig: Quelle and
    Meyer, 1925.

Spranger, E. Types of men: The psychology and ethics of person-
    ality. Halle: Niemeyer, 1928.

Staats, A.W. Psychology's crisis of disunity. New York: Praeger,
    1983.

Staddon, J.E.R. Asymptotic behavior: The concept of the operant.
    Psychological Review, 1967, 74, 377-391.

Staddon, J.E.R. (Ed.). Limits to action: The allocation of in-
    dividual behavior. New York: Academic Press, 1980.

Stumpf, C. Tonpsychologie. 2 vols. Leipzig: Hirzel, 1883-1890.

Stumpf, C. Beiträge zur akustik und musik Wissenschaft. 9 parts.
    Leipzig: Barth, 1898-1924.

Sullivan, H.S. The interpersonal theory of psychiatry. New York:
    Norton, 1953.

Suppes, P., and Atkinson, R.C. Markov learning models for multi-
    person interactions. Stanford: Stanford University Press,
    1960.

Suzuki, D.T. Zen Buddhism. Garden City, N.Y.: Anchor Books, 1956.

Sweetland, R.C., and Keyser, D.J. (Eds.). Tests: A comprehensive
    reference for assessments in psychology, education, and
    business. Kansas City: Test Corporation of America, 1983.

Szasz, T.S. The myth of mental illness. New York: Harper and Row,
    1961.

Szasz, T.S. The manufacture of madness. New York: Harper and Row,
    1970.

Szasz, T.S., and Hollender, M.H. A contribution to the philoso-
    phy of medicine: The basic models of the doctor-patient re-
    lationship. Archives of Internal Medicine, 1956, 97, 585-
    592.

Taylor, C. The explanation of behavior. London: Routledge and
    Kegan Paul, 1964.

Temkin, O. Gall and the phrenological movement. Bulletin of the
    History of Medicine, 1947, 21, 275-321.

Terman, L.M. The measurement of intelligence. Boston: Houghton
    Mifflin, 1916.

Thorndike, E.L. The elements of psychology. New York: Seiler, 1905.

Thorndike, E.L. Animal intelligence. New York: Macmillan, 1911.

Thorndike, E.L. The law of effect. American Journal of Psychology, 1927, 39, 212-222.

Thorndike, E.L. Reward and punishment in animal learning. Comparative Psychology Monographs, 1932, 8 (39).

Titchener, E.B. The postulates of a structural psychology. Philosophical Review, 1898, 7, 449-465.

Titchener, E.B. Experimental psychology: A manual of laboratory practice. 2 vols. New York: Macmillan, 1901, 1905.

Titchener, E.B. The schema of introspection. American Journal of Psychology, 1912, 23, 485-508.

Tolman, E.C. Purposive behavior in animals and men. New York: Appleton-Century-Crofts, 1932.

Turing, A.M. Computing machinery and intelligence. In A. Anderson (Ed.), Minds and machines. Englewood Cliffs, N.J.: Prentice-Hall, 1964.

Turner, M.B. Philosophy and the science of behavior. New York: Appleton-Century-Crofts, 1967.

Turner, M.B. Realism and the explanation of behavior. New York: Appleton-Century-Crofts, 1971.

Underwood, B.J. Psychological research. New York: Appleton-Century-Crofts, 1957.

Underwood, B.J., and Schulz, R.W. Meaningfulness and verbal learning. Philadelphia: Lippincott, 1960.

Von Eckardt, B. The scientific status of psychoanalysis. In S. Gilman (Ed.), Introducing psychoanalytic theory. New York: Bruner/Mazel, 1983.

Walters, C.G. Consumer behavior: Theory and practice. Homewood, Ill.: Irwin, 1978.

Watson, J.B. Psychology as the behaviorist views it. Psychological Review, 1913, 20, 158-177.

Watson, J.B. Behavior: An introduction to comparative psychology.
    New York: Holt, 1914.

Watson, J.B. The place of the conditioned reflex in psychology.
    Psychological Review, 1916, 23, 89-116.

Watson, J.B. Psychology from the standpoint of a behaviorist.
    Philadelphia: Lippincott, 1919, 1924, 1929.

Watson, J.B. Behaviorism. New York: Norton, 1925, 1930.

Watson, J.B., and Raynor, R. Conditioned emotional reactions.
    Journal of Experimental Psychology, 1920, 3, 1-14.

Watson, R.I. Psychology: A prescriptive science. American Psy-
    chologist, 1967, 22, 435-443.

Weber, E.H. Der Tastsinn und das Gemeingefühl, 1846. In R. Wag-
    ner (Ed.), Handworterbuch der Physiologie. 4 vols. Braun-
    schweig: Vieweg, 1842-1853.

Weiner, B. Human motivation. New York: Holt, Rinehart, and Win-
    ston, 1980.

Weizenbaum, J. Computer power and human reason. San Francisco:
    Freeman, 1976.

Wertheimer, M. (Max). Experimentelle Studien über das Sehen von
    Bewegung. Zeitschrift für Psychologie, 1912, 61, 161-265.

Wertheimer, M. (Max). Untersuchungen zur Lehre von der Gestalt.
    Psychologische Forschung, 1922, 1, 47-58.

Wertheimer, M. (Michael). Fundamental issues in psychology.
    New York: Holt, Rinehart, and Winston, 1972.

Wertheimer, M. (Michael). Humanistic psychology and the humane
    but tough-minded psychologist. American Psychologist, 1978,
    33, 739-745.

Wheeler, H. (Ed.). Beyond the punitive society. San Francisco:
    Freeman, 1973.

White, R.W., and Watt, N.F. The abnormal personality (4th ed.).
    New York: Ronald Press, 1973.

Whitney, L.R., and Barnard, K.E. Implications of operant learn-
    ing theory for nursing care of the retarded child. Mental
    Retardation, 1966, 4, 26-29.

Williams, J.B.W. (Ed.). DSM-III: Diagnostic and statistical manual of mental disorders (3rd ed.). Washington, D.C.: American Psychiatric Association, 1980.

Woods, P.J. The psychology major: Training and employment strategies. Washington, D.C.: American Psychological Association, 1979.

Woodworth, R.S. Imageless thought. The Journal of Philosophy, Psychology, and Scientific Methods, 1906, 3, 701-708.

Woodworth, R.S. Dynamic psychology. New York: Columbia University Press, 1918.

Woodworth, R.S. Psychology. New York: Holt, 1921.

Wright, D.S., Taylor, A., Davies, D.R., Sluckin, W., Lee, S.G.M. and Reason, J.T. Introducing psychology: An experimental approach. Harmondsworth, England: Penguin, 1970.

Wundt, W.M. Grundzüge der physiologischen Psychologie. Leipzig: Engelmann, 1873-1874.

Wundt, W.M. Über psychologische Methoden. Philosophische Studien, 1883, 1, 1-38.

Wundt, W.M. Grundriss der Psychologie. Leipzig: Engelmann, 1896.

Yerkes, R.M. (Ed.). Psychological examining in the army. In Memoirs of the National Academy of Sciences (Vol. 15). Washington, D.C.: U.S. Government Printing Office, 1921.

Zilboorg, G. A history of medical psychology. New York: Norton, 1967.

NAME INDEX

Wheeler, H., 13, 101, 111
White, R.W., 243, 279, 284
Whitney, L.R., 309
Williams, J.B.W., 276
Woods, P.J., 271
Woodworth, R.S., 65, 71, 77
Wright, D.S., 280
Wundt, W.M., 4, 10, 27, 32, 50, 59, 60, 63, 64, 65, 112, 122,
    123, 130, 131, 223, 246, 259, 270, 304, 326, 352

Yerkes, R.M., 295

Zilboorg, G., 274, 275, 277, 338

SUBJECT INDEX

Logical behaviorism, theoretical cycles of, 213-214
        macromodel, 214
        macrotheoretical, 213
        micromodel, 214
        microtheoretical, 213-214

Logical positivism, 5, 184, 318, 323, 327, 328

Machine mentation, 192, 202-203, 205, 265

Machine representation of mentation. See Functionalism (approach
        to mentation), functional state identity version

Maladaptive behaviors, 277, 280, 289

Mand, 351

Manic-depressive psychosis, 278

Marxist-based psychology. See Critical psychology; Riegelian
        dialectical psychology

Marxist philosophy, 267, 318, 355, 357

Materialism, 180, 181-190, 192, 193, 196, 203-205, 266
        central state identity: type and token, 181, 186-188, 190,
                204
        eliminative (descriptive behaviorism), 181, 182-183,
                189-190, 203-204
        emergentist, 181, 188-189, 190, 205
        reductive (logical behaviorism): weak and strong, 181,
                183-186, 190, 204.
        See also Monism, materialism

Meaning, in humanistic psychology, 144, 228, 362

Mechanism, 171

"Mechanism become drive" concept, 77

Mediate conscious experience, 61-62, 81

Mental activity. See Conscious experience, in classical schools,
        functionalism; Conscious experience, in contemporary sys-
        tems, cognitive behaviorism; Mind, contemporary concep-
        tions of

Mental events, in relation to the content of observation,
        179-180

Mental representation, 201-203, 205
        classic Humean resemblance view of, 202
        contemporary functionalistic causal role view of, 202, 203

Mental states, nature and status of. See Mind, contemporary
        conceptions of

Multiprediction, in Freudian depth psychology, 225-226

Nativism, 124

Neuroses, 134, 135, 136, 138-139, 279, 280

Nineteenth century French psychopathological movement, 278-279

Nineteenth century German psychiatry, 277-278

Nineteenth century German science, 58

Nominal explanation. See Circular explanation

Nomothetic approach/systems, 7, 100, 101, 135, 262, 320

Normal behavior, contrasted with abnormal behavior. See Abnormality, existential reality level of

Objectively oriented psychology versus subjectively oriented psychology, 4-5, 34-35, 303, 349, 350

Objectivity versus subjectivity, as properties of behavior and conscious experience, 251-256

Object of study, 26, 27. See also Content of observation

Occurrent states, 196, 197, 199-201

Operant conditioning, 10, 32, 77, 100, 106, 108, 236

Operant rate, 237

Operants, 105, 106, 107, 108, 258
    criteria for, 253

Oral stage, 137

Organism, as an information processor, 115-116

Oriental psychology, 17

Orientation(s), 303-304, 347-350
    arbitrariness of, 303-304
    heterogeneous subclass of, 347, 348
    historical progression of, 348-349
    homogeneous subclass of, 347-348
    popularity of mixed type of, 348, 349-350
    subjective, objective polarity of, 348, 349

Orientations, types of, 47-55
    combined objective x subjective, 53-55
    mixed (quasi-objective), 51-53
    objective, 48-49
    subjective, 49-51

Other mind problem, in philosophy, 254

Psychological universe, components of, 42-47
    externally resolvable phenomena, 46
    inferable objects, 45-46
    internally resolvable phenomena, 46
    objects of direct observation, 44-45
    physical environment, 42-44
    self, 42-44, 303
    significant other, 42-44, 303

Psychology and ethics (morality), 342-344
    liberal view, 342-344
    strict view, 342

Psychology and ideology. See Critical theory

Psychology and the meaning of life, 344-345

Psychology, as a component of the economic system, 14-15, 16,
    272-273

Psychology, as a cross-classificational endeavor, 21, 328, 362,
    363

Psychology, as an adjudicative endeavor, 358-359

Psychology, as a science, 323-327
    biological, 326-327
    humanistic, 325
    physical, 326
    possible criteria for, 324-325
    psychiatric, 325
    social, 327

Psychology, as a sociological endeavor, 358-359

Psychology, as related to other endeavors, 266, 267, 327, 328,
    332-342
    humanities: art, literature, theatre, 333-334
    law, 174, 336-338
    medicine, 338-339
    philosophy, 335-336
    psychiatry, 338-339
    religion, 334-335
    social sciences: economics, history, political science,
        sociology, 339-342

Psychology, autonomy of. See Psychological reductionism

Psychology, contemporary focus of, 39, 358-359

Psychology, creative focus of, 39-40

Psychology, cultural relativism in. See Psychology, national
    character of

Psychology, existential reality level of, 3-5, 15

Psychology, generic nature of, 9-11, 15-16

Psychology, infinite nature of, 9-11, 15-16

Psychology, national character of, 315-316

Psychology, possible cultural/social impact of, 329-332

Psychology, provinciality of, 8-9, 15

Psychology, recipient status of, 317-318

Psychology, status in society of, 38-39, 358-359

Psychometrics, 271, 296

Psychopath, 243

Psychophysical fields, 82-84

Psychoses, 278
    functional, 280
    organic, 278

Psychotherapeutic techniques, 286-290
    behavior modification approaches, 277, 287, 288-290
    medical model approaches, 287-288

Qualia, 197, 199-201, 202, 203, 205, 254-255, 260-261, 263, 265
    absent, 200
    differential, 200, 201
    inverted, 200

Qualitative content of a mental event. See Qualia

Rational explanation, 209, 230, 243-244
    and the advocate position, 244
    as related to descriptive scientific explanation, 243
    in an applied context, 244

Reasonable explanation. See Rational explanation

Reference psychological situation/activity, 35-37, 58, 100
    in cognitive behaviorism, 119-121
    in Freudian depth psychology, 136-139
    in functionalism, 75-78
    in Gestalt psychology, 85-87
    in humanistic psychology, 144-146
    in Piagetian structural psychology, 129-132
    in Riegelian dialectical psychology, 151-153
    in Skinnerian radical behaviorism, 107-112
    in structuralism, 67-69
    in Watsonian behaviorism, 93-94, 96-98

Reflex, 37, 105